HARLAN LEBO

Casablanca

behind the scenes

A Fireside Book   Published by Simon & Schuster
New York London Toronto Sydney Tokyo Singapore

F

FIRESIDE
Simon & Schuster Building
Rockefeller Center
1230 Avenue of the Americas
New York, New York 10020

Your comments about this book are welcome. Write to
Harlan Lebo, P.O. Box 641164, Los Angeles, CA, 90064

Designed by Caroline Cunningham
Manufactured in the United States of America

10 9 8 7 6 5 4 3 2 1

Library of Congress Cataloging in Publication Data
Lebo, Harlan.
Casablanca : behind the scenes / Harlan Lebo.
p.   cm.
"A Fireside book."
Includes bibliographical references and index.
1. Casablanca (Motion picture) I. Title.
PN1997.C3523L4   1992
791.43′72—dc20   92-19916
                                              CIP

ISBN 978-0-671-76981-9

To my parents

Acknowledgments

With so many thanks to the very special people who helped make this book possible:

· To my wife, Monica Dunahee, for her patient editing and review of the manuscript, and for her endless reserve of patience, tolerance, and support. Her comments, suggestions, and revisions—some delicate, some otherwise—provided a voice of reason that touches every page of this book.

· To Neil Helgeson, for his doggedly determined yet completely irreverent assistance conducting research and gathering background material from literally hundreds of sources.

· To Kara Leverte and Emily Remes, my two valiant defenders at Simon & Schuster and Fireside Books, for the integrity and conviction that made this project possible.

· To Leith Adams, Stuart Ng, and Ned Comstock from the University of Southern California, for their ever-patient, always-supportive guidance.

· And as always, to my family and friends, who somehow manage to tolerate me during the disordered, disjointed, and disarrayed endurance test that always manages to accompany the writing of my books. Thank you all!

Harlan Lebo
Los Angeles, California
February 1992

Contents

Contents

8

Foreword:
A Conversation
with Julius Epstein

"It was sheer youth and energy."

During nearly fourteen years at Warner Bros., Julius Epstein, a former press agent who came to Hollywood in 1933, wrote or adapted with his brother Philip such studio standards as *Four Daughters*, *Mr. Skeffington*, *No Time for Comedy*, *The Man Who Came to Dinner*, and *Arsenic and Old Lace*.

After Philip died in 1952, Julius continued writing, both in partnerships and independently. Among his works are *The Tender Trap*, *Kiss Them for Me*, *Tall Story*, *Send Me No Flowers*, *Pete 'n' Tillie*, *House Calls*, and *Reuben, Reuben*. Epstein was nominated for four Academy Awards; he won an Oscar, along with his brother and Howard Koch, for writing the screenplay for *Casablanca*.

—H.L.

You worked in Hollywood in the 1930s, and you now work in Hollywood in the 1990s. How do the two eras of moviemaking compare?

Working at Warner Bros. was a very friendly atmosphere during the days of the studio system. For the writers, it was a club. There were seventy to seventy-five writers at Warners—it wasn't called the motion picture *industry* for nothing. It was like an assembly line. We had a writers' building, and in the commissary, only the writers could sit at the writers' table.

But you have to realize that today it's a whole different ball game. The whole contract system is dead. In 1935, I had five released movies in my first year at Warner Bros. It goes without saying that they were all terrible, but there were five of them. Such a thing today would be impossible because in those days, we were under contract, and as soon as you finished one, they shoved another one at you.

The contract system gave you a sense of security, because doing so many pictures, if you batted .500, or even .300, you were in pretty good shape—like a ball player. Today, you more or less live or die on each picture. Instead of five in one year, you're lucky to get one every five years.

The main thing that affected our work in those days was that we were so handcuffed by censorship—remember, the nation shook when Clark Gable said "damn" in *Gone With the Wind*. For instance—this is hard to believe—when my brother and I wrote *My Foolish Heart*, the Breen office [the movie industry's own censors] said we could not show a woman getting divorced in a movie. We fought and fought and fought— threatened lawsuits and everything. Finally they said, "You can have your divorce, *but* we suggest that after the divorce that she gets hit by a truck or a car or gets killed to show that divine providence was punishing her for her divorce."

I think motion pictures today are much better, because you can say something truthful. In some cases, freedoms are being overused, but it's still preferable. You can't really compare motion pictures then and now, and you can't really compare screenwriters today to screenwriters then.

Speaking of censorship, if you go back and look at your early drafts of Casablanca *(see page 106), you and your brother tried to sneak some great material past the censors.*

Well, we tried all the time. Everybody tried, but with very little success.

I always had the feeling that if you threw enough material at them, the censors would miss something.

Yeah, if they were asleep at the switch.

Or, they would bargain down the excess and still give you what you really wanted.

I remember after a long time we could finally say "hell." But it had to be sparse use of "hell." So what we would do was write fifty "hells," and then bargain with them. We'd say "How about twenty-five?" We'd wind up with two or three.

Tell us a little bit about about the working conditions for writers who worked at Warner Bros.

Jack Warner wanted all of his writers to be at the studio from nine to five, which we all resented, so we just didn't come in nine to five. We would have been happy if they wanted to fire us, but they never did.

We'd come in for lunchtime, because the writers' table in the Warner Bros. dining room would be a lot of fun. In around 1940, Warren Duff, Seton Miller, Richard MacCauly, Norman Reilly Raine, Sig Herzig, Casey Robinson, my brother, and I—everybody was there.

It sounds like the West Coast version of the Algonquin Round Table.

Exactly. We took two or three hours for lunch. We would occasionally allow a nonwriter to join us (I can't remember ever inviting a producer to our table). We did allow Errol Flynn to join us when he had just started out, and Flynn would regale with us with his previous night's activities. . . .

After *Casablanca*, the studio tore up our contract and made us producers [on *Mr. Skeffington*], and then for a while we ate in the executive dining room. But we soon gave that up because it was pretty dull compared to the writers' table.

Did the pressures of the studio system inspire you to create good work, or were you put in the position to crank out material?

Well, the first few years, we cranked it out, as evidenced by the five movies in one year. After that, we could say, "No, we don't want to do this, we want to do that."

After we got out of Warner Bros. and went to other studios, we often suggested what we would like to do. By that time, the studio system and the contract system was on its last legs. It became a whole different world, and everybody was free-lancing.

You're one of the few people I've interviewed who worked at that time who prefers making pictures now to making pictures then.

Well, the pictures may be better now, but it was more fun to make them then.

Why?

Each studio was a family—there were a lot of people who spent their whole career at one studio. We had a studio softball league, a studio basketball league. Then, I would say about fifty writers did about 90 percent of the movies. Today, each picture has a new name, a strange name. Sometimes they go on, but many times you never hear from them again. But among the writers then, forty or fifty credits was not unusual.

Do you look back on it now and wonder how you could ever work like that?

It was sheer youth and energy—instead of a sex life, right? I devoted my energy to movies. That's where all the energy went.

* * *

If you think about Jack Warner this many years after the "golden age" of the studios. . . .

It wasn't "golden" then. Only in retrospect.

True. But what about Jack Warner comes to mind for you?

In 1973 I did a symposium for Boston University on the transition from silent to sound film. I wasn't in Hollywood during the silent days, but I didn't miss it by much. For five days there were representatives from every branch of the business. The directors were Frank Capra and Rouben Mamoulian. I was there as a writer together with Walter Reiss. Jean Arthur was there, too, and we were all at the same hotel, and they had a little bar, and a round table at the bar, and every night for five nights we sat around the bar until two or three in the morning and talked about the business.

One of the main topics was: What did the moguls have that made them successful? What did Jack Warner, Darryl Zanuck, Harry Cohn, Louis B. Mayer, and David O. Selznick have? And no one could pin it down. Most of these men were practically illiterate and uneducated. They weren't creative. But they had something.

Casablanca

12

I think what they had was tremendous desire, and showmen's instincts. They were gamblers. Today, heads of studios are lawyers, accountants, former agents—they're a different breed.

In those days, the studios could make a picture a week. Today, if a major studio makes six or seven features plus pickups, it's a gala year for them. So there's no reason for a bad picture today, because they can pick and choose and wait. When you had to make one picture a week, you shoved it into production whether it was ready or not.

Casablanca is a classic case. We didn't have a finished script, which wasn't uncommon at the time. Today, they should never go into production without a finished script because there's plenty of time.

You mentioned that the moguls were all natural showmen. Jack Warner was more of a showman than most.

Well, Warner ran a movie chain before he started making pictures, didn't he? I think Louis Mayer was an exhibitor, too. So they sort of had a sense for what the public wanted. I'm not pretending to know what they had, because Capra didn't know, Mamoulian didn't know, and Jean Arthur didn't know, either.

Did you like Warner?

Yes and no. Nobody likes the boss. Somebody summed him up in two words: affable arrogance. There's a famous saying that Warner would rather tell a bad joke than make a good movie. He certainly tried. You could always tell him if he told a bad joke, which most of his jokes were. He didn't mind. But you also had to know when to laugh.

What about Hal Wallis [the producer of Casablanca]?

He was a great executive. I'm not talking about his creative aspects, but he was a great executive to be able to manage so many pictures and to run a studio the way he did for so many years. When Wallis was there, the films usually started on time and finished on time, and that was terribly important.

I know that Casablanca *isn't your favorite work, but I hope you can still appreciate the enjoyment the film will always bring to audiences.*

Well, it's like no one can explain what the moguls had, I can't explain why *Casablanca* succeeded. First, there wasn't a word of truth in the picture. There were no Germans in Casablanca, certainly not in uniform, no letters of transit, there was nothing. And it was slapped together. For example, I don't know what would have happened if my brother and I hadn't come up with "round up the usual suspects" for the ending. And it wasn't the result of a lot of thought either; it was just one of those flashes. I don't know what the ending would have been—it would have been milk and water, I guess.

But it all worked.

There's a lot of serendipity in there.

One last question: Do you have any favorite stories about Humphrey Bogart that you'd like to share?

Bogie had a reputation of being tough, but we never found him so. Our impression was that his work was secondary to getting out on the boat on the weekend, but I'm no authority.

I just wanted to give you a chance to recollect—I've heard that everyone who was around the studio when Bogart was there has a favorite story about him.

They do? Maybe I should make up something.

The Warner Memos

"Verbal Messages Cause Misunderstanding and Delays
(Please Put Them in Writing)"

Sometimes, as historians and police will tell you, the last person to ask about how an event occurred is an eyewitness. Memories fade, opinions grow, and the decades transform reality into a vision far more attuned to how we *want* to remember than how we *should* remember.

True, personal narratives provide the life and color of history—especially in accounts of the motion picture industry—but many other guideposts still remain from the golden era of the Hollywood studios that provide a more balanced description of the events in the motion picture industry as they transpired.

These troves of material are found in the production files and correspondence from the major film studios that are now housed in university archives scattered across the country, and at the Academy of Motion Picture Arts and Sciences in Los Angeles. These files supply solid evidence—for those who are willing to take the time to look and not rely on previously published, potentially inaccurate sources—about how the tumultuous events that often surround the frantic production schedule of a motion picture actually occurred.

Among the most extensive of these records is the information found in the archives of Warner Bros. Pictures, which are housed at the University of Southern California School of Cinema-Television in Los Angeles. The Warner Bros. organization placed a high priority on written communication—at the bottom of every memo form were the words "Verbal Messages Cause Misunderstanding and Delays (Please Put Them in Writing)"—and the studio meant it. Even in an era when motion pictures were produced with the seeming ease of an industrial assembly line, each project generated thousands of pages of material: correspondence, legal paperwork, contracts, script drafts, publicity material, and, most important of all, the internal memoranda of producers, performers, and studio executives and administrators.

This treasure trove of paper—including most of the written records of the studio's operations from 1915 to 1968—provides a fascinating view of the workings of a movie studio at the height of its productivity—the victories and defeats, the anger and the enthusiasm, and the extraordinary level of creative cooperation that produced this most unusual of art forms: the motion picture of Hollywood's golden age.

These archives are accessible by anyone interested in studying Warner Bros. Pictures, including, of course, individuals who were once associated with the studio. Yet strangely enough, the memoirs written by several former Warner Bros. performers or production staff members, as well as an assortment of biographies written by others, chose to rely on recollections of events as those involved remember them rather than by examining the archives to determine how events actually occurred. In some instances, misinformation has then spread through other works, eventually creating a chain of legends that are assumed to be facts.

With that in mind, let the reader note that every statement presented here as fact about the production of *Casablanca* was confirmed in virtually all cases by using the information found in the Warner Bros. Archives. All other material was checked, whenever possible, with at least two independent sources.

Casablanca:
You Must Remember This

With the spread of World War II across Europe, thousands of
desperate refugees sought the safety of neutral Spain and Portugal, and the promise of a new life in America. But direct travel across
occupied France to Spain was often impossible; instead, many European
refugees were forced to travel a tortuous trail south through unoccupied
France, across the Mediterranean to Oran in Algeria, and then along the
northern coast of Africa to Casablanca in French Morocco. In Casablanca, refugees needed cash, political influence, or good fortune to
acquire exit visas and a trip to Lisbon, where freighters or planes to
America awaited.

Among the refugees traveling to Casablanca are Victor Laszlo, an
influential underground leader trying to escape to America to continue
his freedom fighting efforts, and his companion, Ilsa Lund. Hot on their
heels is Major Heinrich Strasser, a Gestapo officer determined to stop
Laszlo.

Along the refugee trail, two German couriers are murdered. Stolen
from the couriers are letters of transit, which can be used to provide
unchallenged movement across international borders.

In Casablanca, Richard Blaine, an American with a mysterious past
and a track record of antifascist activities, runs Rick's Café Americaine,
a gathering place for refugees. On December 2, 1941—five days before
the United States enters World War II—a black marketeer named
Ugarte comes to the café with the letters of transit, and asks Rick to hide
the papers until they can be sold. Rick hides the letters, but Ugarte is
arrested for the murder of the German couriers.

Laszlo and Ilsa arrive at Rick's café to purchase the letters only to
learn of Ugarte's arrest. Later, Rick and Ilsa "meet," but their introduction is clearly not their first encounter.

Later that night, Rick, in a hateful drunken stupor, recalls his carefree romance with Ilsa in Paris during the days before the Germans invaded France. As the Nazi advance approached the City of Lights, Ilsa agreed to escape with Rick. Instead, at the railroad station, Rick received a letter from her, telling him she could not leave Paris, and she would never see him again—breaking Rick's heart and spirit.

As Rick awakens, Ilsa returns to the café to explain why she didn't leave Paris with him. She begins to tell him of her near-worship of Laszlo, but she is so offended by Rick's anger that she leaves without explaining what happened in Paris.

The next morning, Laszlo and Ilsa meet with Captain Renault, the prefect of police, and Strasser to discuss the implications of the underground leader's presence in North Africa. The Nazi offers Laszlo exit visas in exchange for the names of the leaders of the underground. Laszlo declines.

Next, Laszlo meets with Ferrari, chief of the Casablanca underworld, while Isla explores the outdoor market. There she encounters Rick, who apologizes for his behavior of the night before. But he also says that one day she will leave Laszlo as she had once left Rick. Ilsa says that the prediction won't come true because she is married to Laszlo, and had been, even during her romance with Rick in Paris.

Ilsa joins Laszlo in the Blue Parrot, where Ferrari tells the couple that he cannot supply them with visas; instead, he recommends that they negotiate with Rick, since Ferrari suspects he possesses the letters of transit.

That night in the café office, Laszlo asks Rick for the letters of transit. Rick refuses, and tells Laszlo that his wife knows the reason. Laszlo returns to the café and responds to Strasser and his men singing "Watch on the Rhine" by leading the other patrons in an overpowering rendition of "La Marseillaise." Angered by the outburst, Strasser orders Renault to close the café; as the Nazi departs, he warns Ilsa that Laszlo's options are limited: return to occupied France, imprisonment in a concentration camp, or death.

Later that night, while Laszlo attends a meeting of the underground, Ilsa returns to the café to ask Rick for the letters of transit. Ilsa begs, Rick refuses; she threatens him with a pistol, and he moves closer to make her aim easier. Finally, Ilsa breaks down and confesses her continuing love for Rick. She tells him that during their Paris affair she had thought Laszlo was dead, and only the discovery that he was still alive prevented her from leaving the city with Rick.

Ilsa asks Rick to give Laszlo the letters of transit so he can go on to America alone. Rick points out that if the deeply devoted Laszlo left without his wife, he would lack the driving force he needed to continue his work. Ilsa asks Rick to plan for all of them, and he agrees, just as

Laszlo and Carl, the café's head waiter, return to the café after barely escaping arrest at their meeting.

While bandaging a wound, Laszlo tells Rick that he knows about the Paris affair, and asks that if Rick won't give up the letters of transit, then he should use them to take Ilsa to safety. Before Rick can reply, the police break into the café and arrest Laszlo.

The next morning, Rick plots with Renault to implicate Laszlo in the murder of the couriers, and as part of the "plan" Laszlo is released. That night, Laszlo and Ilsa arrive at the café, and as Rick gives them the letters, Renault arrests the couple. But Rick's plan is a trick; he holds Renault at gunpoint, and orders him to call the airport to clear the way. Instead of notifying the airport, Renault calls Strasser and warns him of Laszlo's impending escape.

At the airport, Rick orders Renault to complete the letters of transit by filling in the names of Mr. and Mrs. Victor Laszlo. Ilsa, expecting to stay with Rick, is shocked, but Rick explains that she is the driving force in Laszlo's life, and their personal problems are unimportant compared to the bigger issues of the world at war. Sadly, Ilsa agrees to leave, but acknowledges that they had revived the everlasting memories of their Paris romance.

As the plane carrying Laszlo and Ilsa taxis down the runway, Strasser arrives and tries to stop the escape by calling the radio tower. Rick orders the Nazi to stop; Strasser shoots at Rick and misses. Rick returns the fire and kills Strasser moments before other police arrive.

Inspired by Rick's newfound patriotism, Renault protects Rick by ordering his men to arrest other suspects. As the plane carrying Laszlo and Ilsa flies toward freedom, Renault and Rick walk off together, planning their own departure from Casablanca and a return to the fight.

o n e

"Whose Name Is
on the Front of
the Building?"

*C*asablanca was born of an era—the epoch of Franklin Roosevelt, big band music, and the *Saturday Evening Post*, of cars that were streamlined and Dodgers that played in Brooklyn. Those years that ended the 1930s and tipped slightly into the 1940s, when the Great Depression was still a recent memory and the nuclear age was a part of the unfathomable future, marked a simpler time in America—or so the distance of passing decades has made it seem—a period jarred from complacency by the smoldering wreckage and raging fires that cast a forbidding glow over the Pacific on the first Sunday in December of 1941.

Part of that era—indeed one of the creators of it—was the Hollywood studio system, the term of convenience that described the formidable collection of motion picture studios scattered across Los Angeles and then humming at their peak. In the unlikely context of the make-believe world of Hollywood confronting its first day immersed in a real-life war, *Casablanca*—a movie set in war but telling a story about ideals loftier than any conflict—was born.

In December 1941, *Casablanca* wasn't yet called *Casablanca;* on December 8, the day after the "date which will live in infamy," it was merely an unproduced play called *Everybody Comes to Rick's* that had been shipped to Hollywood—one proposed script among thousands reviewed by the studios in the harsh winnowing that separated the kernel of a marketable story from the chaff of ideas that arrived by the carload.

While the nation settled down to the grim business of waging war, the home front—and after one day at war, Americans were already learning to call it the home front—geared up for the conflict ahead, but also tried to sustain the normal pace of life. Hollywood was no exception. The motion picture industry would soon be immersed in the creation of war-related features, documentaries, propaganda, and training films designed to aid the defense effort. But war or no war, the Hollywood studios had their own battle to fight: feeding the endless demand of film production and distribution that in only a few years had transformed a sleepy resort and farming town into a bustling industrial center and home of the eighth-largest business in the United States.

The story of how an untested theatrical script became one of the most beloved films of all time begins with an understanding of the rise of Warner Bros. Pictures during the golden age of the Hollywood studio. For without the distinctive style that stamped Warner productions of the 1930s and 1940s—each created with the careful meshing of personalities chosen from a versatile stable of stars, fast-paced directors, and iron-handed producers, all lorded over by a nefarious chief executive—*Casablanca* would not exist. *Casablanca* is the brightest product of Hollywood's most dynamic studio at its fruitful peak; the history books often pigeonhole a motion picture as a "director's film," or a "producer's film," or an "actors' film." *Casablanca* is—primarily for better but a little for worse—a studio's film.

The evolution of Warner Bros. Pictures into a formidable filmmaking power was not unlike the path followed by the other Hollywood studios: the result of fortuitous timing, forceful personalities, and plain old-fashioned good luck. Born out of a film-exhibiting company founded by four of the brothers Warner—Harry, Albert, Sam, and Jack—Warner Bros. Pictures developed when the ambitious siblings realized that the big money in movies came not from merely projecting films on screen but rather from creating and distributing them.

The Warners produced films sporadically throughout the late 1910s, first in New York and then in Los Angeles. On the West Coast, they struggled through the early years of the 1920s, slowly and carefully building the foundation of a moviemaking empire by producing films, acquiring theaters, and shaping a distribution system of theaters across the country. Each brother developed a distinct role in the family operation: Harry emerged as the somber financial wizard who directed the

The mammoth studios of Warner Bros. Pictures as it appeared in the late 1930s—part "country club" and part "Alcatraz."

company's financial operations, first in New York and later in Los Angeles. Albert ran the theater chains and other distribution-related issues. Sam, the innovator, worked on the filmmaking side and tinkered with the technology of making movies. Jack, the flashy, temperamental showman, operated the studio in Los Angeles.

The great Hollywood studios can point to junctures that marked their evolution into cinematic giants; for Warner Bros., that turning point was hiring a dog. In 1923 the Warners produced a film starring Rin-Tin-Tin, a German shepherd found in a World War I trench. The dog became the studio's first box-office smash, and his appearance in nineteen films helped the studio thrive during the mid-1920s.

The success of these films was partly responsible for attracting to the fledgling company influential investors from West Coast banks as well as East Coast financiers; the counsel provided by the moneymen showed Harry Warner how to diversify the organization into a colossus of the entertainment industry.

"By 1928," *Fortune* magazine wrote of the Warners, "they were a $16,000,000 corporation. Within two years, they were to be a $230,000,000 corporation. There has never been anything quite like that, even in the movie industry."

Jack Warner, always on the lookout for young talent, had buttressed his own studio leadership by recruiting two handpicked aides. Darryl Zanuck and Hal Wallis both came to Warner Bros. as filmmaking novices in 1923, yet each would have a lasting impact on the motion picture industry—both at Warner Bros. and elsewhere in Hollywood.

Zanuck, hired at age twenty to write scenarios for the Rin-Tin-Tin films, rose with lightning speed through the Warner ranks. By age twenty-six he was named studio manager, and the next year became Warner's chief of production. Wallis, recruited to the studio as a twenty-four-year-old manager of the Garrick Theater in downtown Los Angeles, came into the Warner fold through an assistant's job in the publicity department. By 1928 he managed Warner's First National Studios.

The year before Wallis took over the reins at First National, the arrival of sound brought Warner Bros. into the limelight as a potent Hollywood force. The studio bet its financial future on the technology of synchronizing sound with pictures; the result, *The Jazz Singer* in 1927, took audiences by storm and started the studio on a creative course that would position it among the leaders of the golden age of the Hollywood studios.

The brothers Warner in the mid-1920s. The brother with the flashing smile second from the left is Jack; Harry is on the far left. Sam second from the right, and Albert (Abe) on the far right. Sam, the mastermind behind the studio's work in film with sound, didn't survive to see his family's company lead the industry into the sound era.

In 1930, Warner Bros. Pictures merged operations with First National, and Jack Warner named Zanuck to lead both. But continuing squabbles with Warner, which peaked with a salary dispute, forced Zanuck out in 1933—and into the waiting arms of 20th Century-Fox. With Zanuck gone, Wallis was elevated to the head of all Warner filmmaking.

Wallis would later become a versatile and durable independent producer whose filmmaking career spanned six decades. (In 1941, exhausted after years at the helm, he began a new phase in his career by stepping down as chief of all Warner production, and instead served as the studio's lead in-house "independent" producer, with first choice of projects and talent on the lot. Despite a complete transformation of the studio era he had helped to create in the 1920s and 1930s, Wallis outlasted the changes and continued to produce durable hits for several studios into the 1970s.)

In 1933, as the driving force second only to Jack Warner at the studio, Wallis shepherded Warner Bros. into a period of productivity unique in the history of motion pictures, releasing scores of films that would be remembered as some of the classics of the era: costume adventures (*Captain Blood, The Adventures of Robin Hood, The Sea Hawk*), action-packed crime pictures (*The Roaring Twenties, Angels with Dirty Faces*), high-powered drama (*Dark Victory, Anthony Adverse, Confessions of a Nazi Spy*), and lavish musicals (*42nd Street, Footlight Parade*).

Warner Bros. could be bold at one extreme—the studio faced head-on the taboo subject of syphilis in *Dr. Erlich's Magic Bullet*—and brassy at the other, such as its star-studded version of *A Midsummer Night's Dream* with Mickey Rooney as Puck and James Cagney as Bottom. Where other studios might be noted for "sophistication" or "polish," the watchwords at Warner Bros. were "action," "fast-paced," "innovative," and "hard-hitting." Jack Warner had another phrase for it: The three most important words that described his motion pictures, the studio chief said, were "entertainment, entertainment, entertainment."

But the creative furor on the West Coast could never conceal that the driving force behind the studio's production were the financiers in the east, and their unending drive to cut costs and boost profits.

"A picture, after all, is just an expensive dream," said the normally stone-faced Harry Warner, who amused studio insiders when caught smiling for a photo in a business magazine—and appeared happy only because he was talking about profits. "Well, it's just as easy to dream for $700,000 as for $1.5 million."

To perform in Warner productions, the studio assembled an acting corps of talented and charismatic stars; such legends as Bette Davis, James Cagney, Edward G. Robinson, Errol Flynn, Olivia De Havilland, Ann Sheridan, John Garfield, and Paul Muni were among more than a hundred actors under contract—all top-flight leading players and versatile character performers who, as Warner liked to say, "made up the brightest constellation of stars in the sky." Warner stars were not always stylish leading men or classic Hollywood beauties; rather, they possessed the more valuable commodities of personality, character appeal, and raw screen presence.

Lording over all on the lot was Jack Warner—aggressive, explosive, charming, irritating, egomaniacal, emotional—always scheming to push the studio forward into new filmmaking adventures, and cajoling his stars and staff to excel in the whirlwind of motion picture production. Warner was a charming dictator known as much for shrewd studio leadership as for petty despotism. Milton Sperling, Warner's own nephew, described him as "fundamentally self-centered, an endearing personality—treacherous, hedonistic, and a tyrant."

But Warner could also be genuinely captivating, a natural ham who sang on studio-owned KFWB radio under the stage name Leon Zuardo, and was brash enough to look out upon a dinner audience of Chinese dignitaries visiting the studio and say, "Holy cow, this reminds me that I forgot to pick up my laundry." The nemesis of money-hungry stars—he called top studio star Bette Davis "an explosive little broad with a sharp left"—the enemy of every agent, a man with a quick temper and a penchant for shooting from the hip, Warner could kill an argument in an instant—and often did—with the discussion-closing question, "Whose name is on the front of the building?"

Recalled Errol Flynn of the studio chief in 1959, "Outside his office Jack Warner has an endearing sense of humor and can out-comic most of the comedians I know. I stress *outside*, because inside his office you are confronted with all the ruthlessness of business in Hollywood. That's Jack."

While Warner probably never completely understood the full impact of his personality on his stars and staff, he didn't apologize for his actions either. Noting that Bette Davis once said, "I do not regret one professional enemy I have made," Warner countered by saying, "I have made many enemies in my time, but I am not sure I want to use the word *regret*. I am what I am, and I will probably never change. I would not kid myself by saying that everyone likes me, or everyone hates me. But I do say: Such is life in a big city."

Warner fostered an environment of frenzied productivity on the lot: a six-day work week where writers were expected to clock in at 9:00 A.M. and punch out at 5:00 P.M. (and sometimes the studio chief himself would check their comings and goings); film crews often worked fourteen-hour days; and even the top Warner stars were immersed in the grind of shooting four to eight films each year—sometimes appearing in more than one production at a time.

In Warner Bros.' heyday, the studio was as vigorous and creative as it was frustrating and exhausting; the lot was called "Alcatraz" by some, and "a country club" by as many others; "machine-belt" or "haven," "factory" or "family"—all were terms used by Warner insiders to describe the studio.

Despite Warner's strict studio leadership and personality quirks, he left a rich legacy unlike any other in Hollywood history—some 570 films during the 1930s alone. Many have tried to capture the essence of Warner and the key to his success as sovereign ruler over Hollywood's most dynamic studio; perhaps the best description of Warner's triumphs came from Wallis, who owed the start of his career to the studio chief but departed in a storm of controversy after more than twenty years on the lot. "Jack was a showman who played his hunches," Wallis said. "I never saw him read a script, let alone a book. Just from glancing at

Jack Warner—his own nephew called him "an endearing personality—treacherous, hedonistic, and a tyrant."

a title or riffling through a few pages, he could sense whether a property would interest millions of people all over the world. He was usually right."

It was in Jack Warner's caldron of creativity—part energetic colony of actors and artisans, part frantic production mill—that was Warner Bros. Pictures in December 1941. In this turbulent setting, as a fearful but determined nation faced the prospect of global conflict, the spark of an idea that would soon become *Casablanca* arrived at the studio.

Casablanca began the long journey into production as the brainchild of Murray Burnett, a New York City high school teacher who dabbled in writing for the stage. While visiting Europe in 1938 while the Nazi advance spread through Austria, Burnett and his wife witnessed first-hand the terrifying menace that only a year later would plunge the world headlong into war. One issue in particular moved Burnett: the plight of the thousands of refugees desperately trying to flee the Nazi threat.

On the same trip, the Burnetts visited France. In a café near the Mediterranean called La Belle Aurore, they listened to a black pianist entertain a colorful crowd of patrons. Included among the customers were refugees from countries across Europe, all en route to Casablanca in French Morocco, one of the principal escape routes to freedom.

After returning to America, and inspired by the memories of Europe on the brink of war, Burnett decided to write a play based in part on his observations; in 1940 he teamed with Joan Alison, a socialite, heiress, and occasional playwright, to create the first draft of a three-act play called *Everybody Comes to Rick's*.

The Burnett-Alison play contains many of the same story lines and characters (although some with different names) that would become so familiar in *Casablanca*. Rick Blaine, an apolitical man of mystery, operates a café in Casablanca (in the play, all of the action occurs in the café). Rick's true background is known only by Rinaldo, the French prefect of police: Rick was a lawyer in Paris; after a passionate affair in 1939 he deserted his wife and children and disappeared.

A black market operative named Ugarte asks Rick to hide two letters of transit until he can sell them later in the evening. The prospective buyer is Victor Laszlo, a wealthy Czechoslovakian who is fleeing a Gestapo agent named Strasser. Rick agrees to hold the letters, but Ugarte is arrested just as Laszlo arrives at the café with a companion, a beautiful American named Lois Meredith—Rick's paramour from two years before.

Strasser meets with Laszlo at the café and threatens that unless he transfers his fortune in foreign banks to Nazi Germany, Laszlo will die. Laszlo refuses. Later that night, Sam, the café's entertainer and Rick's close friend, tries to convince Rick to avoid a renewed encounter with Lois. Rick ignores the advice, and when Lois returns to the café, she sleeps with Rick.

The next morning, Lois explains that although she loves Rick, she also admires Laszlo. Lois begs Rick to help Laszlo escape, and Rick agrees. But Rinaldo convinces Rick that Lois plans to deceive him, so Rick harshly rejects her.

That night, Laszlo and Lois return to the café to meet with Ugarte and buy the letters of transit, only to discover through Rinaldo that Ugarte has "killed himself." Rick, who has begun to drink, meets Jan and Annina, two recently married refugees escaping Bulgaria. After Annina tells Rick that she will trade her virtue to Rinaldo for exit visas, he gets a sense of how Lois wanted to help Laszlo. To prevent Annina from succumbing to Rinaldo, Rick hides the newlyweds, and an angry Rinaldo closes the café.

The following day, Sam buys tickets for Jan and Annina to fly to Lisbon. Lois arrives at the café and tells Rick that she plans to leave Laszlo and stay with him. She agrees to help Jan and Annina escape. As part of the escape plan, Rick lures Rinaldo to the café. He offers the police chief a trade: Rick will trap Laszlo, in possession of a letter of transit, if Jan and Annina can use the other to escape. Rinaldo accepts the plan, and Jan and Annina leave for Lisbon. Rick contacts Laszlo, who arrives at the café to get the letter. When Rinaldo starts to arrest Laszlo, Rick stops him by holding a gun on him. Rick persuades Lois to leave with Laszlo, even though their escape will probably cost the café owner his life. Lois begs to stay, but Rick refuses to let her. After Laszlo and Lois depart, Rick surrenders to Rinaldo and Strasser.

Everybody Comes to Rick's was optioned by Broadway producers Martin Gabel and Carly Wharton. But the play went nowhere; Gabel and Wharton believed that the script needed substantial rewriting before it could be produced—in particular by changing the plot point of Lois sleeping with Rick as part of her plan to obtain visas. Instead, Burnett and Alison looked to Hollywood (even though the writers knew that the issue of Rick and Lois sleeping together would fare no better under the watchful gaze of the studio censors). Burnett and Alison withdrew *Everybody Comes to Rick's* from consideration as a theatrical production, and instead distributed the script to several motion picture studios.

Late in 1941, *Everybody Comes to Rick's* found its way to the New York office of Warner Bros., which forwarded the script to the story office at the studios in Burbank. There on December 8, it was assigned to story analyst Steven Karnot; his analysis and recommendations gave the material its first test.

Karnot was sufficiently impressed with the romance and intrigue in *Everybody Comes to Rick's* to write a lavish recommendation and story synopsis for Hal Wallis to review. Karnot described the story in a staccato burst of descriptive words in his memo to Wallis: "Excellent melodrama. Colorful, timely background, tense mood, suspense, psychological and physical conflict, tight plotting, sophisticated hokum." Always on the lookout for material for the studio's top stars, Karnot described the Burnett-Alison script as "a box office natural—for Bogart, or Cagney, or Raft in out-of-the-usual roles and perhaps Mary Astor."

Decades after he left Warner Bros., Wallis would call *Casablanca* "the most famous picture I ever made, and a legend that has lasted until this day." But in the same breath, and after a half century in the film business supervising or personally producing more than four hundred movies, Wallis also remembered the picture as "my toughest assignment." In the last month of 1941 and the early weeks of 1942, that appraisal must have seemed an understatement.

Wallis and his crew would soon face a mountain of obstacles: casting an all-star production, writing an acceptable version of the script, and, in general, juggling the increasingly formidable problems of creating a film during America's all-involving war. But in December 1941, Wallis faced only a simple question: whether or not he should pursue a film project based on an untested theatrical script that had never seen the footlights of Broadway.

T W O

"A Very Obvious Imitation
of Grand Hotel"

It may be said that the journey that led to the creation of Warner Bros.' greatest triumph began in the wake of swelling war clouds, cutthroat business decisions, and the landslide success of the film story about a backwoods pacifist turned national hero.

Perhaps more than any other studio in Hollywood, Warner Bros. Pictures was uniquely qualified to bring the stories and drama of World War II into the theaters of America. Although all of the Hollywood studios had produced pictures about war in historical settings since the dawn of the moving picture, Warners—ever the filmmaking trend-setter and the studio most capable of moving quickly into new ventures—brought to the screen the first major movie that illuminated the spreading menace that plagued the world in the late 1930s. The studio's 1939 production of *Confessions of a Nazi Spy*, with Edward G. Robinson portraying an FBI agent who uncovers Nazi operations in the United States, brought American audiences their initial taste of the Axis advance.

In fact, *Confessions of a Nazi Spy*, produced in strictest secrecy on the Warner lot and ballyhooed as a massive exposé, delivered little more than a fairly standard crime plot intertwined with villains who happened to be Nazis. However, the massive publicity campaign that accompanied the release of the film did much to boost American interest in the problems bubbling overseas.

The Warners had reasons both personal and professional to decry the Nazi threat. Harry and Jack Warner were both vocal Nazi haters and understood the growing danger of the earliest days of the Hitler regime. Those feelings were magnified considerably when the head of the studio's office in Germany was beaten to death by brownshirts in Berlin. During production of *Confessions of a Nazi Spy*, Jack Warner and his wife received death threats, including one written warning that included a floor plan of his house. A Warner theater was damaged by anti-Semitic vandalism, and the studio itself had been scarred with pro-Nazi slogans painted on the walls of stage buildings.

When the movie industry was threatened by isolationists in Washington who accused filmmakers of warmongering, it was Harry Warner who went to Capitol Hill and blasted Senate hearings with an eloquent defense of the studios—and then capped his scorching comments with an invitation for the entire Congress to attend the premiere of *One Foot in Heaven* a few days later.

But the Warners' interest in war films transcended personal conviction, even beliefs as well-founded as the brothers' contempt for Adolf Hitler. Dollars and cents were the paramount issue at the studio, and making movies with war-related themes simply made good sense. Warners earned a well-deserved reputation for leading the industry in new directions—the *Hollywood Reporter* once said the studio was "long known throughout the industry and the world as the bellwether in the motion picture field in expounding the American creed of life." Warner Bros.' tradition of fast-paced, action-oriented pictures had already served the public well in times of peace; throughout 1941, with most of the world already at war, Warners produced some of the industry's best action-oriented pictures with military themes, months before the United States entered the conflict.

When, in July 1941, Warners screened eight new films at its annual sales convention for its exhibitors, four of the eight were war-related: *Navy Blues*, *The Flight Patrol*, *Dive Bomber*, and the most important of all war pictures to date, *Sergeant York*. No picture better proved the studio's belief in the financial good sense of making war pictures than the summer 1941 release of the adventures of Sgt. Alvin York, starring Gary Cooper in an Oscar-winning role. The Howard Hawks–directed story of the World War I Medal of Honor winner took the filmgoing public by storm, and helped set Warners on a financial and creative course that would give the studio the direction it needed to produce a new generation of motion pictures, including *Casablanca*.

Sergeant York became the biggest money-maker in the studio's history up to that time; with more than $6 million in profits, it would be surpassed by only one other picture—*This Is the Army*—through the 1940s, and wouldn't be touched by any other film until *A Star Is Born* and *The High and the Mighty* reached the same plateau in 1954. (When *Sergeant York* became the studio's most profitable film, it passed *The Fighting 69th*—another war picture—to take the top spot.) At a time when the United States was the sole lifeline to countries fighting a losing battle against the Axis, the picture also shifted views among many Americans about isolationism—much to the anger of many on Capitol Hill.

But *Sergeant York* meant far more to Warner Bros. than money in the cash register; the success of the picture provided the final evidence that Warner needed in 1941 to justify his shift into a fresh direction of filmmaking. The studio's interest in both action and war pictures would soon move into a new era, and again Warner Bros. would lead filmmakers in a change of philosophy that would alter the motion picture industry forever. In October, Jack Warner abruptly killed the studio's production of "B" pictures, the low-budget productions designed for double-bills, and thus eliminated an entire production unit on the lot that had created more than a dozen pictures a year. Instead, the studio shifted its efforts into a production schedule that stressed a smaller number of productions each year, virtually all designed to be high-quality and high-budget pictures.

Warner's reason for the change was simple: With its corps of top-flight stars and a huge backlog of producible stories, the studio had far more to gain by producing fewer pictures that generated bigger returns than by relying on dozens of lower-cost pictures that each turned a small profit. (An even more dramatic version of the same philosophy dominates Hollywood today, where some studios rely on one or two blockbusters released during the summer or at Christmas to generate most of the year's earnings, and offset losses by many other films.)

Although Warners would continue to make some lower-cost pictures and would offer a select number of double features, the studio's announcement would abruptly slash the routine production of low-end films (within a few years, most of the other studios would follow suit).

Hand-in-hand with the death knell of the "Bs," the studio also announced plans to move even more deeply into production of top-of-the-line features. "*Sergeant York* has set the pace for the coming year, not only for us but for the entire motion picture industry," said Gradwell Sears, the studio's sales manager.

It was no wonder that Warners chose to jettison the "B" picture and move the studio's production to a higher plane. In the summer of 1941, the studio was looking forward to some of the most exciting and dynamic films it had ever produced. Upcoming from Warners was the Frank Capra–directed version of the Broadway smash play *Arsenic and Old Lace*, with an all-star cast topped by Cary Grant; *They Died with Their*

Boots On, starring box-office magnet Errol Flynn as George Armstrong Custer; *The Maltese Falcon*, with an emerging star named Humphrey Bogart playing a hard-nosed detective; *Yankee Doodle Dandy*, the blockbuster story of composer George M. Cohan that would win James Cagney his only Oscar; and nearly two dozen other top-flight hits either ready for release or soon to be completed. Clearly, Warners had a line-up to envy, and a future that seemed very bright.

Of course, in the summer of 1941, none of these plans involved *Casablanca;* when Warners planned its production schedule for 1942, the studio's first knowledge of the project was still months away. Considering the high-powered production schedule the studio had already planned, it remains a minor miracle that *Casablanca* was appraised, purchased, and shifted into production at such a rapid rate. Only the involvement of an executive with the power and influence of Hal Wallis—the former second-in-command on the lot who had the power as an autonomous producer to choose his own projects and ramrod them into production—could have penetrated the Warner schedule with a new project, especially when the line-up was already crammed with heavy hitters.

However, even if *Casablanca* had been brought along at a somewhat less frenetic pace without the backing of Wallis, the film probably would have fit into the studio's schedule. (However, had *Casablanca* been produced at a later date, the picture would not have been ready to release in November 1942, when it burst upon the scene with an incredible stroke of luck and timing.) As Jack Warner vividly demonstrated by killing the "B" picture and boosting production of "A" features, the studio was clearly looking to make bigger and better pictures—especially films that could showcase the top talent on the lot in dynamic settings, preferably with war-related themes, romance, and a little action thrown in for good measure. Wallis probably would have been mildly intrigued by *Everybody Comes to Rick's* under any circumstances during his years as chief of production at the studio; however, by the time the Burnett-Alison script arrived, the play featured precisely the sort of story that the studio's newly designated lead producer was seeking.

Throughout 1941, the entire motion picture industry beyond Warner Bros. had reason to be enthusiastic as well. In an era when the summertime was considered an off-season for the movie business—a far cry from today—ticket sales through the summer had skyrocketed. "The year 1941 will be remembered as the year in which the nation's motion picture theaters kicked into a cocked hat the producers and distributors' old alibi, 'We must save our big pictures for Fall,' " cried the *Hollywood Reporter*.

For the movie business, the stampede started with the Fourth of July business and didn't stop for the rest of the year. Profits in some of the theater chains actually ran double the earnings of the hot months of 1940. The Census Department reported that the United States had one theater for every 8,700 people—some 15,115 theaters generated $670 million in revenue in 1940. Motion pictures were the biggest money makers in the amusement field, and they were growing even bigger. Although ticket sales would fall slightly during the first weeks of the war, and earnings would slide temporarily with the final closing of most markets overseas (including the entire Pacific region), the film studios would remain hale and hearty throughout World War II. In fact, in the fall of 1941, one of the few threats to the industry's success came from the growing popularity of that peril of theater owners, gin rummy.

"Gin rummy has captivated many of the picture addicts who formerly rushed from their dinner table to the box office, but now shove the dishes aside, grab a deck of cards, and deal out the game," wrote a film industry analyst. Theater owners added the card game to their list of dreaded competition, along with radio, bowling, miniature golf, dog races, and night baseball. After years of concerns in the motion picture business caused by the depression and the shadow of war spreading across the globe, the specter of gin rummy must have seemed a welcome change.

Behind the Scenes

33

By the time the war exploded on the United States, Warner Bros. and most of the other studios were ready for the fight. For months, Warners had done its part to support the nation's growing defense program (a phrase that would be changed to "war effort" beginning December 7). The company's theater chains donated idle scenery and backstage equipment once used in their stage programs to army camps for their camp shows. Before the school year began in September 1941, New York City school authorities arranged with Warners to book the studio's two-reel Technicolor national defense and historical shorts in the curriculum of the New York public schools. The pictures were shown to 1.5 million pupils in New York's nine hundred public schools, and included such patriotic titles as *Service with the Colors*, *Meet the Fleet*, *March on Marines*, *Here Comes the Cavalry*, *Wings of Steel*, *Young America Flies*, *Teddy the Rough Rider*, *The Bill of Rights*, *The Declaration of Independence*, and *The Man Without a Country*. The same films were also made available for free bookings across the nation under sponsorship of the Veterans of Foreign Wars.

The *Warner Club News*, the employees' monthly newspaper, featured notes about the growing number of studio employees who had been drafted or enlisted (the staff voted to give a watch to each new soldier or sailor). The paper featured a column called "Serving with the Colors"; the column grew longer and longer each month as hundreds of studio staff departed for armed service. A huge bronze plaque honoring all Warner servicemen was installed under the flagpole in front of the

ALL THE NEWS ALL THE TIME

LARGEST HOME-DELIVERED CIRCULATION
LARGEST ADVERTISING VOLUME

MAdison 2345
The Times Telephone Number

Los Angeles Times

EQUAL RIGHTS — LIBERTY UNDER THE LAW — TRUE INDUSTRIAL FREEDOM

IN THREE PARTS — 36 PAGES

Part I — GENERAL NEWS — 18 Pages

TIMES OFFICE
202 West First Street

VOL. LXI — CC — TUESDAY MORNING, FEBRUARY 24, 1942. — DAILY, FIVE CENTS

SUBMARINE SHELLS SOUTHLAND OIL FIELD

Noble Pleads Jap Case at Hearing Here

Attack on Pearl Harbor Justified, He Says at Un-American Acts Inquiry

Inured to shocking testimony by months of hearings on un-American activities, the Assembly investigating committee at its hearing in the State Building yesterday was all but floored when they heard from the lips of Robert Noble, founder and leader of the Friends of Progress, a declaration that he thought that in their attack on Pearl Harbor "the Japanese did the proper thing under the exigencies of the time."

Prior to that the committee had wrung from Noble the admission that he had received a dishonorable discharge from the United States Navy after he ran away and had been arrested for desertion.

DESERTION EXPLAINED

He shrugged it off, however, with an explanation that he then was only 18, was ill and, anyway, he did not want to fight against the Germans in the first World War. He was really a pacifist then, he said.

Another statement credited to Noble by an earlier witness was that Gen. MacArthur and his men were "not heroes but fools."

PRESIDENT "TRIED"

Noble later denied a statement credited to him in which he urged people not to buy Defense Bonds or Stamps. He said it would have been foolish for him to have done so because it would not have done any good. Asked if he had purchased any himself, he said he had not.

Ellis O. Jones, a codirector with Noble in the Friends of Progress meetings, held weekly in a downtown hotel auditorium, admitted that the organization had conducted a mock trial of President Roosevelt on charges of being "traitorous to the American people and had gotten them into war." Jones acted as "chief justice" and at the conclusion of

Turn to Page 13, Column 3

President Pledges to Take Offensive

Roosevelt Assures Nation Pacific Fleet Intact and Engaging Foe; Promises Destruction of Jap Militarism

BY KYLE PALMER
Times Staff Representative

WASHINGTON, Feb. 23.—On a rugged note of confidence, with a certain promise that the nation's enemies soon will be on the defensive, in a pledge to victory that held no proviso or reservation, President Roosevelt tonight gave his answer to critics of his administration and told the American people what they must face in the way of sacrifice and service before the war is won.

Speaking from the White House to a radio audience that listened throughout the world and encompassed the vast spread of oceans and continents which he discussed, the President analyzed the war strategy of friend and foe, told of the mighty preparations that are being made for victory, and spiked many of the false rumors which are being circulated about our war efforts and losses.

Turn to Page 6, Part I, for full text of President Roosevelt's talk.

LOSSES SUFFERED

Reiterating a pledge he made to the people on Dec. 9, in which he said the government would keep the public informed of events, good or bad, Mr. Roosevelt said on their part the people must have confidence that the government will keep nothing from them which can be published without aiding the enemy.

We have suffered and will continue to suffer losses in the Atlantic and in the Pacific, Mr. Roosevelt said, but, he added:

"Speaking for the United States of America, let me say once and for all to the people of the world: We Americans have been compelled to yield ground, but we will regain it. We and the other United Nations are committed to the destruction of the militarism of Japan and Germany.

STRENGTH INCREASING

"We are daily increasing our strength. Soon we, and not our enemies, will have the offensive; we, not they, will win the final battles, and we, not they, will make the final peace."

Germany, Italy and Japan, he pointed out, "are very close to their maximum output of planes, guns, tanks and ships," while "the United Nations are not—es-

Turn to Page 5, Column 1

Desperate Stand Taken in Burma

Last Line of Defense Before Rangoon Pounded With Terrific Intensity

LONDON, Feb. 23. (U.P.)—Burma's defenders are making a desperate stand east of the Bilin River, last defense barrier before Rangoon, but the Japanese are pressing their attacks with "utmost intensity" and are aided by reinforcements fresh from the conquest of Singapore, Far East advices said today.

CLAIM NEW LANDINGS

(Vichy and Rome radio reports said that Japanese reinforcements had landed on the west coast of the Gulf of Martaban, south of Rangoon. If true, the troops could have come by sea from Singapore through Malacca Strait and Martaban Gulf and would be in position to flank Rangoon by driving up one or more mouths of the Irrawaddy River.)

(Chungking advices said Saturday that a large Japanese convoy had been observed steaming up the gulf.)

(An American Volunteer Group officer told United Press Correspondent Karl Eskelund at A.V.G. headquarters in Southwest China that telegraphic communication with Rangoon had been cut and that fall of the city was a matter of days.)

R.A.F. REPORT

The All-India Radio heard an R.A.F. communique broadcast from Rangoon today saying that the military situation was unchanged but that violent fighting continued between the Bilin and

Turn to Page 2, Column 7

Japs on Bali Shut Off From Fleet

Enemy Ships Smashed by Bomber Assaults; Drive Deeper Into Burma

Times Pacific War Summary

Three Japanese columns, reinforced by divisions released by the fall of Singapore, were driving deeper into British Burma yesterday but in the Netherlands Indies the Nipponese appeared to have been stopped, for the moment at least, on their partly won bases off the eastern and western ends of Java.

Batavia said that planes and warships of the United Nations had smashed a Japanese invasion fleet which landed troops on Bali, off the tip of Eastern Java, and Washington reinforced this by announcing that the United States Army Air Force in the Netherlands Indies since Jan. 1 has sunk at least 9 enemy vessels and damaged 24 others. The Bali invaders were cut off by the Jap fleet losses.

It was admitted, however, that the Japanese held the important Denpasar Airdrome and other strategic points on Bali and that their conquest of Southeastern Sumatra is virtually complete.

The situation in the Far East yesterday as summarized from United Press and Associated Press dispatches was:

EAST INDIES—It seemed certain that the Japanese invasion fleet suffered heavily. Estimates ranged from 5 to 15 Jap ships were sunk, most of them victims of airplanes. The Japanese apparently captured the Denpasar Airdrome in good condition since the communique said that American planes bombed it yesterday, damaging the runways and field.

BURMA—London admitted the prospects in Burma were gloomy but it was asserted that combined forces of Indian, British and American-volunteer fighter planes had established air superiority over the battle front, which apparently was along the Sittang River, just west of the vital Rangoon-Lashio Railway.

PHILIPPINES—There was little change in the situation on the Bataan Peninsula where Gen. Douglas MacArthur's durable Filipino and American troops again had fought the Japanese to a standstill.

Japanese Make Direct Hit North of Santa Barbara

No Lives Lost and Little Damage Inflicted by First Enemy Assault on Soil of United States Since War Started in December; Witnesses Declare Submersible Fired 16 Shots From Mile Offshore

In the first attack upon United States soil since this war began, an enemy submarine rose out of the sea off the rich oil fields at Ellwood, 12 miles north of Santa Barbara, shortly after 7 p.m. yesterday and pumped 16 shells into the tidewater fields, but caused only superficial damage.

A single oil well derrick was reported by eyewitnesses to have been hit, but there were no casualties in human life.

Choosing the dramatic instant of the halfway mark in President Roosevelt's fireside chat, the commander of the presumably Japanese submarine opened fire from his deck guns at 7:15 p.m.

Three of the shells dug up the sands off the Bankline Oil Co. refinery. The only damage in the raid was the destruction of rigging and pumping equipment of a well about a quarter of a mile from the beach. Loss was estimated at several thousand dollars.

NAVY BEGINS HUNT FOR SUB

One of the shells whistled three miles inland to the Tecolote ranch where it exploded. Another missile gouged out a five-foot-wide crater on the Staniff ranch near by. The other salvos fell short of their marks, it was asserted, and dropped into the sea.

Navy planes roared over the channel a short time later and counteroperations were begun.

Four Japanese and one Italian were taken into custody

Illustrated on Page 9

by Ventura County Sheriff's authorities last night shortly after the attack. Two Japs were said to have been riding around the city during the blackout in a station wagon, armed with guns. For more than two hours after the raid, brilliant yellow flares burst over darkened Ventura. Authorities said it was clearly an effort to signal the enemy.

RAIDER LAST SEEN HEADED SOUTH

When last reported, about 8:30 p.m. by a minister at Montecito, the submarine was slipping out of the Santa Barbara Channel in the direction of Los Angeles. The clergyman, Rev. Arthur Basham of Pomona, who was visiting there, said he observed the "pigboat" flashing signal lights, apparently to someone on shore.

The Ventura County Sheriff's office received reports that flares had been sighted lighting the skies at several points along the coast in Ventura County near Hueneme.

At 7:58 p.m. upon orders of the Fourth Interceptor Command all radio stations in Southern California abruptly left the air. A few minutes later the coast line was completely blacked out from Carpinteria to Goleta. The blackout area covered a distance of about 25 miles. The yellow alert flashed simultaneously in police headquarters in Los Angeles.

The "all-clear" signal light was flashed in Los Angeles at 12:11 a.m., four hours and 13 minutes later.

SANTA BARBARA BLACKED OUT

Air-raid sirens screamed in Santa Barbara and within a few moments the entire city was dark.

At 12:20 a.m. today the all clear was sounded.

First report of the submarine reached the Sheriff's office from Mrs. George Heaney on San Marcos Pass, northwest of Santa Barbara. She informed authorities that she heard the first gun report shortly after 7 p.m. With field glasses, she said she sighted the submarine. It was lying about a mile offshore.

The next report came from Bob Miller of the Bankline Oil Co., who gave a similar report. By this time, the guns of the submarine were speaking repeatedly and shells shrieking overhead.

F. W. Borden, superintendent of the Bankline plant, gave this eyewitness account of the raid to the 11th Naval District.

"At 7:10 P.W.T., one large submarine came to the surface

Turn to Page A, Column 8

Shelling of Oil Field Described by Eyewitness

Restaurant Man First Believed Explosions Caused by Army Conducting Target Practice

"Their marksmanship was rotten."

Thus did Lawrence Wheeler, proprietor of a roadside inn situated in the heart of the Ellwood oil fields, describe the shelling of the fields by enemy submarine deck guns last night.

"It started about 7:15 p.m.," he said. "I know it was about that time because we were serving dinners to customers and listening to the President's speech, and he was about halfway through.

HEARD LOUD REPORT

"Suddenly we heard a loud report, followed in a few moments by another. Some soldiers who were in my place said it was probably just target practice.

"We heard a bit later that the oil fields were being shelled. I went outside and ran over to a point whence I could see the ocean. It looked like a submarine, about a mile offshore, cruising slowly down the coast and firing at regular intervals.

"I could see the flashes as the gun went off.

AIMED AT PLANT

"The submarine seemed to be aiming at the Barnsdall Oil Co.'s main absorption plant, located almost on the beach.

"They missed with all their shots at this plant, though some of the shells landed fairly close, throwing up geysers of dirt and sand near the building.

"One shell hit a well and blew the pumping plant and derrick to bits.

"That was the only real damage they did.

"There must have been 20 or 25 men working in the field at the time. Nobody was injured.

NOTIFIED SHERIFF

"One of their shots whistled over my inn, which is a good mile from the shore line, and burst up the canyon on the Hollister estate across the highway.

"We notified the Sheriff's office and they said planes would be here in 10 minutes.

"It seemed to me as if the enemy vessel was firing a 5 or 6-inch gun. Their shooting wasn't very good, because that absorption plant was a beautiful target and they didn't hit it."

CUSTOMERS CALM

Mrs. Wheeler added this account:

"I saw the explosions. At first they were very faint. I thought it was the Army practicing but then I heard a shell fly overhead and strike in a canyon inshore from our place."

Wheeler said there was no panic among his customers.

"We immediately blacked out the place," he said. "One shell landed about a quarter of a mile from here and the concussion shook the building but nobody was scared much."

Suspicious Lights Flashed Here After Submarine Attack

Flashlights in the hands of suspicious persons, possibly signalers, were reported to police last night shortly after a Japanese submarine dropped shells near Santa Barbara.

Six calls were received by the police complaint board, telling of the blinking flashlights in various parts of the city. One witness said he saw one or two persons at the end of the Venice pier with flashlights.

Policemen were dispatched to the locations given, but in all instances the suspicious persons were gone.

During the radio blackout coincident with the shelling, hundreds of phone calls were received by the board inquiring whether residence lights should be doused. Callers were reminded that one of the rules during an alert was not to use the telephone.

IN THE 'TIMES' TODAY

TUESDAY
FEBRUARY 24, 1942

RADIO. Page 11, Part II.
COMICS. Page 17, Part I.
FASHIONS, CLUBS, SOCIETY. Pages 5, 6 and 7, Part II.
PUZZLE. Page 12, Part I.
FRANK KENT. Page 8, Part I.
MOTION PICTURES AND THEATERS. Pages 14 and 15, Part I.
BIRTHS, DEATHS AND MARRIAGE NOTICES. Page 14, Part I.
PICTORIAL PAGE. Page 9.
FINANCIAL. Ryan will build new type airplane. Steel operations expand. Domestic markets resume today following holiday. Oil news. Page 12, Part I.
THE SOUTHLAND. Ten persons meet death in Southland traffic. Page 10, Part I.
SPORTS. Jackie Wilson favored to defeat Ceferino Garcia this evening. Page 8, Part II.
Angels open spring drills at Ontario. Page 9, Part II.
Pastor and Franklin in heavyweight clash tonight. Page 9, Part II.
Clark Shaughnessy admits he's Yale coaching possibility. Page 8, Part II.
THE CITY. Jap submarine shells Ellwood oil field north of Santa Barbara. Page 1, Part I.
Noble tells un-American acts hearing Jap attack on Hawaii justified. Page 1, Part I.
Japanese exodus under way at harbor. Page 10, Part I.
Rationing of retread tires goes into effect in Southern California. Page 1, Part II.
Draft official tells of men having teeth pulled in attempt to get deferment. Page A.
Log of lifeboat tells tragedy of Pacific war. Page 2, Part II.
America must conquer or die, Pepper declares. Page 6, Part I.
Raiders charge mixed party dancing in nude. Page 3, Part II.
Southland plane factories and shipyards ignore holiday. Page 1, Part II.
Mt. Wilson astronomer discovers new "hot star." Page 1, Part II.
Federal intervention asked to prevent threatened tie-up of milk supply through strike. Page 2, Part II.
Six hundred in County Jail volunteer blood for country. Page 1, Part II.
Total of bonded indebtedness in county dropping. Page 1, Part II.
GENERAL EASTERN. Willkie repeats belief MacArthur should be returned. Page 8, Part I.
THE WEST. Demand for extra pay on holiday keeps 17,000 West Coast workers idle. Page 10, Part I.
WASHINGTON. President, in broadcast, gives nation pledge of certain victory. Page 1, Part I.
Mrs. Roosevelt reports she is out of O.C.D. but has not forsworn public office. Page 8, Part I.
Draft boards warned farm labor supply must not be depleted. Page A.
THE WAR. United Nations' airmen blunt Japs' pincers on Java. Page 1, Part I.
Fight for Burma turning sharply against British. Page 1, Part I.
Russians reported within 80 miles of Smolensk. Page 8, Part I.
United States warship sunk off Iceland. Page 8, Part I.
MacArthur holds on in Bataan as fighting lulls. Page 2, Part I

Japs Control Bali Airport

BANDOENG (Dutch East Indies) Feb. 23. (AP)—The Japanese enemy has overrun part of Bali and controls the airport at Denpasar, on the southeast of the island near its only good harbor, but his entire invading fleet has been destroyed, damaged or dispersed and his landing troops are isolated, the Dutch announced tonight.

Thus was summed up the first phase of the invader's thrust at the near approaches to the Java keystone in the Allied arch—a thrust in which Japanese sea power suffered, under co-ordinated American-Dutch bomber and warship fire, its gravest wounds

Turn to Page 8, Column 3

administration building. The staff had spruced up its rifle range in Lopez Canyon so prospective inductees and defenders of the home front could brush up on their marksmanship. (Marksmen were reminded that the range provided facilities "for the comfort of the wives of members who desire to accompany their husbands.")

The *Warner Club News* even included safety tips on how to dispose of an incendiary bomb if one landed nearby. "Should one of these things drop into your yard, don't get excited and run out and start squirting the hose on it," said Warner employee Paul "Doc" MacWilliams, "for brother if you do, it would have been better for you to have had a 100-pound bomb smack you right on the back of the neck, for your departure from this land of sunshine would have been much quicker and a darn sight less painful. These bombs contain magnesium, and when burning, if water in any large amount is brought into contact with it, results in a terrific explosion. If you have to use water, use it in the form of a fine spray. Better still, use sand."

From the moment the war began for America on December 7, the studios were immersed in defense of the home front. When the state of California needed emergency transportation to defense positions in the early morning after the attack, the studios responded with 150 trucks and drivers. Warner Bros., as always, took the lead for the film industry in the war effort. Harry Warner was named to head the Red Cross effort at all of the studios; in April 1942, Jack was appointed a lieutenant colonel in the army, with responsibility for public relations operations (for the duration of the war, all memos addressed to the studio chief had to be directed to "Col. Warner"). The studio supported entertainment shows for military camps, and led drives to collect scrap, sell bonds, and recruit blood donors. Hundreds of Warner workers completed crash courses as air-raid wardens, spotters, firemen, auxiliary policemen, and first-aid workers.

Nearly every Warner employee participated in the studio's payroll deduction plan for war bonds—"Let's 'Bond' the Hell out of 'em," cried the bond-drive banners. By May 1942, 2,525 of the 2,600 regular Warner employees were buying war bonds every week. Warners also encouraged its performers to participate in bond drives along with stars from other studios; actors under contract to Warner Bros. were responsible for generating hundreds of millions of dollars in bond sales.

Bette Davis and John Garfield, two top Warner stars, were instrumental in creating the Hollywood Canteen, a restaurant and nightclub exclusively for servicemen; like its East Coast cousin, the Stage Door Canteen, the Hollywood Canteen was staffed in large measure by entertainment figures. Soldiers and sailors on their way to overseas duty

Even in idyllic Southern California, the war came home to haunt residents.

might hear Bob Hope entertain the crowd while Lana Turner or Greer Garson served dinner and Edward G. Robinson cleared their table—and all for free.

But the biggest contribution that Warners could offer to the war effort was continuing the work the studio knew best: making movies. The shock of the war's first days did little to slow the pace of production at the studio.

"Production of all kinds is vital to the success of our country's effort to rid the world of a horrible danger," wrote Harry and Jack to all employees at Warners a few days after the United States entered the war. "This applies, we believe, to the work of making and exhibiting motion pictures as it does to every vital industry in America. Ours is an important link in the chain America seeks to forge around the forces of evil.

"We are working now with a double purpose and it is necessary, we believe, that every loyal American employed by Warner Bros. recognize this and have a hand in building entertainment that will help keep up the courage of the workers at home as well as of the troops in the field. This is the time for every man and woman to consecrate themselves to the serious business ahead of us and to give freely of his time and strength and courage to the Victory we will all sometime celebrate. The word is *courage*."

While the motion picture industry was prepared for the challenge of producing films to support the war effort, after Pearl Harbor one question lingered for weeks: Would the government impose censorship on films? On Christmas Eve, President Roosevelt provided the answer.

"I want no censorship of the motion picture," Roosevelt said. "I want no restrictions placed thereon which will impair the usefulness of the film, other than those very necessary restrictions which the dictates of safety make imperative.

"In the months to come world conditions may cause the motion picture industry to play an even larger part in the war against Axis tyranny. I know that the responsibility this presents will be cheerfully and completely fulfilled, because no one has a greater stake in victory than you whose profession is so bound up with the maintenance of the American tradition of free communications."

The government would impose no direct censorship during World War II—at least not on films released only in America. But as the film industry would quickly discover, the federal government would have plenty to offer the studios in the form of "guidance"—stopping just short of direct intervention—that would "encourage" filmmakers to work more closely with the government than ever before.

As America's first month at war came to a close, and Wallis mulled over the script of *Everybody Comes to Rick's*, Warners prepared for 1942 determined to move ahead. On New Year's Eve, the studio placed an ad in *Variety* wishing the entire entertainment industry a Happy New Year. The words *NEW YEAR* were spelled with a letter from each of seven blockbuster titles in the studio's current crop:

SergeaNt York
They DiEd with Their Boots On
The Man Who Came to Dinner
You're in the ArmY Now
All Through thE Night
The MAle Animal
King's Row

War or no war, with winning pictures like these in circulation, a bushel of equally attractive projects waiting in the wings, and an as-yet-unknown project that would ultimately become *Casablanca* just around the corner, for Warner Bros., 1942 would be a very Happy New Year indeed.

Soon after receiving Karnot's seven-hundred-word brief and twenty-two-page story synopsis, Wallis was sufficiently interested by the combination of romance and exotic locales in *Everybody Comes to Rick's* to inquire about its price. At the same time, he decided to "shop" the script around the studio and solicit reactions and opinions about the play from his trusted associates and staff writers. On December 22, Wallis asked Irene Lee, the Warner Bros. story editor and one of the few women in senior management at the studio, to distribute *Everybody Comes to Rick's* around the lot and "get reactions on it from three or four people."

Opinions about the play were, to say the least, mixed.

"I think this story has definite possibilities for a motion picture," said David Lewis, a trusted Wallis associate producer with such films as *Dark Victory* and *King's Row* to his credit. "The background is colorful and modern, and the characters romantic. I think the story needs work, but it is an attractive setup."

However, Robert Lord, another respected production aide who worked on such box-office hits as *Dodge City, Confessions of a Nazi Spy,* and *The Private Lives of Elizabeth and Essex,* couldn't muster much enthusiasm for the Burnett-Alison script. "I suspect with enough time and effort," Lord sniffed, "a picture could be got from this very obvious imitation of *Grand Hotel.*"

But it was Jerry Wald, one of the rising stars of the writing corps who had recently been promoted to producer, who agreed with Karnot's assessment about the "tough guy possibilities" for the script and provided just the right voice of inspiration that Wallis needed.

"This story should make a good vehicle for either Raft or Bogart," Wald told Lee three days before Christmas. "I feel it can be easily

STAGE PLAY
Rec'd Ms from NY
12/8/41

EVERYBODY COMES TO RICK'S
Reader: Karnot
12/11/41

EVERYBODY COMES TO RICK'S
by
Murray Burnett & Joan Alison

Rick Blaine, American owner of de luxe Rick's Cafe in Casablanca,
French Morocco, is a taciturn man of mystery to his patrons --
wealthy French expatriates; refugees; French, German and Italian
officers. Cynically indifferent, Rick enforces an atmosphere of
strict neutrality in his powderkeg of political tension. Only
Rinaldo, French Prefect of Police, Rick's professed friend, knows
of his background as a famous criminal lawyer in Paris, his affair
with a woman, his divorce from his wife and children in '39, his
abandonment of career and flight into oblivion. But only Sam,
Rick's devoted Negro entertainer, knows what's in Rick's embittered
heart. Ugarte, peddler of stolen exit visas, asks Rick to hold a
pair of priceless letters-of-transit signed by Weygand. He plans
to sell them for a fabulous sum this evening, and quit Casablanca
and the racket. Rinaldo enters with Strasser, Gestapo agent, seek
ing to prevent recently arrived Victor Laszlo -- wealthy Czech
patriot hunted by the Nazis for his fearless underground activity
-- from buying the letters from Ugarte. Rick plays dumb, but
Ugarte is arrested. On their exit enters Laszlo, accompanied by
beautiful Lois Meredith. Rick is almost visibly shaken by her pre
sense -- their casual greeting betrays their past connection.
Strasser privately gives Laszlo an ultimatum. Unless he signs
over his foreign-banked millions to Germany, he will never leave
Casablanca. Laszlo calmly defies him. Later, after all have left
Sam begs Rick to avoid re-entanglement with Lois. But Rick cannot
She soon returns alone, and spends the night with him. In the
morning, torn between unquenchable love and deep distrust, Rick
challenges her motives. Frankly admitting admiration for valiant
Laszlo, she insists she loves Rick, wants to stay with him. But
she owes Laszlo a debt. Rick promises to help Laszlo. Rinaldo
enters, and with one remark makes it clear to Rick that Lois is
playing him for a sucker. Rick tersely, viciously, rejects her re
assertion of love. That evening, when Laszlo, followed by Lois,
comes seeking Ugarte, Rick, now drinking heavily, insults them
both. Rinaldo brings news of Ugarte's suicide -- bluntly charges
Rick with possession of the letters, but Rick outbluffs him.
Rinaldo introduces Jan and Annina Viereck, young, bewildered,
newly-wed Bulgarian refugees. When Annina confides to Rick she
has agreed to yield to Rinaldo for the sake of an exit visa for
Jan, Rick's cynicism is pierced; he begins to understand Lois.
Rinaldo makes passes at Annina, Jan knocks him down. As he screams
for his gendarmes, the lights go out. When they come on, the
Vierecks have disappeared. After a vain search, Rinaldo summarily
closes the cafe, promising Rick trouble. Later Rick brings the
Vierecks from hiding, refuses to let them leave. In the morning,
as Sam brings plane tickets for Lisbon, Rinaldo appears, warning
Rick he is closed and will not leave town until the Vierecks are
found. On his exit Lois appears; she is leaving Laszlo for Rick.
Without explanation he demands her aid in helping the Vierecks.
She agrees. He calls Rinaldo, offers to surrender the Vierecks.
Rinaldo arrives to find Rick and Lois in rapturous embrace. Rick
makes another offer; he will trap Laszlo for him, with one of the
letters, if the Vierecks are allowed to leave with the other.
Convinced by the lovemaking, Rinaldo agrees, calls off his police,
and the Vierecks leave with the letter and plane tickets. Rick
then calls Laszlo, who comes immediately for the letter. Rinaldo
emerges to arrest him as he takes the letter, but Rick covers
Rinaldo with a gun. Just realizing that Rick is practically committing suicide, Lois frantically tries to prevent him, but Rick
insists that she accompany Laszlo. Despairing, she does. Rick,
his self-respect redeemed, surrenders to Rinaldo and furious
Strasser.

tailored into a piece along the lines of *Algiers*, with plenty of excitement and suspense in it."

Wald's comparison of the Burnett-Alison script to *Algiers*—the 1938 United Artists romance-thriller starring Charles Boyer and Hedy Lamarr—struck a chord with Wallis. As he prepared to bet a sizable fee on an unproduced play with few features beyond a superficial romance and an exotic locale, Wallis was forced to justify his risky purchase by comparing the play to a proven film hit.

"Jerry had gotten to the heart of the matter," said Wallis. "This could indeed be another *Algiers*—a romantic story in an exotic setting."

Wallis was convinced by Wald's analysis of the play (the same comparison of the *Casablanca* plot to *Algiers* would later persuade producer David Selznick to lend Ingrid Bergman to Warners for the production) and bought the rights to *Everybody Comes to Rick's* for $20,000—at the time the largest fee ever paid for an unproduced play. With only an untested script and mixed reviews from his own colleagues to bank on, the best Wallis could hope for was that his new pet project might rehash the success of a desert potboiler produced three years before by another studio.

While Wallis's purchase of *Everybody Comes to Rick's* may be remembered as a bold financial move, the buy marked only one gamble among many risky ventures that were standard operating procedure at Warner Bros. in the early 1940s. In the final days of 1941, the studio was clearly in a buying mood; on December 18, for example, the studio announced the purchase, for $12,500, of "Aloha Means Goodbye," a *Saturday Evening Post* serial by Robert Carson that explored spies and intrigue in the Hawaiian Islands (the serial was soon loosely adapted for *Across the Pacific*, with John Huston directing Humphrey Bogart and Mary Astor). If the studio could afford to purchase a magazine yarn for $12,500, it could certainly ante up that amount plus another $7,500 to gamble on a plot filled with intrigue, drama, and romance—especially if the project had the potential, as Karnot suggested, to be a "box-office natural" and a possible vehicle for the top stars on the lot.

Nevertheless, spending five-figure sums for untested properties was not a decision to be taken lightly; the price of the purchase—enough to pay the salaries of at least a half dozen typical Warner employees for a year in the early 1940s—was the principal reason why Wallis sought advice from so many colleagues at the studio before he ultimately decided to buy *Everybody Comes to Rick's*.

Karnot's summary of Everybody Comes to Rick's *was accompanied by his recommendation, "a box office natural—for Bogart, or Cagney, or Raft in out-of-the-usual roles and perhaps Mary Astor."*

Throughout Hollywood's heyday, the pressure at all the film companies to keep preproduction costs to the absolute minimum was nearly overwhelming—especially at ever thrifty Warner Bros.—but the urgency to slash costs was greatly magnified during the wildly uncertain early days of World War II. (Later, when principal photography on *Casablanca* was scarcely hours away from beginning, the studio heads would force changes in the casting of several bit players simply because the cost difference between one performer over another was a few dollars a week less.)

With a cost-conscious attitude prevailing at Warner Bros., even an industry heavyweight such as Wallis had to think twice before purchasing a property, especially when the studio could choose from the spectrum of more successful theatrical productions, books, short stories, and original ideas produced by the writers on the lot. While the price paid for the screen rights to *Everybody Comes to Rick's* seems a mere trifling by today's standards, Wallis's first major decision involving the project illustrates the constant tug-of-war between philosophies that marked the studio system operating at its peak: on one hand, to produce the highest quality productions using the best material available, but, on the other hand, doing so only at the price of working under constant pressure to trim expenses to the bone.

As Wallis mulled over his new purchase, he prepared for the arrival of the new year by requesting another round of opinions from associates at Warner Bros. But before Wallis left his office on New Year's Eve, he completed one final housekeeping chore: "The story we recently purchased entitled *Everybody Comes to Rick's,*" he informed all departments at Warner Bros., "will hereafter be known as *Casablanca.*"

The straightforward choice of the title surprised some industry observers who knew that Warners devised some of Hollywood's catchiest titles—the studio was legendary (or notorious, depending on how you viewed the subject) for such melodramatic titles as *Each Dawn I Die, I Was a Fugitive From a Chain Gang*, and *King of the Underworld*—title verbiage as colorful as the Warner films they described. Studio insiders could also note with amusement some near-disasters in title choices; earlier in 1941, for example, *The Maltese Falcon* came within a whisker of being called *The Gent From Frisco*.

Wallis's rationale for renaming his project simply *Casablanca* remains forever unknown. However, as the producer would discover less than a year later, the title of his new production would not only prove acceptable to audiences, but it would become one of the most fortuitously well-timed decisions in Hollywood history.

As 1942 began, Wallis found few new supporters at Warner Bros. for his latest acquisition. Robert Buckner, one of the studio's most reliable writers who wrote or co-wrote *Yankee Doodle Dandy, Dodge City*, and

Knute Rockne—All American, voiced dissent even stronger than Wallis had heard in his first harvest of opinions.

"I do not like the play at all, Hal," Buckner told Wallis early in January. "I don't believe the story or the characters. Its main situations and the basic relations of the principals are completely censorable and messy, its big moment is sheer hokum melodrama of the E. Phillips Oppenheim variety [a British mystery writer of the early 1900s]. This

Hal Wallis, second-in-command at Warner Bros., during the studio's most creative period Wallis outlasted friends and foe alike to produce films for more than fifty years.

guy Rick is two-parts Hemingway, one-part Scott Fitzgerald, and a dash of cafe Christ."

Screenwriter Aeneas MacKenzie saw the possibilities in the Burnett-Alison script but also recognized that "it isn't a pushover."

"I think we can get a good picture out of this play," MacKenzie wrote to Irene Lee. "Certain characterizations need very definite strengthening and certain basic situations present problems from the censorship angle.

"These, however, can be overcome, I believe," MacKenzie said. "Because behind the action and its background is the possibility of an excellent theme—the idea that when people lose faith in their ideals, they are beaten before they begin to fight."

But MacKenzie's confidence in his initial cursory appraisal didn't last long. After looking at the script more closely a second time only three days later, "the result caused me to revise the favorable impressions left by my first reading of the play," he confessed. "It presents some very serious problems indeed, and has certain defects which are slurred over in its present form but which will become very apparent in a picture. This is a tough job for anyone to whom it may be assigned."

Fellow writer Wally Kline found similar flaws.

"In taking this apart I find that when the highly censorable situations, relationships, and implications are removed, we have left an American ex-lawyer in Casablanca who owns a cafe—the reasons for which are lacking. It will be a tough job to get a satisfactory picture out of this material, but I believe it can be done."

Apparently Wallis respected those who voiced negative opinions—on January 9, he assigned Kline and MacKenzie to write the first draft of *Casablanca*.

Even before initial work on the screenplay progressed under the guidance of Messrs. Kline and MacKenzie, Wallis had announced his new pet project to the world. On January 7, the Warner Bros. Hollywood News Press Service reported that "Ann Sheridan and Ronald Reagan will be teamed by Warner Bros. for the third time in *Casablanca*." The announcement had already appeared in the *Hollywood Reporter* two days earlier.

Dennis Morgan was named as "the third member of a starring trio," presumably for the still-developing role of underground leader Victor Laszlo. (Some film historians later assumed that Reagan had been chosen to play Laszlo, and not café owner Richard Blaine, soon to be even better known as "Rick"; however, because the two romantic leads were Blaine and Lois Meredith, the character who would eventually become Ilsa Lund, Reagan was undoubtedly being considered for the Blaine role.)

But was Ronald Reagan really the studio's first choice to play Rick? The Warner publicity release would provide one of the few moments in the spotlight for Reagan, Sheridan, and Morgan in the saga of *Casablanca* (although Sheridan's role in the production would survive for the time being). While the three actors will be recalled by some as "the actors originally cast for the leads in *Casablanca*," the Hollywood News announcement only served publicity purposes. Wallis, in fact, had not really cast anyone to play the leads. With the ink still fresh on his new agreement to make pictures at Warner Bros. under the banner "Hal B. Wallis Productions," his pick of any project and player at the studio, and with memories still fresh of Karnot's assessment of *Casablanca*'s potential as a star vehicle, he began to hunt the biggest game on the lot.

Within hours the studio changed its public announcement of the cast, and on January 8 said that because of shuffles in production, Reagan, Sheridan, and Morgan had been reassigned to appear in *Shadow of Their Wings*. But Reagan didn't appear in that movie either; the Lloyd Bacon–directed picture was eventually retitled *Wings for the Eagle*, and starred Morgan, Sheridan, and Jack Carson. *Casablanca*, the studio explained, "is hung back on the hook"—an interesting choice of phrases considering that the picture had been a Warner property for less than two weeks, and MacKenzie and Kline weren't assigned to the script until the next day.

Instead, on Valentine's Day 1942, Wallis told Warner executive Steve Trilling to "please figure on Humphrey Bogart and Ann Sheridan for *Casablanca*." The public release of Bogart's assignment was not published until April 10, when the trades carried the story that Bogart replaced Reagan, "who goes into service April 19."

U.S. Army Reserve Lt. Ronald Reagan—who had just turned thirty-one in February and for years had been neatly pigeonholed at Warners as the handsome supporting character or the lead in "B" productions—had indeed been called into the army, possibly costing him a role in *Wings for the Eagle*. However, Reagan's reporting for military duty was probably not the most convincing factor in the decision to assign Bogart to *Casablanca*.

The role of Rick was clearly destined to be played by a hardened romantic worn by years and experience; whatever strengths or weaknesses Reagan possessed as an actor, creating the character of a mysterious saloon keeper with a shady past was not perceived by the studio as a performance within his range. Army service or no, Reagan was hardly the ideal choice for the role. And as Wallis's Valentine's Day memo to Trilling indicated, he had Bogart in mind all along; in April, Wallis told Jack Warner that the part "is being written for him" (sees pages 79–80). No matter the explanation, and regardless of whether he could have carried the role with the same impact as Bogart, Reagan, who had a moderately successful stint in both motion pictures and television before taking a somewhat higher profile in the political arena, missed the opportunity to appear in what would have been the most important role of his film career.

Instead, Bogart was given the opportunity. Wallis's near-casual request to assign Bogart to the production in a role that was clearly developing into a strong romantic lead, followed six years of studio buildup for the actor, and intertwined with the rise and fall of several of the most tempestuous personalities in movies. For Bogart, the time had come for a breakthrough—and the leap into the top ranks of Hollywood stars.

Casablanca

44

t h r e e

"I Don't Know
What My Fans Who Love
to Hate Me Are Going
to Think"

$\mathcal{I}$n the gloomy postdepression year of 1931, predicting that a new-comer to movies named Humphrey DeForest Bogart—a young actor of medium stature and moderate good looks who had achieved only limited success on Broadway and practically none in Hollywood—might one day emerge as a legendary icon of the silver screen would have stretched the imagination of even the most optimistic Hollywood soothsayer. Bogart, who would eventually rise to the pinnacle of Hollywood box-office stars playing the cynical hero with a cast-iron will and an unwavering personal code, had originally found his niche as an actor playing a succession of supporting roles, first on stage as second fiddle pretty boy, then later on screen as a psychotic killer or amoral gangster.

That Bogart would find his way into show business at all seemed more unlikely than his eventual rise to stardom. Born in New York to a doctor-father and illustrator-mother, Bogart freely admitted "there wasn't a drop of theatrical blood in me." Instead of college, Bogart opted for a stint in the navy in the closing days of World War I. The naval experience spurred in Bogart a love of the sea that would last throughout his life—and would also earn him a scarred lip that would later add to his "tough guy" film persona.

(The source of Bogart's scar would provide the basis for two stories that became entrenched in Hollywood lore, yet only one could be assumed true. Warner publicity reported that Bogart suffered a lip wound caused by a flying wooden splinter during battle action at sea aboard the troop ship *Leviathan*—an improbable tale since the war had been over for more than two weeks when Seaman Bogart reported for duty. Another more plausible account said that the wound was caused by a prisoner Bogart was transporting to Portsmouth Naval Prison. Regardless, the "wood splinter story" has endured in virtually every account of Bogart's life.)

After leaving the navy, Bogart took his first step toward an acting career by accepting an offstage job in the theatrical production office of William Brady, the father of a childhood friend. Bogart soon found his way into acting, appearing on stage for the first time in 1920 in *The "Ruined" Lady*. His first night on stage was anything but pleasant.

"It was all a horrible fiasco," Bogart recalled. "In one scene, an actor was supposed to be mad at me, and I thought he was really mad; he scared the hell out of me. It was the first time I had been face-to-face with actors at work. I didn't realize how convincing they could be. After that experience, I thought, 'never again.'

"What changed my mind was finding out I'd never get rich as a stage manager. I was young and I wanted to get ahead in the world, so I went to Mr. Brady and told him my problem. He said, 'Why don't you become an actor? Actors earn good money.' So, to make a fortune, I became an actor."

A succession of minor stage appearances followed that momentous decision, but Bogart, who would eventually become notorious for playing the rock-hard screen villain, soon found himself typecast as a superficial supporting actor in plays like *Meet the Wife*, *Cradle Snatchers*, and *Baby Mine*. In fact, Broadway legend recalls that Bogart may have been the first actor to bounce onstage in sports garb and chirp, "Tennis anyone?" Bogart later recalled his early acting with the amused ease of a seasoned professional who fondly remembered the journeyman's days; for many years after Bogart appeared in *Swifty* in 1922, he carried Alexander Woollcott's review of his performance, which read, "the young man who embodies the aforesaid sprig is what is usually and mercifully described as inadequate."

But Bogart persisted in the acting trade through his durability as a co-star, and he assembled a string of moderately successful theatrical appearances throughout the 1920s. In 1930, he acted in his first "film"—a ten-minute short for Vitaphone called *Broadway's Like That*. Over the next four years came a succession of second-tier roles in pic-

Humphrey Bogart, at the peak of his success as he looked in the mid-1940s, at home and at ease. A pretty boy during his stage years, a tough-guy during his early years on-screen, his career would evolve in a direction unlike any other Hollywood actor's.

tures for Fox, Universal, Columbia, and a first stab at Warner Bros. Bogart played a cowboy here, a sailor there, an aeronautical engineer in one feature—and even a few minor gangster parts that foreshadowed much nastier roles to come (in Mervyn LeRoy's *Three on a Match*, for instance, he played a character known as "The Mug").

But by 1934, when Bogart appeared in *Midnight* (playing a gangster named Garboni who is killed with his own gun by star Sidney Fox), he had grown weary of the studio grind and missed the lure of the stage. He returned to the theater, supposedly vowing never to return to the screen.

But a second shot at Hollywood was soon to come, an opportunity made possible by his most formidable stage role yet.

While appearing in *Invitation to a Murder*, Bogart was noticed by powerhouse theatrical producer Arthur Hopkins, who would soon be casting the Broadway version of *The Petrified Forest*. Hopkins wanted Bogart for the role of the murderous gangster Duke Mantee in the new Robert Sherwood play. Although the actor had established himself as a stage softy, Hopkins must have spotted Bogart in one of his on-screen "mug" roles, because the producer believed the time was ripe for Bogart to break type.

"When I dropped into his office," Bogart remembered of his meeting with Hopkins, "Robert Sherwood, who was a friend of mine, was there. Hopkins said to me, 'I've got a good role for you. A gangster role.'

Sherwood said, 'Why, you must be crazy. He doesn't fit that part at all! What he ought to do is the part of the football player.'

"They argued back and forth, and I thought Sherwood was right. I couldn't picture myself playing a gangster. So what happened? I made a hit as the gangster."

Indeed, *The Petrified Forest*, with Leslie Howard in the starring role as Alan Squier and Bogart as Duke Mantee, was a smash on Broadway. Some viewers recall audible gasps from the audience when Bogart, once the pretty boy in tennis clothes, shuffled onstage as Mantee, slackjawed and glowering. Bogart had arrived as a Broadway star, but his stage persona—transformed literally overnight by *The Petrified Forest*—would haunt the development of his career for years to come.

The success of *The Petrified Forest* on Broadway immediately attracted the attention of Hollywood, and Warner Bros. bought the screen rights to the play in 1935. The studio desperately wanted Howard, who had already amassed a strong screen record following appearances in *The Animal Kingdom, Of Human Bondage,* and *The Scarlet Pimpernel,* to recreate his role as Alan Squier, but the studio bosses were less than enthusiastic about Bogart.

Years later, Jack Warner blithely remembered that he brought "the whole cast of *The Petrified Forest* out to Hollywood"—and conveniently forgot that he used his own star Bette Davis in the female lead. In fact, Howard had to fight to get Bogart into the cast. (Bogart never forgot Howard's friendship, and the break that reignited his film career. Nine years after Howard's tragic death during World War II, Bogart named his daughter Leslie Howard in his memory.) Only Howard's threat of "no Bogart, no me" finally convinced Warner Bros. that signing Bogart for the role was a wise move. Thus Bogart, who had departed Hollywood two years before, swearing never to return, left the Broadway stage forever.

Bogart repeated his electrifying stage performance as Duke Mantee in the 1936 Archie Mayo–directed screen version of *The Petrified Forest*. Gone forever was the pretty-boy style of Bogart's Broadway days; when the new Bogart blasted onto the screen with a three-day growth of beard, a dull psychotic stare, and a hunched-over profile, he brought a fresh dimension to the notion of the antisocial screen demon. Bogart's character depicted a different kind of mobster than the Warner Bros. gangster films had popularized throughout the early 1930s; in Bogart's Duke Mantee audiences found no lust for a gangster's glory or riches as portrayed by Edward G. Robinson or James Cagney; instead, they discovered evil personified.

"Humphrey Bogart can be a psychopathic gangster more like Dillinger than the outlaw himself," wrote the *New York Times* in its review of *The Petrified Forest*.

After six years of struggles in film, Bogart had arrived in a hurry, and Warners immediately molded the actor into a valuable cog in the studio machine. The studio quickly cast its new contract player into a nonstop series of pictures. After *The Petrified Forest*, Bogart appeared in four more movies in 1936, seven in 1937, and another six in 1938. Two years after his return to films, Bogart became one of the hardest working actors on the Warner lot.

Although loaded with work, Bogart was moving forward but not upward. True, he was gaining a solid reputation as a hard-working and seasoned acting professional, but not as a full-fledged star. In the thirty-five pictures he made under contract at Warner Bros. before *Casablanca*, Bogart played gangsters, underworld figures, or other unsympathetic characters twenty times. He also "died" on-screen more frequently than any other leading actor at the studio—some eighteen times—and his frequent demises were often at the hands of Cagney, Robinson, or the other more established stars of the Warner stable.

"In those days," recalled Robinson of the studio pecking order while working with Bogart in their first four films together, "I would play the leading role, and Bogart would be opposite me, and we would shoot at each other perhaps a reel before the picture finished. Since I happened to be the so-called star, Bogart would die a reel ahead of me, and I would go on with a bullet in me right up to the last scene." (More than a decade after the early gangster period came to a close, Bogart and Robinson would appear together once more—this time in John Huston's *Key Largo*. Except in 1948, with Bogart at the pinnacle of success, the tables would be turned; not only would Frank McCloud, Bogart's character, gun down Robinson playing the psychotic gangster Johnny Rocco, but he would survive the battle unscathed.)

While Bogart occasionally drew a starring role, more often than not he was wedged into the convenient Warner cubbyhole as the doomed killer, the second gun to Cagney or Robinson, or the amoral heavy. Bogart wasn't entirely relegated to typecasting, however. He did play a smattering of sympathetic parts, including a second-billing in *Marked Woman* as a district attorney opposite top Warner star Bette Davis—and he actually got the girl occasionally in his more sympathetic roles. But through the late 1930s, the typical Bogart character was, as the actor himself said, "a bad man with a capital 'B.'"

Bogart remained a good sport, to say the least, as he watched colleagues like Cagney and Robinson take the leading roles in high-profile films while he played supporting roles—and machine-gun fodder. Never one to blame his problems with the studio on his fellow performers, Bogart also remained silent when George Raft, formerly under contract to Paramount, came to Warner Bros. in 1939 and began gobbling up choice appearances that would have suited Bogart perfectly.

Bogart as Duke Mantee in The Petrified Forest—*evil personified.*

Even worse for Bogart was the artistic indignity of being tossed cast-off roles that Raft refused to play. Bogart played so many parts rejected by Raft that he began to refer to his hard-nosed character roles as "George Raft parts." In retrospect, Raft's stubborn refusal to appear as a tough guy—roles he called "dirty heavies"—would cost him some of the choicest appearances the studio had to offer. Over the course of only two years, Raft refused assignments in such solid box-office hits as *High Sierra, The Maltese Falcon, The Sea Wolf,* and many others—and most of those roles went to Bogart. Had Raft appeared in these hit pictures, his star status would have no doubt increased rather than declined, and he might have surpassed Bogart as the actor on the rise at Warner Bros. in the early 1940s.

Bogart's fellow actors noticed his plight. Friends and friendly rivals at the studio sympathized, including Cagney, the top star on the lot who had no love of Jack Warner, the studio, or the studio system.

"Endlessly the studio required him to show up without his knowing what the script was, what his dialogue was, what the picture was about," said Cagney of Bogart. "On top of this he would be doing two or three pictures at a time. That's how much they appreciated him."

Incredibly, even the studio's own publicity releases admitted that Bogart was trapped by his success. "Bogart started his current picture career as a hunted criminal," reported a studio press release, "and the taint of *The Petrified Forest* role stuck with him more or less through all the time he has worked in pictures."

By 1939, Bogart was no longer tossed crumbs, but the choicest morsels were still few and far between. He was upgraded into a near-romantic role for *Dark Victory*, playing the unrequited lover opposite Bette Davis. But he was soon returned to the old mold, and he pressed out the same antisocial persona again and again.

Within weeks of *Dark Victory*, Bogart was back in gangster pictures, playing two of his nastiest parts ever as a bootlegging racketeer in *The Roaring Twenties* and a crime-hardened parolee in *Invisible Stripe* (he was killed in both pictures). By this time, dying on screen had practically become a Bogart trademark; in between the two gangster pictures, for example, Bogart "died" twice in one film. He appeared in *The Return of Doctor X* as, of all things, an evil scientist resurrected from the dead who searches for a rare blood type to sustain his afterlife. Needless to say, Bogart's character—adorned with a streak of white hair that resembles nothing less than a human version of a skunk—is killed before his quest for blood leads to heroine Rosemary Lane.

In spite of the seemingly endless typecasting and career backslides, Bogart remained the consummate professional he strived to be throughout his career—the seasoned, versatile actor who did his job, and did it well. Other more high-strung stars may have squabbled with the studio over dressing rooms or on-screen credits; when Bogart fought with Jack Warner, the quarrels concerned characters and the quality of his roles.

"I've never forgotten a piece of advice [a friend] gave me when I was a young squirt and I asked him how I could get a reputation as an actor," Bogart said. "He said, 'Just keep working.' The idea is that if you're always busy, sometime somebody is going to get the idea that you must be good."

That work ethic was precisely the attitude the studio wanted from Bogart, and if his roles weren't as substantive as he might have hoped, they were certainly frequent. By 1940, Bogart had worked under contract at Warner Bros. for more than four years, and he had appeared in twenty-nine pictures. Yet he was still seeking a solid direction for his career. Finally, in 1940, a part came along that truly excited him: the lead in Raoul Walsh's production of *High Sierra*.

Although the part of Roy "Mad Dog" Earle was another cast-off role (Paul Muni had originally been slated to appear as the escaped criminal on the run), Bogart recognized the character potential in the ruthless but sympathetic criminal—a convict with a heart and depth to his personality.

"You told me once to let you know when I found a part I wanted," Bogart telegrammed Wallis in March 1940. "A few weeks ago I left a note for you concerning *High Sierra*. I never received an answer so I'm bringing it up again as I understand there is some doubt about Muni doing it."

Bogart won the part—second-billed to newcomer Ida Lupino—and earned acclaim for his performance. "Bogart is tops as the graying gangster," *Variety* reported, "he's properly silent and hard, with an underlying tenderness that's incongruous with his ability to kill."

Bogart—debonair, but still slightly diabolical.

With *High Sierra*, Bogart had risen nearly to the first rank of Warner stars. After the film's release in 1941, Bogart was top-billed on every picture, and would remain so for the rest of his life. By 1941 he was ranked fourth on the Warner roster of its top stars, behind only James Cagney, Bette Davis, and Errol Flynn (the other stars among the Warner top ten in 1941 were Ann Sheridan, Edward G. Robinson, Ronald Reagan, Joan Leslie, Olivia de Havilland, Priscilla Lane, and John Garfield). But even with his climb up the studio ladder, Bogart's salary didn't reflect his box-office sock. His new contract, signed in late 1941, paid him a "paltry" $3,750 per week—a pittance compared to the stratospheric sum of $368,333 paid to Cagney, or $213,333 paid to Flynn. Later, when Bogart's success in *Casablanca* skyrocketed the actor's box-office appeal, Warner's penny-pinching would cost the studio dearly, in the form of a renegotiated contract at a substantially higher amount.

But *High Sierra* alone didn't transform Bogart's career—he was still a gangster, although he had proven he could play a gangster with a heart. The Bogart image of rugged individualist was still to come. It was 1941— post–*High Sierra*—that would mark the turning point; a series of events at the studio would land him on the top of the heap.

Bogart's rank in the Warner star hierarchy finally came to a head during the April 1941 filming of *Manpower*, a turgid love triangle involving high-voltage powerline workers and café hostess Marlene Dietrich. Originally slated to appear opposite George Raft, Bogart, fresh from his success in *High Sierra*, was fired from *Manpower*, and was replaced by Edward G. Robinson in part because of incompatibility on the set with Raft.

As events unfolded during the shooting of *Manpower*, Raft had even less luck with Robinson. Raft so resented Robinson that he sparked several needless arguments on the set, at least one of which resulted in a near-brawl between the two high-priced stars, who had to be physically separated by cast and crew. Raft's attack, reported Warner legal counsel Roy Obringer to the Screen Actors Guild, "was wholly uncalled for and actually brought about a very serious disturbance."

Raft and Robinson cooled their tempers long enough to complete *Manpower*, but not before Raft had worn out his welcome at the studio —no wonder Wallis later recalled that "our association with Raft was a constant battle from start to finish."

Regardless of how events at Warners affected the careers of others, Bogart was fed up with the squeaky wheels at the studio. The week after he was removed from *Manpower*, Bogart finally exploded.

With memories still fresh of two uncomfortable appearances as western badmen in *The Oklahoma Kid* in 1939 and *Virginia City* in 1940, Bogart refused yet another horse-mounted appearance—this time after being asked to play outlaw Cole Younger in *Bad Men of Missouri*—thus violating his contractual obligation to play any role the studio chose for him, and setting up a battle royal between the actor and studio chief Jack Warner.

On March 13, the studio sent Bogart a copy of the Charles Grayson script for *Bad Men of Missouri*. Four days later, he returned the script to Warner aide Steve Trilling with a scathing note. "Are you kidding?" cracked Bogart. "This is certainly rubbing it in. Since Lupino and Raft are casting pictures, maybe I can. Regards, Bogie."

While Jack Warner had more than his share of feuds—both public and private—with stars like Cagney, Bette Davis, and Errol Flynn, his tussles with Bogart were few and far between. In his memoirs, Warner, who recalled most other stars with little fondness, said of Bogart, "I really liked this ornery genius because he had a heart under the crust."

Although Warner claimed victory in nearly all of his clashes with contract players, one of his favorite defeats involved Bogart, and an argument that the studio chief gladly conceded. Once, when Warner ordered Bogart to appear in a boxing picture, the actor refused the part despite Warner's direct order. Finally, Bogart removed his sport coat, unbuttoned his shirt and pulled it open, revealing his decidedly slender physique. "Look," Bogart said to Warner, "make me a fighter and everyone will laugh." Warner was relieved at the rationale; "I thought he was going to kill me," sighed the studio chief.

Boxing pictures and skinny chests notwithstanding, it was a different matter entirely for Bogart to turn down a role of the sort that he had already played successfully in pictures that kept the turnstiles spinning. While *Bad Men of Missouri* was no potential blockbuster, the studio viewed the solid action picture as perfect grist for the ceaseless demands of the Warner production and distribution mill. Simply, Bogart appearing in *Bad Men of Missouri* was money well spent, no matter how the actor viewed the role; refusal made him just one more high-priced expense on the studio's books until another role could be found for him. A clash was unavoidable.

After returning the script to the studio, Bogart was ordered to appear on the set the next day. He refused, instead remaining blithely and stubbornly at sea aboard his boat.

Bogart's instincts about *Bad Men of Missouri* were soon proved correct. The picture opened to so-so box-office business and mediocre reviews; one critic titled his review of *Bad Men of Missouri* with the phrase, "Much too Bad." The review went on to report that "Warner Bros.' *Bad Men of Missouri*, with the accent on the first word of the title, starts with the rifle shots and the thunder of pounding hoofs and begins its action with a Civil War battle. There are few interruptions from the mood in its opening titles set. It may qualify as the noisiest picture of the year."

Regardless of a picture's potential quality or actors' personal preferences, the studio word was law. For his refusal to appear in *Bad Men of*

Missouri, Bogart was immediately suspended from the payroll; Dennis Morgan replaced him on the picture. Bogart attempted to return to work on April 2, but the studio continued the suspension without pay until Morgan finished work on the film.

Fortunately, the Bogart-Warner feud cooled quickly, and not a moment too soon—Bogart's act of defiance would nearly cost him the choicest part of his career thus far, and would be followed soon after by the role that would firmly establish the actor among the top stars in Hollywood.

While Bogart cooled his heels in Newport Harbor during his suspension in the spring of 1941, John Huston, a vagabond writer-director and the son of veteran character actor Walter Huston, was putting the finishing touches on the script for the third film version of Dashiell Hammett's *The Maltese Falcon*. The film revolved around the characterization of Hammett's streetwise and scheming private detective Sam Spade, and Huston knew that Bogart could generate the ideal combination of cynical charm, hard-edged persona, and leading-man screen appeal.

But the studio had other ideas for the role of Sam Spade, once again in the form of George Raft. While the studio's confidence in Raft had waned, Warners was still determined to make good its investment in the actor by finding work for him in top roles—despite months of infighting and a succession of turned-down parts. Raft was again offered a plum assignment, and again he refused it. While the film would eventually be ranked among the definitive detective thrillers, in 1941, Raft doubted the "importance" of the film.

"I strongly feel that *The Maltese Falcon*, which you want me to do, is not an important picture," Raft told Warner in June. "I must remind you again, you promised me that you would not require me to perform in anything but important pictures. I understand that you are quite agreeable to use someone else in *The Maltese Falcon*, provided you get an extension of my time."

Bogart stepped in, and with his appearance as Spade, he found his niche in the Warner fold.

"Of major importance is the stand-out performance of Humphrey Bogart, an attention-arresting portrayal that will add immeasurable voltage to his marquee value," said *Variety* in its review of *The Maltese Falcon*. "Bogart not only dominates the proceedings throughout, but is the major motivation in all but a few minor scenes."

Said Bosley Crowther in the *New York Times*, "Bogart is a shrewd, tough detective with a mind that cuts like a blade, a temperament that sometimes betrays him, and a code of morals which is coolly cynical."

As Spade, Bogart for the first time personified the character that generations of audiences would grow to adore: the no-nonsense loner

who lived by his own rules—a hero with appeal enough to woo his leading lady but one so committed to a personal moral code that he could send her to the death house when he discovers she is a murderer. Bogart's character, under Huston's able guidance, became a screen personality immensely appealing both to men who admired him, and, much to the amazement of the studio bosses, to women who were attracted to him.

Bogart's attractiveness to women provided a surprise bonus for Warners, although it shouldn't have, after several "semi-romantic" roles and a mob scene of adoring female fans at public appearance at a New York theater. Bogart had "gotten the girl" before—in fact, in his first appearance in a full-length film in 1930 he won over Mona Maris in *A Devil with Women*. But usually Bogart's screen romances were mere sidelights to other action—or his getting shot.

By the summer of 1941, Bogart was slated to appear in a meaty role as a gangster-turned–Nazi hunter in *All Through the Night*. The role was

Bogart in **The Maltese Falcon**. *"A shrewd, tough detective with a mind that cuts like a blade," said the* New York Times *of Bogart's performance as Sam Spade.*

solid, but the old pattern of casting remained; while the release of *The Maltese Falcon* was only a few weeks away and the studio already knew it had a potential hit on its hands, he was appearing in his second picture in a row in a "George Raft part." Although Bogart took the role of Gloves Donohue, "he is unhappy about the idea of doing a role only because George Raft refused to do it," wrote Sam Jaffe, Bogart's agent, to Warner aide Steve Trilling.

"My point in writing you about it is only that I think you should bring this matter to the attention of Jack Warner," Jaffe said. "Point out to him that a story should be prepared for which they have Bogart in mind and no other actor because it seems that for the past year he's practically pinch-hitted for Raft and been kicked around from pillar to post."

The studio dug up another starring role for Bogart—a minor box-office success but a giant step backward professionally. In *The Big Shot*, Bogart played yet another gangster—a three-time loser with good intentions who stages a prison break and gets himself and his co-stars killed in the process. At the same time, the studio's advertising for *The Maltese Falcon* refused to release Bogart from his past. Even though Bogart plays a sympathetic character who never fires a gun, some advertising for the film described him with the puzzling phrase, "He's a killer when he hates!"

After *The Big Shot*, Bogart rebounded strongly—again directed by John Huston and teamed with Mary Astor and Sydney Greenstreet—in *Across the Pacific*, playing a court-martialed officer (actually an army intelligence agent on special assignment) who foils an Axis plot to blow up the Panama Canal.

Bogart's appearance in *Across the Pacific* further honed the sympathetic side of his individualist screen personality. While his character, Richard Leland, is hard as nails when the action gets hot, he was also developing a new softer image. This erstwhile screen gangster had proven his worth as a romantic star as well; in *Across the Pacific*, he flirted with co-star Mary Astor in scenes of playful banter and managed to flirt his way into a perfectly credible romantic kiss from his leading lady scarcely fifteen minutes into the motion picture.

Even more important, Bogart was being groomed to become the on-screen hero facing a new kind of on-screen adversary: Axis villains. Although he would still play the occasional mob boss fighting cops or rival gangsters, Bogart's screen personality was fast transforming into an American screen icon: the solid-steel hero who could stand up against the evil empire that was the Axis powers in 1941. "Bogart is as tough and sharp a customer as ever faced the world with bitter eyes," wrote the *New York Times*.

As Warners would soon discover in *Across the Pacific*, *Casablanca*, *Action in the North Atlantic*, and many other wartime dramas, the gritty hero as portrayed by Bogart would provide both the Nazis and the Japanese empire with the ultimate on-screen adversary.

"You guys have been looking for a war, haven't you?" says Bogart as Rick Leland in *Across the Pacific*, to Victor Sen Yung, playing Japanese-American turncoat Joe Totsuiko.

"That's right, Rick, that's why we're starting it," says Joe.

"You may start it, Joe," cracks Leland, "but we'll finish it."

Or, after Bogart arrests spy Sydney Greenstreet when the rotund actor's character hasn't the will to kill himself. "If any of your friends in

The tough villain turns gritty hero. "You may start it," his character tells a Japanese spy in Across the Pacific, *"but we'll finish it."*

Tokyo have trouble committing hara-kiri," Bogart says, pointing to a wave of American planes flying to protect the Panama Canal, "those boys will help them out."

Tough talk for dark times. But in the grim days of World War II, with the United States reeling from the shock of surprise attack in the Pacific, and gearing up to fight on a second front against the Nazis, American movie heroes—their defense of Allied honor and promises of better times to come—provided some of the few psychological lifts available to a nation that was temporarily flat on the canvas.

Changing actors who were formerly gangster specialists into rock-solid American heroes seemed a natural progression in the development of screen characters. However this new kind of movie hero also provided Warner Bros. with a solution to the problem of how to recycle actors who had made their careers playing criminals as gangster pictures waned. The answer? Make them even more dangerous *heroes*.

In the months before *Casablanca*, Warner Bros. began the rapid transformation of Bogart's screen personality from antisocial villain into hard-boiled wartime hero. Bogart's appearance in *All Through the Night*—in which he plays a gambler who tracks down a scheming Nazi spy played by Conrad Veidt and stops him from blowing up a battleship in New York Harbor—marked an odd balance point between the two screen types: Warner Bros. advertisements for the film display Bogart grinning his tough-guy grin while gripping two .45s pointed straight at the viewer. "He's Gunning After the Gestapo!" the ads read. "Me and the Mob don't like you rats," Bogart's caption growled at the Nazis. "Here's the payoff!"

This genesis of this screen personality was, quite happily for Warner Bros., a natural course of evolution. World War II, the end of the gangster cycle in films, and the rise of Humphrey Bogart all fit neatly together as the result of an odd combination of international politics, changing film viewing tastes, and one actor's rise to the pinnacle of his career.

While the transformation of Bogart, Cagney, and others into heroic characters may have seemed a sensible transition at Warner Bros., no one at the studio could have predicted how potent and impactful these screen heroes would become. The tough loner was a potent figure in time of war, but was also just as effective when later applied to characters on the home front.

The personality of the hardened wartime hero would outlast the conflict, persevering in countless incarnations—cowboys, detectives, and many other screen versions of the man alone, confronting seemingly stronger forces, and emerging victorious. The image of the tough hero would become one of the most appealing screen images in cinema, and rising to the top of the list of these enduring screen personalities would be Humphrey Bogart.

While Bogart was building his acting career, by 1941 he was also establishing a voice for himself within the film community on political issues that moved him deeply. Later, Bogart would be active in opposing the hearings held by the House Subcommittee on Un-American Activities on "subversive activities" within the film industry, and he would stand strongly in defense of the Hollywood Ten.

In 1941, Bogart, backed by his studio, took an active stance on behalf of the entire motion picture industry against film censorship; in a signed article that eerily foreshadows current-day demands for censorship in both films and music, Bogart decried those who called for increased restrictions on motion pictures, especially restraints that would neutralize the gangster pictures that had made him famous.

"The blanket of censorship covers practically every country in the world these days except our own," Bogart wrote in the *Hollywood Reporter*'s annual issue just before America's entry into World War II. "And judging from the editorials, whenever the threat of censorship rears its head in this country, most of us seem agreed it is the number one enemy of a free democracy.

"This is where my pet peeve comes in. While people are always quick to take up the cudgels against censorship of the press or radio, any crackpot can advocate new forms of censorship for the movies, and not a voice is lifted in protest. There's something illogical about this indifference to censorship of the movies. After all, it's just as much a medium of public expression as are the radio and newspaper.

"My own type of film has shown me how wrong and unfair advocates of censorship can be. For several years now, various groups have urged the banning of crime pictures on the grounds that they influence youth to turn to crime. I have never heard of any youngster going wrong, turning to crime, because of the movies. It simply isn't possible. Our relation to crime is, in a sense, the same as the prison warden's. We don't create it. We deal with it after it has happened, and we always make the criminal look bad.

"Movies don't cause crime any more than prison wardens cause crime. It has been charged against the motion picture industry that we take a sympathetic attitude toward gangsters, thugs, racketeers, and criminals. I deny that. After the things that have happened to me and my fellow screen heavies, I don't see how they can say that.

"There are groups that would like us to show the criminal always outmatched, poorly armed, and all policemen a good six inches taller, armed with tear gas and tommy guns, while the poor, dear, miserable rat of a gangster has to fight it out alone with only one measly little pistol. The object would be to deglamorize the gangster. That's all right, but it seems to me they are asking us to go about it in the wrong way. It seems to me that disarming the gangster tends to add glamour rather than remove it, and in some instance even make him seem gallant. What these critics forget is that the sympathies of the crowd are always with the underdog.

"It is better, I think, to de-glamorize His Excellency the Rat as we do it at Warners, by showing him well-armed, with an up-to-date arsenal, with smokescreens for his automobile, expensive short-wave radios, and other good equipment for the art of murder and arson. When we show a criminal on the screen like that, there is no doubt in the mind of the weakest low-grade moron who the hero is. The hero is unquestionably your friend and mine, the cop.

"I have dealt with only one phase of the attempt to impose censorship on the movies. It is the phase with which I am most familiar. But there are men who advocate even more dangerous types of film censorship, and if America is to continue to have freedom of the press and radio, as well as every other type of freedom, these insidious enemies of freedom must be emphatically discouraged. Because once the movies are gagged, these men will move on to the other means of public expression. We have seen it happen in other countries, and it can happen here."

Casablanca

62

With *Across the Pacific*, Bogart had completed three solid performances since his suspension. His star was rising—albeit slowly—but the studio's confidence in his appeal was growing. Bogart on-screen made the triumphant transition from immoral brute to the hard-edged hero. The time had come for both actor and studio to take a giant step.

Bogart's rise as a star in the Warner constellation was the happy result of both good luck and painstaking planning, just at the time when the studio was looking for a fresh face among its top rank of stars. By the beginning of 1941, Warners clearly needed to build its stock of leading men; Cagney, though still a box-office giant, continued to clash with the studio, and he would soon leave to form his own production company, thus depriving Warners of its top contract player.

Paul Muni, once the principal player in Warner "prestige" films, had left by mutual agreement. Edward G. Robinson, approaching fifty, remained the dependable character actor, but he was not a romantic box-office draw. Raft's star was already tarnished as far as Warners was concerned, and he would soon depart to work at other studios.

While the other leading actors at Warners—Ronald Reagan, Dennis Morgan, and George Brent among them—could provide reasonable box-office results, only Errol Flynn could approach the box-office firepower of Clark Gable, James Stewart, Cary Grant, or the other top draws of the day. And even if a potential shining new star loomed on the Warner horizon as World War II erupted, chances were quite likely that he was being whisked away for military service by Uncle Sam. Clearly, Warners needed a new first-rank talent, and Bogart was the most likely candidate.

Bogart had certainly proven himself as a reliable performer in action features, westerns, crime thrillers, espionage dramas, and virtually every other type of role that contract players were expected to play. Only one question remained about his long-term screen potential: Could he create the screen personality required to establish him as a top romantic star?

Looking back on the career of Humphrey Bogart over the distance of decades, it's difficult to imagine that the actor's unique style and on-screen personality could have been questioned. But at the time, in spite of years of patient apprenticeship and star grooming, Bogart remained an unlikely—and risky—romantic screen prospect. Few at the studio could imagine Bogart as a film lover, let alone a popular heartthrob, even after *The Maltese Falcon*, New York mob scenes, and favorable appraisals in the press of his unorthodox screen charm. In February 1942, Bogart had just turned forty-three years old—middle aged by Hollywood standards—and his looks were questionable, at least to the studio chiefs. His staunchest fans had to admit his stature was shortish, his voice nasal and gruff, his teeth slightly crooked, and his face was often marked by the sour expression of a man wearing shoes that were too tight. Errol Flynn, he was not.

But executives and actors at *other* studios certainly saw Bogart's appeal as a romantic leading man; screenwriter Casey Robinson, one of the leading writers on the lot, recalled that on a train trip with Wallis they met producer Pandro Berman, formerly production chief at RKO. "Pan astonished Wallis by saying that he thought the man at Warner Bros. who had the most appeal to women was Humphrey Bogart," Robinson said. Jack Warner, in the presence of Ingrid Bergman, reportedly once asked the rhetorical question, "Who would want to kiss Bogart?" Bergman is reported to have replied, "I would." At the time, Bogart's appeal may have been difficult to understand, but it was certainly undeniable.

So, for whatever their reasons, whether auspicious hunches, faith in untested abilities, or serendipitous decisions forced by other events at the studio, Wallis and Warner gave Bogart his final boost into stardom, and a place in Hollywood legend, by choosing him to play Richard Blaine in *Casablanca*, his first romantic starring role.

Later, before the film was released, even Bogart himself expressed doubts about a two-phase switch in his screen persona from bad boy and gangster to romantic and hero.

"This gangster stuff is old-hat to me," Bogart "said" in a Warner Bros. press release—no doubt a dose of studio hype blended with some elements of the actor's true feelings. "I've been playing mobsters and gunmen for eight years in more than thirty pictures. I've handled everything from a rod to a sawed-off shotgun in movies and would feel at home inside an arsenal any day. I'm what they call a 'super-heavy' in the trade.

"I've greeted beautiful women with an uppercut in the jaw and mowed down more rival mobs than Central Casting could round up in a week. Audiences have despised me with a deep and burning hate. And I've been happy about it because villainy on the screen pays off a lot better than virtue.

"But look what's happening to me now. All of a sudden I'm a hero. In *All Through the Night,* me and my mob mopped up on a nest of fifth columnists. In *Across the Pacific,* I kept the Japs from blowing up the Panama Canal.

"In this *Casablanca,* I'm a tough American up against a batch of fascists in French Morocco. I don't know what all my fans who love to hate me are going to think about it."

While publicly unsure of his changing screen image, privately Bogart must have felt that the studio's growing faith in him was a deeply satisfying challenge. After years mired in the morass of the Warner mill, Bogart, the onetime second-fiddle who took the cast-off roles of the studio's higher profile talents, had finally emerged as a candidate for top star. Still, Bogart's trial by ordeal would not be easy; in *Casablanca,* he would receive the biggest test of his career.

Casablanca

64

Bogart at the peak of his star power, as Richard Blaine in Casablanca.

four

Cigarette Smoke
and Guitar Music

*B*y early February, when discussing plans for *Casablanca*, Hal Wallis
could say only two things with certainty: he owned an idea, and he
had a star assigned to the project.

That was all. Everything else—cast, crew, script, sets—was a loom-
ing question mark, and no doubt a daunting prospect, with cameras
scheduled to roll in scarcely three months. And Wallis would soon discover that even his leading actor was not secure for his budding production.

Whatever weaknesses can be found in the filmmaking goliath that
was Hollywood of the 1940s, its greatest strength—and the envy of every
filmmaker outside the United States—was a studio's remarkable ability
to swing an entire motion picture production into action—literally at a
moment's notice. In his new role as a quasi-independent producer with
first choice of everything at Warner Bros., Wallis could pick and choose
from all of the studio's departments, selecting the best writers, the top
stars, the ideal supporting performers, and the most talented off-screen
technicians, artists, and directors.

However, the biggest problem, and the most time-consuming issue, remained the script. In the era of the long-term studio contract, stars could be assigned to a production with a phone call, and sets or props could materialize on soundstages overnight. But no weight of studio power could formulate a script without hundreds, often thousands, of hours of creative effort; in the case of *Casablanca*, even optimistic assessments found little but the sparest of plots worth salvaging from the Burnett-Alison script; weeks of work lay ahead before the first frame of film could be shot.

Over the next seven months, for Wallis and his staff shaping the script would become a battle of details large and small—a step forward here, a setback there—an added burden that hampered the always complex process of assembling all of the creative elements that would eventually become *Casablanca*. Wallis's work entered two distinct phases: first, the producer assembled his creative team and started the production cycle as if planning any routine Warner picture as it moved smoothly into production. At the same time, the producer and an assortment of writers wrestled with a stubborn script that would only grow more difficult to complete as time passed.

So in February 1942, while the world faced the grimmest months of its grimmest years at war, the American home front, including the Hollywood studios, tried to carry on with life as normally as possible. Throughout the winter, Wallis and company proceeded with the production of several projects: the last stages of preproduction of the Bette Davis vehicle, *Now, Voyager*, the principal photography for *Yankee Doodle Dandy* (which would win James Cagney his only Academy Award), and the writing of draft after draft of a script that would, come the first weeks of May, go before the cameras as *Casablanca*.

Soon, the two phases of work would clash, but the final result would become a tribute to Wallis's effectiveness as a producer—a master mechanic of the mammoth studio machine. In spite of all the obstacles, Wallis would eventually achieve virtually all of his goals for the project.

However, the first tentative steps toward creating the script were rocky. While both Wally Kline and Aeneas MacKenzie could boast strong track records at Warner Bros. and together wrote the Errol Flynn showpiece *They Died with Their Boots On*, their luck with *Casablanca* was far more limited. The writers produced little on the script that satisfied Wallis, and he soon replaced them with contract writers Julius and Philip Epstein, a brother writing team with a host of screenwriting hits to their credit, including such Warner winners as *The Bride Came C.O.D.*, *The Male Animal*, and *Daughters Courageous*, as well as uncredited contributions to such classics as *Yankee Doodle Dandy*.

The Epsteins, Wallis recalled, "were enthusiastic and tremendously excited by the idea. And I liked everything they suggested."

Simply stated indeed, but controversy has simmered ever since over which writers on the Warner lot were "most responsible" for the script of *Casablanca*. Seven writers would be logged onto the budget of the production: The Epsteins were first assigned to the project, and completed the first substantial work on it; soon to follow was Howard Koch, who had made his mark in radio working on Orson Welles's Mercury Theatre and was the writer credited with adapting the script for the infamous *War of the Worlds* radio broadcast on Halloween Eve 1938. Later, Casey Robinson, Wallis's favorite staff writer, would also be called in to consult and write crucial elements of the production. (Other writers assigned temporarily to the production were MacKenzie, Kline, and *Four Daughters* scenarist Lenore Coffee, who contributed material to early drafts.)

The individual writers and the Epstein team would each contribute their own unique elements to the script, sometimes working in groups, often working independently and consulting with Wallis. The crush of deadlines would weigh so heavily that revised material would often reach the *Casablanca* sets mere hours before those scenes were shot.

But in February 1942, the Epsteins seemed the perfect team to begin writing in earnest. Wallis liked everything about the Epsteins working on the project—everything, that is, except their availability. Even though the brothers were under contract to Warners, they felt a higher calling to their country.

Director Frank Capra, who had recently joined the U.S. Army Signal Corps to serve the war effort, had moved to Washington to plan the production of his mammoth documentaries *Why We Fight*, a series that would provide much of the world with its first detailed glimpse of the Axis menace. Capra invited the Epsteins to work on the project, and, in spite of their commitments to their assignment and protests from Warners, they agreed to join the director in the nation's capital.

"The studio said, 'No, you've got to do this picture,' " said Julius Epstein of Wallis's concerns about the brothers' sudden departure during preproduction. "We said, 'We're going anyhow.' We never did a line on *Casablanca* before we went to Washington. And we went."

So only a few days into production, Wallis became an early victim of manpower drains caused by the war effort, losing two of his best writers for more than a month. In the meantime, he continued to let other studio writers tinker with the project.

Wallis wasn't having much luck luring a suitable director to the project either. He fished around among several Warner directors, but wasn't impressed by his first round of meetings with the available on-lot talent. So while he could have assigned any director at Warner Bros. to the production, he had another candidate in mind—and he was not at the studio.

The year before, Warners had, for the first time, begun the routine use of directors not under contract. These projects by outside directors—Sam Wood for *King's Row,* Howard Hawks for *Sergeant York,* and William Wyler for *The Letter*—were handled with great success; for *Casablanca,* Wallis set his sights on Wyler. To lure the director to the project, Wallis shipped a copy of the script to him while he vacationed in Sun Valley with 20th Century-Fox production chief Darryl Zanuck.

But Wyler, who was also being wooed by Sam Goldwyn, didn't have time for anything except Zanuck and their mutual passion for cards. Zanuck and Wyler "play gin rummy until 2:30 A.M., which, you can see, leaves little time for anything else," Wallis heard from writer Norman Krasna, who had accompanied the pair to the Idaho ski resort. "Wyler hasn't read Goldwyn's story either," said Krasna, "so you can't feel slighted."

Wyler missed his chance. Instead, Wallis returned to the studio corps, and selected Michael Curtiz, "my favorite director," the producer said, "then and always."

In Michael Curtiz, Wallis chose a tall, imposing personality who maintained a country squire's life-style filled with skeet shooting and polo on a ranch not far from the studio—and a director with a well-earned reputation for being a hard-nosed workaholic with a dictatorial on-set disposition.

Curtiz is often remembered in film history as a contract director who lacked the individualistic personal style of some of his better-known colleagues, such as Howard Hawks, George Cukor, or John Ford, and he seldom receives the same reverence granted to the other directing legends of Hollywood's studio era. But Curtiz's personal and artistic "flaws" are eclipsed by cinematic achievements that include a range of films so successful and broad in scope that, when measuring sheer entertainment value, his work easily equals the creative output of any other director of his era.

With some of Hollywood's favorite films among the more than 165 movies of his legacy—including costume adventures (*Captain Blood, The Adventures of Robin Hood, The Sea Hawk*), musicals (*Yankee Doodle Dandy, White Christmas*), westerns (*Dodge City, Virginia City*), comedies (*Life with Father*), drama (*Mildred Pierce, Angels with Dirty Faces*), and his Academy Award–winning direction of *Casablanca*—Curtiz is classified quite differently from his peers. No visionary who sought to inject higher meaning into his cinematic themes, Curtiz found his niche for success in Hollywood as the consummate studio director, a filmmaker who meshed perfectly with the Hollywood machine of the golden era of movies, and a forceful manipulator of the studio methods who could shape performances and projects to fit his unique fast-paced style.

Born Mihaly Kertesz in Budapest, Hungary, on Christmas Eve 1888, Curtiz received his directorial training on the stages of Europe in the early years of the twentieth century. After shifting to films in the late 1910s, he was soon directing motion pictures in his native Hungary as well as France, England, and Scandinavia. (Accounts of Curtiz's early career are sketchy; for example, he may have guided Greta Garbo in one of her early silent appearances, but complete records of his credits during these years is lacking.)

When Curtiz fled to Vienna in 1919 after the Communist dictatorship of Bela Kun nationalized the Hungarian film studios, he quickly earned a reputation as one of the top directors in Austria and Germany. It was his production of *Moon of Israel* that attracted the attention of the brothers Warner.

"We were laid in the aisles by the impact of Curtiz's camera work," Jack Warner recalled of *Moon of Israel*. "We saw shots and angles that were pure genius."

Harry Warner himself brought Curtiz to America in 1926. His first big success for Warners was *Mammy*, the fourth Al Jolson film, in 1930; the review of *Mammy* that appeared in *Variety* summarized the picture with words that would describe many of Curtiz's future efforts: "a lively picture, playing fast."

Accumulating a string of briskly paced hits throughout the 1930s, Curtiz soon joined the upper echelon of the Warner directors. He would eventually direct some eighty-eight films for the studio, and during some extraordinarily fruitful periods averaged as many as five films per year.

Curtiz became known as a "money director"—one who made his pictures on schedule, within the budget, and much more often than not with tremendous box-office appeal. (After *Casablanca*, seven of his pictures would be ranked for decades among the top-grossing films of all time, and by 1946, he had been the biggest money-making director in Hollywood three years in a row.) Curtiz's value to the studio was reflected in his salary; when production of *Casablanca* began, the director's $183,000 salary made him the fifth-highest paid employee at Warners, behind only James Cagney, Wallis, Edward G. Robinson, Errol Flynn, and fellow director Lloyd Bacon.

While acclaimed throughout his career for entertaining and profitable productions, Curtiz won few points for his on-set behavior. Although perfectly capable of being a genteel charmer, an engaging intellectual, and a sociable partner for chess, riding, or shooting, on the set he was notorious for all-encompassing work habits and a pendulum-swing temperament that soared from calm to rage and back again within seconds.

Curtiz demanded that his sets be run precisely according to his dictates and his orders were followed. During the filming of *Captain*

Blood, for example, Errol Flynn said that Curtiz ordered the removal of the safety tips from swords used in dueling sequences to make the actors' reactions real.

Curtiz could terrorize the most formidable personalities on the lot— especially those who deplored his dawn-to-dusk work style. Said John Barrymore while visiting a dance marathon in Santa Monica just past the two-hundred-hour mark, "You don't know what it is to be tired unless you've worked for Curtiz." Even Wallis, himself intolerant of easygoing work attitudes, once called Curtiz "a demon for work" and "a slave driver."

Referring to Curtiz in a note to Jack Warner, Olivia De Havilland recalled a brief moment of director-inspired turmoil on the set of *The Private Lives of Elizabeth and Essex* in 1939.

"I found that a certain man [Curtiz] who means well, wanted to get this charming scene over in a hurry—and then, bang! he said something very tactless, and to my horror I found myself shaking from head to foot with nerves, and unable to open my mouth for fear of crying—which would never do in front of so many people," De Havilland wrote.

"The man, who meant well, realized he had gone too far, apologized, and dismissed the company, assuring me that he could quite well shoot the scene another day," said De Havilland. "He had said the same kind of thing a few days before to a famous blond actress [Bette Davis] who had gone home with tears streaming down her face."

Curtiz's intense focus on his work kept him as tough on inanimate objects as he was on cast and crew; in fact, the studio's own publicity crowed about Curtiz's intolerance of anyone or anything that stood in the way of filming. For instance, while directing *The Breaking Point* in Newport Harbor, Warner publicity reported, a boat kept bobbing. "Let the boat stand still," Curtiz screamed, presumably to the gods. "Why doesn't the boat move that way? Tell the boat to stop bouncing!" The director ordered the boat nailed to the dock, but when an assistant director told him that the nails might cause leaks, Curtiz gruffly revoked the command.

While directing Gary Cooper, Lauren Bacall, and Patricia Neal in *Bright Leaf,* Curtiz discovered that a pile of tobacco wouldn't "quiver in the breeze" as he envisioned. During the shooting of *Young Man with a Horn* at Ocean Park in Santa Monica, the noise of the waves disturbed the shooting. Finally Curtiz could stand the roaring sea no longer. He stood up and yelled, "Somebody stop that ocean!"—at least that's what the Warner press release claimed.

"It isn't that Curtiz is childlike and doesn't know better when he starts yelling at inanimate objects," the studio's publicity explained. "It's just that he gets so wound up with his direction that he seems to forget his inability to make things do what he can make people do."

Despite more than fifteen years' experience working in the Warner system, Curtiz retained an adversarial attitude on the set with actors, technicians, and producers alike. His unyielding control and strong-willed opinions of the material placed him in frequent conflict with the Warner brass; in a Hollywood era when the producer's word was law, Curtiz followed his own course for a motion picture, often conveniently "forgetting" to shoot dialogue when he thought silent scenes were more appropriate, or skipping shots altogether when he believed they were unnecessary to advance the story. Curtiz clashed constantly with the Warner powers, always taking an argument to the limit of everyone's tolerance—but stopping short of overstepping his bounds so he might be replaced on a project.

While Wallis held Curtiz in high esteem, the director's creative indiscretions usually compelled his producer to watch him like a hawk (a tactic, Wallis would soon realize, that was necessary during the filming of *Casablanca* as well). Over the course of his career at Warners, Curtiz was constantly scolded for his on-set pigheadedness—often in colorfully phrased memos.

"I have talked to you about four thousand times, until I am blue in the face, about the wardrobe in this picture," Wallis screamed in a memo to Curtiz during the production of *Captain Blood* with Errol Flynn in 1935. "We discussed the fact that when the men get to be pirates, that we would not have 'Blood' dressed up.

"Yet tonight, in the dailies, in the division of the spoil sequence, here is Captain Blood with a nice velvet coat, with lace cuffs out of the bottom, with a nice lace stock collar, and just dressed exactly opposite to what I asked you to do.

"What in the hell is the matter with you, and why do you insist on crossing me on everything that I ask you not to do? What do I have to do to get you to do things my way? I want the man to look like a pirate, not a molly-coddle. Let him look a little swashbuckling, for Christ sakes! Don't always have him dressed up like a pansy! I don't know how many times we've talked this over."

Or, during *Charge of the Light Brigade* in 1936, Wallis told Curtiz, "I remember about four months ago when you came to my office and pleaded to be allowed to make this picture and promised me that if you got it you would absolutely behave and do everything that you were told to do, and I would not have any trouble with you on the picture, but I have had just one headache after another.

"I certainly am not going away with any feeling of security over this picture, because every day that you have shot so far there has been something wrong."

Regardless of creative differences large and small with his producer, Curtiz maintained a congenial friendship with Wallis, and a close working relationship with the producer on the lot. In fact, the pair were frequent riding and shooting partners at Curtiz's ranch.

Curtiz rehearses Bogart and Bergman for the Paris flashback sequence, dancing to the tune of "Perfidia."

"Mike Curtiz and I had our differences," Wallis said, "but he was a superb director with an amazing command of lighting, mood, and action. He could handle any kind of picture: melodrama, comedy, western, historical epic, or love story." Warner, too, regarded Curtiz with respect—in between nagging memos and reprimands for shooting too many takes or wasting film—calling him "my friend and one of the truly great directors in the business."

Beyond his somewhat noteworthy professional habits, Curtiz became legendary in Hollywood lore for his use and abuse of the English language. The director frequently spouted verbal blunders so pronounced and unintentionally amusing that they were known throughout the industry as Curtizisms. So celebrated did these spoken gaffs become that *Time* magazine once joked that producer Sam Goldwyn, another frequent word abuser, had a press agent following Curtiz to gather material. These language garblings were noted with such frequency that Curtiz's crew hung signs during a production that read "English Broken Here" and "Curtiz Spoken Here."

Included among the turns-of-phrase attributed to Curtiz are: "Next time I send some fool for something I go myself," "I'm worried because I'm so optimistic," and "Don't do it the way I showed you; do it the way I mean."

Curtizisms were overheard during every Curtiz production: "I don't want yesmen," Curtiz said on the set of *Kid Galahad*. "If you don't agree, say so even though I will fire you." During *Charge of the Light Brigade*, he told extras to "stop standing together in bundles." On the same picture, Curtiz reportedly said, "Bring on the empty horses"—an order so memorable that David Niven used the phrase for the title of his second book.

Curtiz also developed a reputation, noted in private whisperings around the studio, for an unyielding sexual appetite. A flagrant womanizer who reportedly employed a certain blonde extra far more for sexual service than acting talents, Curtiz was legendary at Warners for "nooners" in lieu of lunch. While cast and crew dined, Curtiz was known to retire for a midday liaison, usually in his office but on occasion in an unused corner of the set—an indiscretion that once backfired when crew members working in the rafters of a stage discovered the director and his "colleague" below at the height of passion.

But through a lifetime of Hollywood adventures, and beyond the ballyhoo about his on-set behavior, turns-of-phrase, or sexual adventures, Curtiz retained a surprisingly simple attitude about his profession. He once described his directorial role as "I help out so the actors don't bump into each other." Or, when asked his method for success, he said, "I take a simple story and try to handle it artistically."

Curtiz avoided the normal Hollywood scene, calling studio parties "beautiful bubble talk. I am scared to death of all this honey, this saccharin. Our success—it's so flimsy."

Curtiz instead found diversion at his ranch, or in continuing observation of the American scene. The studio reported that Curtiz wandered through the seamier side of Hollywood life with the insatiable curiosity of a ten-year-old, hanging around street corner conversations and bars to listen to the talk, or roving through juvenile court, night court, pawn shops—anywhere he could gain a stronger grasp of Americans and Americana.

"In places like that you see the emotions of people at a climax," said Curtiz. "You see them suffering through the big moments of their lives, the result of all the little anxieties of the years.

"Perhaps I was more receptive to what I heard because it was all new," Curtiz said of his early explorations as an immigrant in Hollywood. "The average American takes these things for granted. I have never forgotten."

By the spring of 1942, Curtiz, at fifty-three, was an aggressive and successful veteran in a young man's game. Only a few weeks before beginning his assignment on *Casablanca*, he had wrapped photography of *Yankee Doodle Dandy*—yet another blockbuster-in-the-making. Soon after taking over the reins of the latest Wallis production, Curtiz would discover that his new assignment would become, for reasons out of his control, one of the most challenging projects of his career

While the Epsteins toiled in Washington with Capra, and with only a general idea of his characters for *Casablanca*, Wallis proceeded to cast his principal players. With Bogart set for the hero, Wallis's first priority was a leading lady, and he was having second thoughts about assigning Ann Sheridan in the starring role. The Epsteins and Wallis had explored the idea of changing the character of "Lois Meredith" into a mysterious foreigner, so Wallis put out feelers to other studios to try to find the right woman for the part.

First he dickered with MGM to see if he could borrow starlet Hedy Lamarr. But MGM studio chief Louis B. Mayer wasn't dealing for his popular Austrian actress. "Mayer is opposed to loaning her out to anybody," Wallis told Warner aide Steve Trilling.

Instead, the producer turned to MGM's neighbor in Culver City, independent producer David O. Selznick, to entice the creator of *Gone With the Wind* to loan out Ingrid Bergman, his top female star. With appearances in *Intermezzo*, *Rage in Heaven*, *Adam Had Four Sons*, and *Dr. Jekyll and Mr. Hyde* in a span of only two years, Bergman was one of the hottest actresses in Hollywood.

With her natural beauty and gentle accent, Bergman brought a warm, elegant presence to the screen unlike any other leading actress. Before her Hollywood career, she appeared in films in her native Sweden, debuting at nineteen in *The Count From the Monk's Bridge*. With a succession of motion pictures—some eleven films by the time she was twenty-three—Bergman soon rose to the pinnacle of the Swedish film industry.

In 1936, Bergman appeared in her most popular role yet—Gustaf Molander's tragic romance, *Intermezzo*. Her performance caught the eye of Selznick, who brought the actress to America to appear in the English-language version of the film.

After receiving strong critical praise and audience acceptance for *Intermezzo*, Bergman quickly became a popular young star of the American cinema. Although she earned acclaim for romantic roles, early in her career Bergman sought to expand her performances. Asked to play Beatrix Emery, the innocent fiancée in *Dr. Jekyll and Mr. Hyde* opposite Spencer Tracy, she instead sought and secured the role of the "low-life" Ivy Peterson.

Although Warner Bros. maintained a bevy of attractive and talented starlets under contract, Wallis wanted Bergman to play Ilsa; she was, the producer said, "ideal for the foreign girl with a slight accent."

Wallis's turndown at MGM for Lamarr soon faded from memory; Bergman, said Wallis, "was the only actress with the luminous quality, the warmth and tenderness necessary for the role."

Ingrid Bergman. An actress with "the luminous quality" needed to play Ilsa, according to Wallis.

Yet Selznick—"an agent at heart" as Wallis called him—was a hard-bitten negotiator for the use of his prized contract talent, and Bergman was his star in demand. Selznick knew that Wallis was anxious to sign Bergman, so her producer-boss played hard to get. Selznick had no projects scheduled for Bergman, and even though he had told her that he "would rather pay her to do nothing until the ideal part came along," Selznick knew that the lead in *Casablanca*, with a bushel of big stars and a topical romantic subject, could be the part that catapulted her into stardom. Eventually, after some fancy horse trading Hollywood-style and a load of cash, Selznick agreed to lend the services of his starlet.

By early March, the Epsteins were wrapping up their assignment on *Why We Fight*. In addition to their work with Capra, they had been writing brief segments of *Casablanca* while in Washington—working, as was their custom, side by side, contributing equally to every project, and recording the text in longhand for later transcription.

From their suite at the Hotel Lee Sheraton in Washington, the Epsteins sent their first batch of notes to Wallis.

"We'll try to get back as soon as possible," they wrote, "but in any event will keep right on with the pages. While we handle the foreign situation here, you try to get a foreign girl for the part." As an alternative to a foreigner, they wrote, "An American girl with big tits will do."

Finally, the Epsteins returned to Los Angeles and, as promised, began work full-tilt on the script. By the end of March they had finished their first full preliminary draft. Their work on the script would continue, but Wallis had a more urgent assignment of a different sort for his wise-cracking brother team.

Wallis wanted Bergman as his co-star for Bogart, and after experimenting with others for the role of Ilsa Lund, he wanted her badly. He had already tested Michele Morgan, the graceful French actress who had scored a recent success at RKO with another foreign-born actor, Paul Henreid, in *Joan of Paris*. In fact, Wallis actually announced publicly that Morgan would appear in the role—the April 10 release that announced Bogart's assignment to *Casablanca* said that he "takes the male lead opposite Michele Morgan"—perhaps as a not-so-veiled hint to Selznick that other candidates for the role besides Bergman were indeed available. But in spite of the announcement, Wallis was convinced that Bergman was the ideal choice for the role, and he barraged Selznick with phone calls to see if they could arrange a deal.

Selznick, however, wasn't biting, avoiding Wallis's calls and delaying negotiations by weeks. Finally, Wallis arranged for the Epsteins to serve as intermediaries, and the brothers took their "dog-and-pony" show to Selznick's office and tried to sell the producer on the story's merits.

Again, as in December 1941, allusions to *Algiers* saved the day.

"We went to Selznick to tell him the story," said Julius Epstein. "He was in his office having his lunch—soup on his desk. He never looked up from his soup as we started to tell what little story we had. I soon realized that we had told less than a half hour of story and we were floundering. Ingrid Bergman's character hadn't even come into the picture yet, and we wanted her for the starring role! So I said, 'Oh hell, it's going to be a lot of crap like *Algiers*. A lot of cigarette smoke and guitar music.' Selznick said, 'You've got Bergman!' "

Epstein's story remains a marvelous tale in Hollywood lore—and probably mostly true, with only a modicum of embellishment that the passage of years tends to add to such reminiscing. In fact, by the time the Epsteins met with Selznick, they had indeed finished their first draft, and there was a great deal more to the plot than merely "cigarette smoke and guitar music."

When the first half of their draft—dated April 1, 1942—was circulated around the studio, the Epsteins had transformed the original Burnett-Alison plot into a script far more suited to the crisp, hard-edged style that was the Warner trademark in the 1930s and 1940s. The principal plot lines that would become so familiar in the final film were already emerging: the murder of two German couriers, the letters of transit, Rick's adversarial friendship with Louis Renault, the romance between Ilsa and Rick, and many of the memorable lines.

In the early Epstein drafts, Rick is no longer married or a lawyer; instead, his previous employment was unclear and he was left with a foggy past. The Epsteins also downplayed the importance of Jan and Annina's escape from Casablanca, and instead built up Victor Laszlo's importance as a leader of the resistance, rather than as a wealthy potential contributor to the Nazi cause.

One vitally important plot point was already clear: The heroine would not stay with Rick, she would leave Casablanca with her husband. That issue never varied throughout the production of *Casablanca* in spite of the recollections of some of the performers who appear in the film. Only the circumstances surrounding the departure of Lois Meredith—soon to be Ilsa Lund—would change over the course of the writing.

With the Epsteins continuing their work throughout April, by the third week of the month, Wallis had "about sixty-five odd pages," he told production manager Al Alleborn, "and I hope to have a good deal more by the end of the next week." But by the end of April, the Epsteins weren't the only writers working on the script. Writing in tandem with the Epsteins was Howard Koch, who Wallis had also assigned to develop aspects of the plot.

For two sets of writers to be working on a script, often without each other's knowledge, was not uncommon in Hollywood, especially when a production start date loomed only weeks away. Often, the largest studios with the biggest writing stables, such as MGM, assigned several sets of writers to work on a single script (sometimes with individuals writing specific scenes or brief smatterings of dialogue) with all of the pieces mashed together into a seemingly unified whole.

By April, Wallis had no choice but to assign yet another writer to the project. The Epsteins' work proceeded, and with strong results, but the producer realized that he needed additional help with the plot and character development—especially to build the part of Lazlo—that a fresh approach to the writing could provide.

During April and May 1942, four of the studios' best and highest-paid writers: the Epsteins, Koch, and eventually Casey Robinson—who had run up a string of sensational writing hits with *Dark Victory*, *The Old Maid*, *All This and Heaven Too*, *King's Row*, and *Now, Voyager*—would be assigned to *Casablanca*, each working on different aspects of the project. In fact, some question remains about whether the Epsteins and Koch knew the extent of Robinson's involvement in contributing to the script.

With the passage of years, and the rise of *Casablanca* to the status of film legend, some of the recollections of Koch, Robinson, and Julius Epstein (Philip died in 1952), while fascinating studies of writers toiling in the Hollywood studio age, seem to add more questions than answers to the issue of how the script evolved.

Koch, for example, insisted that the Epsteins had been removed from the project early, and he continued on alone to complete the job—a claim disproved by an assortment of comments in the Warner files referring to the brothers' work late in the production. Robinson would assert that he never read the original drafts before he added key elements to the script after the production had already started shooting—a statement that his own memos to Wallis contradict. Julius Epstein, too, would have his share of inexactitudes—all perfectly understandable consequences of recalling work on a single script among dozens of projects at the studio. However, the accumulation of contradictions would add little to understanding the genesis of one of the most famous scripts ever produced in Hollywood.

Fortunately, answers to most questions about the script can be found in the Warner files, which show that the Epsteins, Koch, and Robinson all played critical roles in the production, each with his unique talents. The Epsteins created the original structure of the script and continued to polish material throughout the production; Koch added substantial character development and individual story points; and Robinson built up Laszlo's part and the romantic elements of the plot.

Wallis may have played all four screenwriters against the middle, but not without cause. The results as displayed in the final script show that relying on each writer for individual elements of the plot worked for the producer; without any single piece, the puzzle of the script that became *Casablanca* would not have been complete.

The spring of 1942 also brought some significant casting successes, along with a new assortment of problems acquiring actors. First and foremost among the casting issues was actually more of an annoyance, once again in the form of George Raft's status at the studio. For once, the actor was seeking a role rather than rejecting one, and this time he enlisted the support of studio chief Jack Warner.

On April 2, nearly two months after Humphrey Bogart had been assigned to *Casablanca*, Warner sent a confidential note to Wallis. "What do you think of using Raft in *Casablanca*?" the studio chief inquired. "He knows we are going to make this and is starting a campaign for it."

In his memoirs, Wallis recalled receiving the memo, but he also said that he "discreetly ignored it." Had he checked his own files, Wallis would have found his response to Warner in one of the classic bits of Hollywood correspondence. Wallis, in fact did reply to Warner's inquiry—exactly one day after Warner's confidential note.

On April 3, Wallis replied, "I have thought over very carefully the matter of George Raft in *Casablanca*, and I have discussed this with Mike [Curtiz], and we both feel that he should not be in this picture. Bogart is ideal for it, and it is being written for him, and I think we should forget Raft for this property.

"Incidentally," Wallis continued on the subject of Raft, "he hasn't done a picture here since I was a little boy, and I don't think he should be able to put his fingers on just what he wants to do when he wants to do it." That, indeed, was that.

OFFICE OF
J. L. WARNER

To **MR. HAL WALLIS**   April 2, 1942
    Confidential Correspondence

> **What do you think of using Raft in "CASABLANCA"?**
>
> **He knows we are going to make this and is starting a campaign for it.**
>
>   JACK

(Continued on following page.)

WARNER BROS. PICTURES. INC.
BURBANK, CALIFORNIA

INTER-OFFICE COMMUNICATION

TO MR.___WARNER___   DATE___April 3, 1942___

FROM MR.___WALLIS___   SUBJECT___"CASABLANCA"___

Dear Jack:

I have thought over very carefully the matter of George Raft in "CASABLANCA", and I have discussed this with Mike, and we both feel that he should not be in this picture. Bogart is ideal for it, and it is being written for him, and I think we should forget Raft for this property.

Incidentally, he hasn't done a picture here since I was a little boy, and I don't think he should be able to put his fingers on just what he wants to do when he wants to do it.

HW:og   HAL WALLIS

VERBAL MESSAGES CAUSE MISUNDERSTANDING AND DELAYS
(PLEASE PUT THEM IN WRITING)

By April 24, Selznick finally agreed to lend Ingrid Bergman to Warner Bros., for $3,125 per week. Also part of the deal was a swap of the services of Warner star Olivia De Havilland, whom Selznick desperately sought for another film ever since the actress appeared as Melanie in *Gone With the Wind*. (Surprisingly, after holding out so long to get precisely the deal he wanted for Bergman, and demanding De Havilland as part of the agreement, Selznick never did use the Warner star in another film. Instead, the producer lent De Havilland to RKO, where she starred in *Government Girl*, a modest vehicle that touted war production.) Selznick balked at Wallis's request for a two-picture deal for Bergman, but he did promise an "understanding" that if Selznick arranged an outside deal for his actress again, Warner Bros. would be given first consideration (in fact, Bergman's next role turned out to be her last-minute casting to star as Maria in Paramount's adaptation of Ernest Hemingway's *For Whom the Bell Tolls*; Warners didn't oppose the deal). As part of her contract with Warner Bros., Bergman would also receive star billing with her name above the title, along with her co-stars.

By April 29, just two weeks before the production was scheduled to go before the cameras, Wallis had cast two of the three principal roles; only the part of Victor Laszlo remained. Wallis needed a unique combination of personality traits for the role of the Czechoslovakian underground leader: an actor who could convey a sense of supreme courage and moral standing but who could also be noble enough to win the heroine and not make Rick seem foolish in the process. Considering all the requirements, finding the right man would not be an easy task.

Wallis considered a number of actors for the role of Laszlo, including red-hot newcomer Joseph Cotten, who had recently compiled a string of sensational performances in his first Hollywood appearances, including *Citizen Kane* and *The Magnificent Ambersons*, and *Journey into Fear* for Orson Welles. But Cotten wasn't available, and a number of experiments and screen tests with a series of unknown actors (including a too-young Jean-Pierre Aumont) proved fruitless.

Strangely, with so many foreign-born actors in their mid-thirties floating around Hollywood in 1942, Wallis and his staff could find no other candidates for Laszlo who suited them. "Aside from Philip Dorn, whom we cannot get, and Paul Henreid, who I am sure will not play the part when he reads it, there is no one else that I can think of," Wallis told Curtiz on April 22. "I think you should satisfy yourself on this point; that is, that there is no one available, and then begin to adjust yourself to the thought that we might have to use someone of the type of Dean Jagger, Ian Hunter, or Herbert Marshall, or someone of this type without an accent."

Instead, Wallis decided to focus his attentions on Henreid, the actor *Time* called "Hollywood's likeliest leading man."

Yet another Austrian émigré associated with the project, Henreid learned the acting trade on the stages of Austria and England. Born in Trieste, Henried alternated between a career in publishing and acting before becoming a leading star of the Vienna theater. As the Nazi menace began to threaten Austria, Henreid moved to England, where in 1939 he appeared in MGM's smash hit film adaptation of *Goodbye Mr. Chips*—only his second English-language film. Henreid soon came to Hollywood via Broadway, and was lured to Warner Bros. by a studio contract and a dynamite role: the romantic lead opposite Bette Davis in Wallis's own production of *Now, Voyager*.

Henreid, Wallis said, "had the dignity and integrity the role demanded." Warner aide Steve Trilling agreed with that assessment but also noted that Henreid was "a bit of a ham." In spite of his accessibility on the lot—in April, his work on *Now, Voyager* continued only steps away from the soundstages where the *Casablanca* sets were under construction—Wallis was concerned about the actor's availability. The producer questioned whether the Austrian actor would complete his assignment on *Now, Voyager* in time to start in his new role.

Also, both Wallis and Trilling wondered whether Henreid could be enticed to play the role of Laszlo, a part that would at best portray a noble husband but at worst might be viewed as the ungrateful spouse who stole away the heroine from the romance of a lifetime. Henreid agreed with

Paul Henreid with Michele Morgan, his co-star in Joan of Paris.

their concerns, recalling the part as originally written as being "the second lover."

But when Henreid met with Wallis and company, he began to better understand the role. "Listening to them, I began to see the film as a very exciting melodrama," Henreid recalled, "and although my part was not the real love in Bergman's life, and not even that good a part, it also wasn't that bad."

With general promises to build up the part, assurances that he would indeed "get the girl" in the end, and specific arrangements to receive equal billing to Bogart and Bergman, Henreid agreed to play Laszlo.

Still, the logistical issue remained of whether or not Henreid would complete *Now, Voyager* on schedule. Eventually Henreid's commitments to *Now, Voyager* would bring him into the *Casablanca* production in barely the nick of time, but after he arrived, his health would nearly cost him the most famous role he would ever play.

f i v e

"Our Operation Was a Great Success—the Patient Died."

With his starring roles finally cast, Wallis could turn his full attention to signing outside talent or assigning contract players for the production. Among *Casablanca*'s greatest strengths is its cast, which from top to bottom includes not only some of Hollywood's biggest stars of the 1940s but also a host of versatile co-stars, character actors, and bit performers to round out the group.

"Warners always had a good casting department," Julius Epstein recalled. "In fact, one of the major reasons for *Casablanca*'s success was its casting."

In mid-April, barely a month before the scheduled start date, three critical co-starring roles remained to be filled: Sam, Rick's piano playing friend (called "Sam the Rabbit" in the Burnett-Alison script); Captain Louis Renault, the unscrupulous but charming prefect of the Casablanca police; and Major Heinrich Strasser, the diabolical Nazi officer (at this point in the writing, Strasser's character was still a captain; he was later "promoted" to major, no doubt to avoid confusion with Captain Renault).

Claude Rains: "I was in awe," said Bette Davis of Rains's talents.

As when casting Laszlo's character, Wallis and his staff could choose from the gamut of Warner actors, but they were painstaking in their effort to identify precisely the right actor for each role—whether from the studio roster or not. Easiest of these castings was signing the actor number one on Wallis's list for his co-starring roles. Claude Rains, the veteran actor who had been an established figure at the studio since he appeared in his first Warner vehicle, *Anthony Adverse* in 1936, was the ideal performer to create the role of Louis Renault.

Rains built a career as a solid theatrical actor for nearly two decades before he appeared in his first motion picture in 1933—a blockbuster performance in the title role of *The Invisible Man*. Understated, suave, and genteel, Rains lacked the bearing of a glamorous leading man—a minor shortcoming he more than compensated for with debonair charm and potent acting talents. A shameless scene-stealer with an uncanny knack for dominating any shot with a sideways look or a hooked eyebrow, Rains could outact any other performer on the Warner lot—and often did as deliciously devilish villains such as Prince John in *The Adventures of Robin Hood*. His appearances—whether as the star, co-star, or in a supporting role—provided the perfect complement to the other top players at the studio.

"I was in awe," said Bette Davis of Rains when they appeared together in *Juarez*. "I was thrown for a loop. At the time, he scared the life out of me."

Like Henreid, Rains was working on *Now, Voyager*, playing Bette Davis's psychologist in one of the few purely sympathetic roles of his early film career. Rains was assigned to *Casablanca* for $4,000 a week, but he, too, would present problems of timing because of his work on the other Wallis project in production. (Eventually, because of late arrivals to the *Casablanca* set forced by other filming commitments or ill health, the production schedule would become a juggling act, as Curtiz and his team fought the clock in their struggle to finish shooting the highest-priced talents first to get them off the payroll, while others did nothing and patiently waited for their calls.)

Casting the ruthless Strasser wasn't as simple as choosing Rains to play Renault. The problem wasn't actor availability or talent—this time it was money. Wallis had set his sights on signing one of the two nastiest screen villains in Hollywood: Conrad Veidt or Otto Preminger.

Conrad Veidt, costumed as Major Heinrich Strasser (left). Veidt's diabolical on-screen personality contrasted sharply with his gracious charm in real life (right).

Although both Veidt and Preminger would become legendary Hollywood figures for appearing in the most wicked roles of the day, off-screen they maintained vehemently anti-Nazi views. Preminger, an Austrian-born Jew, had been fortunate enough to leave Europe and was already in America when the Nazis annexed his country.

Veidt, although not Jewish, barely escaped Germany with his life. An outspoken anti-Nazi who left Germany because of the developing horror in his country, Veidt unwisely returned to complete a final film commitment. While in Germany, the Gaumont-British Studio announced his upcoming appearance in the lead in the film version of Lion Feuchtwanger's novel *Jew Suss*. Told by Nazi propaganda chief Josef Goebbels to renounce the role—supposedly on orders from Adolf Hitler himself—Veidt refused. As a result, the actor was held under house arrest by the Nazis, supposedly too "ill" to return to his family in England. Fortunately, his release was secured before he suffered the same fate as other artistic agitators: transport to the concentration camps.

While either Veidt or Preminger—scheming, intelligent, satanically diabolical in appearance—could have provided an admirable foil to Bogart's Richard Blaine, the final selection became a matter of price. Preminger, under contract at Fox, was available on loan-out from Darryl Zanuck for an outrageous $7,000 per week—a ridiculous sum even in the heyday of the studio system. Even Louis Mayer's asking price for Veidt seemed steep: $25,000 for five weeks, plus one week "free" if needed for retakes or other shooting. The budget won out, and Veidt, a tall, debonair gentleman who on-screen projected a smoothly evil presence, was signed to join the cast as the highest-paid performer on the payroll.

Casting Sam, a black character playing an equal to a white leading player, was an especially delicate matter for Wallis. Hollywood's greatest shame for the first fifty years of film production was its treatment of black characters, virtually without exception, as inferior to whites. Black actors were almost never cast in everyday roles, and instead were relegated to wide-eyed servants, shuffling shoeshiners, or criminals.

In Hollywood in the 1940s, after more than five thousand feature films in the sound era, among the very few respectful characterizations written by the studios for a black character in a predominantly white cast was Hattie McDaniel's appearance as Mammy in *Gone With the Wind*. The performance, a powerful, witty, and intelligent portrayal, earned McDaniel the first Academy Award presented to a black actor.

Nevertheless, it was impossible to deny that even an actress as formidable as McDaniel had won her Oscar for playing a slave, and she seldom received the opportunity to play anything but servants. McDaniel, like many of her fellow black performers, took whatever roles she could to earn a living.

Even legendary entertainer Lena Horne, who appeared in tradition-ally white roles in MGM musicals, suffered the indignity of knowing her appearances were often crafted so they could be clipped without harm to the plot when her films were screened in Southern theaters—or any-where exhibitors objected to black actors appearing in anything but subservient roles.

In spite of the dismal track record for black characters in films produced by all of the major Hollywood studios—Warner Bros. in-cluded—no one involved in *Casablanca* ever questioned or attempted to revise the plot point that Sam, while an employee of Rick, was also his closest friend and confidant. Nor did Wallis ever consider not leaving Sam black, even though the character could have been easily changed to white. And no goggle-eyed caricature of the sort Hollywood typically demanded in the thirties and forties would suffice for Sam—Wallis needed a performance by a black actor who could overcome the tradi-tional stereotypes that the studios themselves had created.

At first Wallis considered changing Sam's character to a woman, and pondered testing Horne or singers Hazel Scott and Ella Fitzgerald for the role. Then, after deciding to retain Sam's character as written, Wallis tested several actors, including Clarence Muse, a talented musician,

Dooley Wilson's appearance as Sam was a breakthrough role for black actors.

singer, and actor who had appeared in dozens of films in stereotyped black roles. But in 1942, Muse, a renowned composer, co-founder of the Lafayette Players in Harlem, and one of the first inductees into the Black Filmmakers Hall of Fame, lost the role because he was a victim of casting against type—or rather, casting against stereotype. Muse wasn't hired, Wallis remembered, because "he seemed too much of a caricature of a black type in the test, and we didn't want broad comedy in the romantic scenes played around the piano."

As an alternative, Wallis remembered the performance of an actor named Dooley Wilson, a hoarse-voiced singer and drummer who had appeared in Federal Theater productions created by Orson Welles. Wilson had also originated the role of Little Joe in *Cabin in the Sky* on Broadway before being enticed to Hollywood by Paramount.

Wallis tested Wilson, who was under contract to Paramount, and found his acting performance satisfactory; Wilson played Sam as friendly, loyal, and intelligent, Wallis recalled, and "his personality was just right." But strangely Wallis thought Wilson's rough but well-trained singing voice unacceptable for the picture's musical numbers. Thus the producer only grudgingly agreed to borrow Wilson from Paramount to play Sam, for $500 a week. "He isn't ideal for the part," said Wallis to Curtiz in relation to Wilson's singing voice. "But if we get stuck and can't do any better I suppose he could play it."

Later, Wallis planned to dub Wilson's singing; long after the actor had completed his assignment and recorded all of his own songs, the producer was still not convinced that the performances were adequate. Fortunately, Wallis was convinced otherwise, and Wilson's dusty stylings remained.

As a result of the studio's willingness to let Wilson play Sam's character as originally written, the actor portrayed one of the few nondegrading black roles in any film (other than all-black productions) made in Hollywood to that time. Still, the industry itself would not forget the presence of a black actor among the stars of the film; some reviews of *Casablanca*, especially those in film industry publications, made certain to delicately point out that Sam was a "black piano player," or a "negro find"—discreet notices to those exhibitors who remained on guard against showing to racially insensitive audiences blacks and whites interacting as equals.

Nevertheless, Wilson's portrayal of Sam provided one more demonstration that black characters could be accepted in roles that had been traditionally limited to whites. While war dramas—and the need to portray soldiers of all races—provided more jobs for black actors, Wilson's performance in *Casablanca* marked a major step forward; the next substantial progress wouldn't come for a decade, until the arrival of Sidney Poitier as a major film star.

*   *   *

For the two important supporting roles—Ugarte, the murderer of the two German couriers, and Señor Ferrari, the owner of the Blue Parrot Café and head of the Casablanca black market—Wallis set his sights on a pair of Hollywood's most versatile character actors: Peter Lorre and Sydney Greenstreet.

Lorre, who Jack Warner once called "a plump little fellow with a deceptive baby face," was a Hungarian native who, like Henreid, had trained for an acting career on the stages of Vienna. Lorre also appeared in minor roles in German films before exploding into stardom as a psychotic child murderer in Fritz Lang's powerful thriller *M*.

With a mysterious on-screen disposition, a slight build, and a face dominated by expressive and often bulging eyes, Lorre was ideally suited to play sinister foreigners or shady character roles. He starred in the "Mr. Moto" series for Universal before hitting his stride at Warner Bros.

Peter Lorre found his breakthrough role playing the demented child killer in M—*the forerunner of all psychotic killer roles.*

in a succession of adventure and crime pictures, capped by his immensely popular performance as Joel Cairo in *The Maltese Falcon*.

The embodiment of screen intrigue, Lorre off-screen was the perfect gentleman—polite, debonair, and charming. But his pleasant personality marked only one aspect of his demeanor; Lorre was notorious at the studio, not for prima donna histrionics, but for his ceaseless practical jokes and well-planned disruptions on the set that would provide a welcome break to the otherwise hectic pace of shooting. The *Casablanca* production team would soon discover how much Lorre delighted in disrupting the project.

Lorre's smooth and scheming characters provided the perfect complement to the domineering performances of Sydney Greenstreet. Though a seasoned acting professional, Greenstreet was, in 1942, a newcomer to film. After appearing on the stages of London and New York for more than forty years, Greenstreet, at sixty-two, switched to film appearances only the year before, making an impressive debut as Kaspar Gutman in *The Maltese Falcon*.

An overpowering presence on-screen, off-camera Sydney Greenstreet was a charming gentleman who did his cheerful bit along with hundreds of other actors during the war clearing tables at the Hollywood Canteen, the free nightclub and restaurant for U.S. servicemen.

Topping the scales at nearly three hundred pounds, with a gruff voice and an overpowering screen presence that could dominate any scene, Greenstreet became an immediate hit with both critics and audiences. With Lorre, the two were formidable opponents to Bogart's Sam Spade in *The Maltese Falcon* (the trio would again appear together in 1944 in *Passage to Marseilles*).

Although both Greenstreet and Lorre found great success as character actors, they each expressed surprisingly divergent views about the craft of screen performance. "The lens," said Greenstreet after a lifetime on the stage and scarcely a year in the movie business, "is the actor's best critic, showing his mind working more clearly than on stage. You can get wonderful cooperation out of the lens if you are true, but God help you if you are not. You are at the mercy of the camera angles and the piecemeal technique."

Lorre, with more than a decade of appearances in both silent and sound films, looked upon the business with his customary mild amusement, and even poked gentle fun at Warner's first (and four-legged) star: "Much film acting is not really acting, no matter how successful it may be at the box office," he said. "Often it is a trick of personality, a theatrical gag. Dogs have been box-office bonanzas."

Lorre and Greenstreet are seen in only the briefest of appearances in *Casablanca* (Lorre less than four minutes in all, and Greenstreet barely five). Yet their colorful personalities added even more depth to the already talent-laden cast, and contributed immeasurably to the intrigue-shrouded atmosphere of the production. Lorre and Greenstreet would go on to appear together in several other thrillers for the studio—*The Mask of Dimitrios, Three Strangers,* and *The Conspirators* among them—an unlikely pair of menacing schemers who brought a heightened level of intrigue to some of the most popular productions of the 1940s.

For Warner Bros. to endure complex machinations with casting—horsetrading with independent producers, paying near-extortionate fees to other studios to acquire supporting actors, and finding the lists of players appropriate for a part limited to one or two actors—shows the desperate straits that all of the studios found themselves in during the early days of World War II. When the war brought shortages of resources, first on the list was manpower.

By March 1942, only three months after the United States entered the war, some fifteen hundred film employees had entered military service—5 percent of the total Hollywood work force. By February 1943, one out of every five male employees had left the studios for service in the armed forces. Even worse, many more departed the movie business for high-paying noncombat jobs in the blossoming defense industry in Southern California. The supply of freelance carpenters, painters, and technical workers shrank to such low levels that rather than hold up production because of the inability to acquire needed men, most studios adopted a policy of maintaining a larger labor staff on the payroll continuously, even through slack periods, which reduced the number of freelancers even further.

A year into the war, the studios' concerns about the manpower shortage had become so acute that several companies announced plans to begin training women to take over the technical jobs vacated by men—much to the horror of the trade unions, Warner Bros. led the pack of movie companies eager to find substitutes for the dwindling staffs. "Any day now you may find a woman at the mixing desk on the soundstage, refilling a camera, actually assisting a top cameraman, or doing other necessary work around a stage and in a studio in a takeover to relieve men for essential war work," warned the *Hollywood Reporter*.

Even though jobs for women at the studios were limited almost entirely to clerical positions in the 1940s, Warners was reportedly ready to train a hundred women to pinchhit in male-dominated positions if the worker shortage reached crisis levels. However, if union members were concerned about women invading the top tiers of union-dominated jobs, their angst was unfounded; the planned switchover, reported the trade papers, would take place *in all but the vital key spots*.

While the departure of valued technicians from Warners was certainly a blow, the loss of actors was far worse. In 1942, 60 percent of all actors under contract fell within the age range for draft or enlistment into military service, one industry study glumly reported, and "approximately half are unmarried and practically all of them are extremely healthy A-1 specimens." The trickle of performers leaving the studio soon became a flood; James Stewart and Clark Gable enlisted in the Army Air Corps, depriving MGM of its two most valued male stars; Robert Montgomery joined the navy, and many more would follow. Directors and other creative personnel also departed. Capra was already in Washington working on *Why We Fight* and other military projects, as was John Ford. Hollywood had begun to feel the wartime pinch.

The studios also experienced another form of actor shortage that developed from a shameful chapter in U.S. history: the plight of Americans of Japanese descent. By January 1942, Hollywood experienced an acute shortage of Japanese-American performers; few actors of Japanese heritage were either willing or available to appear in films playing the enemy; some feared that appearing as villains in American films would bring retaliation against their relatives in Japan, and even more were quite rightly concerned about the potential reprisals in their own neighborhoods at the hands of other Americans who sought a convenient scapegoat for the sneak attack treachery that forced the United States into the war.

When 20th Century-Fox filmed *Secret Agent of Japan* with Preston Foster, the cast featured thirty Americans of Japanese descent as extras—one of the few films in which Japanese-Americans appeared after the war began but before the issuance of the federal internment order that uprooted thousands of Japanese-Americans and relocated them into camps. (After the internment order and for the duration of the war, Japanese characters in American films were played by Chinese-Americans.)

Anger in Hollywood about Japanese warmongering spilled over into hatred of Japanese-Americans. The *Hollywood Reporter*, for example, gladly pointed out that before filming began on *Secret Agent of Japan*, clearances had to be obtained from the FBI and Naval Intelligence for each of the thirty Japanese-Americans in the cast; the paper neglected to mention that the background checks turned up nothing. During the filming, the paper reported, police were detailed to keep an eye on the actors "to prevent them from wandering off the set."

But manpower losses to the war effort weren't the only drains on the actor rolls; all of the studios—and Warner Bros. in particular—were short of available performers because the needs of production had become so demanding. While riding high on its crest of success, Warners faced a frustrating double dilemma when casting its pictures: not only were key actors departing, but the company faced additional talent shortages caused by every studio in Hollywood gearing up production of top-flight pictures to unprecedented levels.

Just before the war began, the picture boom had peaked with a vengeance: Ticket sales in the late summer and early autumn of 1941 were the best in the history of the business—some 100 million tickets a week in October, up from 60 million in April and May.

"Theater business is at the tops," wrote one industry analyst, "and exhibitors, distributors and New York sales heads are of the opinion that the boom has just started." No one in the film industry was surprised when, in November 1941, Warners announced that 1940–41 profits had jumped 100 percent to $5.4 million, the best earnings since before the Depression. "The company is in an especially rosy financial condition," an analyst reported, "in better condition than it has known for more than a decade."

Once the war started, the future looked even brighter—at least as far as studio profits were concerned. To a public with shrinking choices for entertainment, movies were more attractive than ever; travel was curtailed by gasoline cutbacks, and luxury items were in short supply because of rationing. Most stores closed at 5:00 P.M. to meet wartime restrictions, thus shifting larger amounts of holiday spending cash into motion picture ticket booths—a point *Variety* described, ten days into the war, as "a ray to shine on the film house operators of this jittery terrain."

The pace at Warner Bros., which usually hummed along near top speed, approached overload levels during the autumn of 1941 and the winter of 1942. In October, Jack Warner announced the heaviest production schedule in the history of the studio, with nineteen features and eight short subjects set to reach soundstages throughout the fall. This production schedule was also the riskiest Warners had yet attempted; because of the studio's new emphasis on producing only "A" pictures, all of these new ventures were considered high-budget films with casts selected from its roster of stars and featured players (the studio categorized its list of performers under contract in a ranking as either "stars" or "featured players"). Talent acquired from off the lot, when it was available, helped fill the gaps.

At the same time that Jack Warner was announcing the studio's soaring production plans, nine films were already in production—at one point, three pictures started shooting on the same day. Not long after, the studio logged an all-time high of eleven features in work simultaneously, while another twelve pictures were winding their way through post production.

By the fall of 1941, the studio announced that it was "so swamped" with filmmaking that the studio's entire roster of nineteen top stars was employed in current pictures or making camera tests for productions scheduled to start (the only Warner stars not working were Wayne Morris, who had left for the navy, and Brenda Marshall, who was recovering from an appendectomy). Most of the studio's seventy featured players under contract were also assigned to productions, along with another twenty-eight off-the-lot artists.

In October, Jack Warner announced that his company's objective for 1942 was to keep six pictures before the cameras on every working day of the year—a hugely ambitious goal that meant the studio had to start filming twelve features within the next two months, as well as prepare screenplays and production of another twelve pictures for the next two-month period.

The prospect of so many productions packed into such a frantic time schedule was nearly overwhelming; for T. C. Wright, who managed the Warner studio facilities and directed the staff of unit managers who worked on each picture, those days must have seemed an unending whirlpool of planning projects and shuffling studio space and staff. Wright, a thirty-year veteran of the motion picture business who was better known as "Tenny" to nearly everyone at Warners, was responsible for ensuring that filming continued at the optimum pace; the studio could ill-afford empty stages going to waste, but even worse was the prospect of production traffic jams caused by shooting schedules that inadvertently overlapped.

The onset of war made no dent in the studio's pace. When preproduction began for *Casablanca* in the winter of 1942, the studio was also preparing two other top-flight features for some of its most important stars: *The Hard Way*, a vehicle for Ida Lupino, Dennis Morgan, and Joan Leslie; and *The Constant Nymph*, a top-of-the-line production featuring

Charles Boyer and Joan Fontaine. Those three films, all key links in Warners' ambitious plans early in the war, meant that the studio was working simultaneously on eight high-budget motion pictures.

All of these grand plans would soon pay off handsomely for the studio. In 1942, Warner profits would again jump—this time to $8.6 million. Earnings would drop slightly to $8.2 million in 1943 and $7 million in 1944—possibly because all of the earnings from its biggest hit of the decade, *This Is the Army*, would be donated to war relief funds— but they grew again in 1945, to $9.9 million. Then profits would sky-rocket, thanks in part to lengthy theatrical runs of such blockbusters as *Saratoga Trunk* in 1945, *Night and Day* in 1946, and *Life with Father* in 1947. Warner earnings nearly doubled to $19.4 million in 1946, and rose again in 1947 to $22.1 million—the highest profits the studio would ever earn while under control of the Warner family.

However, even the brightest silver lining had its dark side. Despite the studio's eagerness to boost production to unheard-of levels, the ambitious plans meant that reducing costs to a minimum was more important than ever. The emphasis on "A" productions may have inspired bigger budgets, but the new policy also demanded even greater need for budget-watching; when Warners reported that 1940–41 profits had increased by $5.4 million, those earnings were based on total income of $102 million, up from $100 million the year before. The totals meant that the studio's profits had increased more than $5 million even though total income grew by only $2 million. Clearly, the budget-cutters at the studio were keeping their axes sharp.

The film industry got a glimpse of the philosophy behind budget cuts at the studio when, in a very public forum, Warners stated its case for "killing" its production of "B" pictures. Two weeks after Jack Warner told his department heads that production of all low-budget second features was canceled, the studio ran an advertisement in *Variety* featuring a graveyard tombstone with scripts of "B" pictures littered in front of it. The ad was topped with the bold headline, "Have You Heard About Our Operation? It was a great success. The patient died." On the tombstone was written, "Here lie 'B' pictures. The 'Bs' are dead and have no mourner, 'Their day is passed,' says J. L. Warner." Below the grave was a boxed condolence card that read, "And we're glad that you're dead, you rascals you! signed, Warner Bros." At the bottom of the ad was the phrase, "That's all there is, we ain't gonna 'B' no more!"

The "death announcement" was no doubt amusing to those within the film industry who thought that the day of the "B" picture was dead, as well as to Warner insiders who believed that the best course for the studio to follow was to focus on "A" productions (considering the studio's success making money with "A" pictures throughout the 1940s, and the fact that "B" production soon declined at all of the other major studios as well, the decision to kill "B" production was no doubt correct).

But the amusing tone of the ad could never disguise the upheaval of staff and talent produced by the new policy; among many losers in the decision to kill "B" pictures was Brian Foy, production chief for all "B" projects and a longtime Warner executive who had directed the studio's first all-talking picture, *The Lights of New York*. After Warner's decision, Foy was forced to leave the company after nearly two decades of service. The studio's dramatic action showed that beneath the glitz and glamour that created Hollywood's veneer was an unrelenting corporate enterprise capable of brutal tactics without hesitation. The business of making movies has always been a cutthroat proposition, and in the war years, the struggle was more hard-edged than ever.

Casablanca

96

"Hitler or No Hitler—
Kiss Me"

*B*y the end of April, both the Epsteins and Howard Koch were working full-tilt on their versions of the script for *Casablanca*. But work
was not progressing as quickly as Wallis had hoped. Although only the
week before the producer had told production manager Al Alleborn that
he would have a "good deal" of the script by the end of the month, on
April 28, Wallis told Jack Warner, "I should judge the Epsteins will be
through in about four weeks."

Wallis seemed optimistic, but he was fighting a losing battle against
the clock. He had hoped to begin production on *Casablanca* during the
first week of May; now, even the more realistic start date of May 18
seemed to be slipping away.

The producer had good reason to be worried. With contract performers assigned to the picture's budget, the first payment dates for outside
talent fast approaching, and an entire production team ready to swing
into action in mid-May, Wallis soon faced the unenviable position of
supporting a cast and crew that was ready to work but with nothing to

do. The meter was running, and unless work on the script proceeded rapidly, Wallis would be forced to watch almost $30,000 a day in unavoidable production costs and salaries go down the drain.

The same day Wallis reassured Warner about his confidence in the Epsteins' progress, Koch was working on his own material a few steps from the brothers' office in a corner room of the writers' building. "I believe I can finish the first act—about twenty-five pages—up to the flashback, by the end of the week," Koch told Wallis. "Now that we have a definite story in mind, I feel there is nothing serious to worry about."

No, Koch had "nothing serious" to worry about—only a start date that loomed three weeks away. By the last week of April, if he hadn't realized it before, Wallis knew that he had only two options: either postpone production, or take the picture before the cameras without a finished script. As it turned out, he chose both.

By May 11, a new script draft circulated around the studio. Although this draft doesn't indicate which writers wrote specific material, the Warner correspondence shows that the Epsteins continued to develop the plot and humor while Koch was proceeding, as he had agreed with Wallis, to flesh out the more serious elements of the drama. Both the Epsteins and Koch massaged the rough material from previous versions into a tighter, more deliberate plot.

The May 11 version of the script contained a host of small changes but none to the basic plot. The character of Lois Meredith, for example, was renamed Ilsa Dorn (only to be renamed Ilsa Lund in later drafts). When Rick refuses to admit an arrogant banker to the gambling room, we discover he works for the Deutsches Bank (in earlier drafts, the banker, to be played by Gregory Gaye, worked for the Bank of England).

The blending of Epstein wit with Koch's dramatic elements produced an entertaining meld of humor with the life-and-death drama of pitiful refugees caught up in world conflict—a combination that might have eluded less-talented writers. The Epsteins delivered much of this humor in deliberate slaps at the Nazis. Nearly all of the anti-Nazi remarks that appeared in the film were preserved from the earliest drafts, such as Renault's line, "Major Strasser is one of the reasons that the Third Reich enjoys the reputation it has today." Or, after searching the café for the letters of transit, Renault tells Rick, "I told my men to be especially destructive—you know how that impresses Germans." Or when Renault asks Carl the waiter to give Strasser's group a good table, Carl says, "I have already given him the best, knowing he is German and would take it anyway."

Not all of the political humor in the early drafts was directed at America's enemies; one satirical phrase came at the expense of the Allies' weak war effort. Early script drafts, as well as the final film, featured the pickpocket played by Curt Bois describing the murder of the two German couriers. But early drafts also included the pickpocket describing the two killings by saying "this constitutes a major allied victory." This nasty shot at the tenuous state of U.S. military affairs was wisely deleted from later scripts.

Some of the Epstein's anti-Axis material would be trimmed as well. Even during World War II, at the height of the vicious feelings in Hollywood toward the Nazis, some attempts at humorous insults were simply too ridiculous to film. For example, in early drafts, Major Strasser and Renault discussed the problem of Victor Laszlo's presence in French Morocco, and Strasser brought up the issue of Renault's preoccupation with women.

"Don't you think," Strasser asked, "that with so much important work to be done, you could devote a little less time to personal matters?"

"Well," Renault shrugged, "you enjoy war. I enjoy women. We are both very good at our jobs."

"I think the German viewpoint is a much healthier one," Strasser said.

"You are probably right," said Renault. "At least your work keeps you outdoors."

This exchange was snipped as the start of the production neared, but barely a week before the revised start date, many other plot elements remained rough. Rick still moped around his café, whining about the past—a far cry from the attractive man of mystery that would emerge in later material. The friendship between Rick and Louis was still hazy, and hadn't focused on the easy camaraderie between two men of the world that would provide some of the film's most endearing highlights.

In fact, in the May 11 draft, one is never quite sure whether Rick and Louis are friends at all; in the final scene, for example, as Laszlo is about to escape, Rick says, "Louis, it would make very little difference to me if I had to shoot you"—a far cry from the line as it eventually evolved, "Louis, I wouldn't like to shoot you, but I will if you take one more step."

Yet the biggest problem remained the ending. Only days before filming was to begin, the climax of the picture as written was, quite frankly, terrible.

All of the *Casablanca* drafts feature the same general conclusion: Laszlo and Ilsa escape by plane, Strasser is dead, and Rick and Louis banter. But the similarities end there; in the May 11 draft, the closing scene plays out inside Rick's café, not at the airport.

With Rick holding Louis at gunpoint, Ilsa tells Laszlo, "Victor, darling, I hate to tell you this way. I hate to do this to you, but I'm not going with you. I should . . . I know I should . . . but I can't go with you."

But Rick refuses to let Ilsa remain with him. "I'm not the Rick you knew in Paris," he tells her. "I serve drinks. I run a crooked gambling table. Every morning I lock myself in a room and drink myself dizzy."

Laszlo's character is no better. "If I had any pride, I'd walk out and leave you here," he tells his wife. "But I'm asking you, Ilsa, come with me."

Soon, Ilsa relents and leaves with Laszlo. Seconds later, Strasser arrives and tries to stop the plane. Rick and Strasser struggle, and Strasser throws Rick, giving the Nazi a moment to get to the telephone. Just as Strasser's call connects with the airport, Rick kills him by emptying a pistol into his back.

Hardly the noble scene as eventually played out in the film with its skillful blending of tender parting and high ideals. So with a week remaining before the start date, Wallis, the Epsteins, and Koch still needed to worry about characters who needed fleshing out, relationships in need of definition, and an ending in search of a resolution. They had a long way to go.

While the May 11 draft circulated throughout Warner Bros., and with lingering thoughts of starting production on May 18 still alive, an anxious Wallis, who was clearly depending on Koch to smooth off the rough

144.

246.   MED. SHOT   STRASSER

on phone in German Consulate.

                    STRASSER:
               (jiggling the receiver
               violently)
          Hello, hello -- what was that?

He hangs up, reaches for his hat, runs out.

                                        CUT TO:

247.   MED. SHOT   RICK, ILSA, VICTOR AND RENAULT

                    RENAULT:
               (with a gesture)
          There you are! You may lower
          that gun a little now.

The roar of the airplane's motor is heard.

                    LAZLO:
               (taking Ilsa's arm)
          Ilsa -- we'll have to hurry.

Ilsa looks quickly at Rick, then turns to Lazlo. Her
face is pale and it is evident she is steeling herself.

                    ILSA:
               (in a strained voice)
          Victor darling -- I hate to tell
          you this way. I hate to do this
          to you, but I'm not going with you.
          I should -- I know I should -- but
          I can't go with you.

                    LAZLO:
          Ilsa!

                    ILSA:
               (almost tearfully)
          I'm staying here with Rick, Victor.
          I love Rick. I loved him in Paris.
          I left him once to go back to you --
          but I can't do it again. For over
          a year I've tried to forget him.
          I've tried to love you -- and I do.
          I do love you, but not the way I
          love Rick. I've got to stay, Victor --
          I belong here with Rick.

                    LAZLO:
               (brokenly)
          Ilsa, I --

                                        (CONTINUED)

(On this page and the following page) Two script pages from the closing scene in the May 11 draft—not exactly the high ideals and powerful romance that all involved in the production were seeking.

247 (Cont.)

                RICK:
           (breaking in, savagely)
It's just talk, Lazlo, this not
staying here! She's going with you!

                ILSA:
Rick!

                RICK:
Do you think I'm going to let you
rot here? I can never get out.
I've got no place to go and nothing
to do when I get there --

                ILSA:
I don't care, Rick. I don't care --

                RICK:
I'm not the Rick you knew in Paris.
I'm not a man you can love any more.
I serve drinks. I run a crooked
gambling table. Every morning I
lock myself in a room and drink
myself dizzy. That's all I'll be
doing every day and night for the
rest of my life --

                ILSA:
Then I'll do it with you.

                RICK:
No, I've got it down to a science
now. I don't need any help doing
it. I don't want you around.
           (pointing to Lazlo)
You go with him. He wants you.
I'm all finished. You belong to a
fighter, not a saloon-keeper --

                ILSA:
           (tearfully)
If you think you can talk me out of --

                       CUT TO:

248.   CLOSE SHOT   RENAULT

                RENAULT:
I beg your pardon, Madame. I do not
like to interfere in this matter --
but the choice is not yours. Rick
will spend the rest of his natural
life in a concentration camp.

                     (CONTINUED)

Casablanca

102

edges from the Epstein material, pleaded with the writer to force the creative pace into high gear.

"I will appreciate anything you can do to speed up the balance of the script," Wallis told Koch. "We are starting production next Monday, and I am very anxious to get as much script as possible.

"I think this next batch of the Epsteins' stuff is for the most part good. There are one or two things that I did not like, but aside from this, I think almost everything of the Epsteins' is useable.

"Will you please step on it as much as possible and get this next batch through to me within the next two or three days if you can."

Later that day, Koch—who hadn't sought assignment to the production, and now found himself in the unenviable position of having much of the burden of responsibility fall on him—replied to Wallis:

"Although the Epstein script follows in a general way the new story line, I feel it is written in a radically different vein from the work I've just finished on the first half of the picture.

"They apparently see the situations more in terms of their comic possibilities, while my effort has been to legitimize the characters and develop a serious melodrama of present-day significance, using humor merely as a relief from dramatic tension. I am not presuming to decide which is the better way to attack the picture, but certainly they are different from the ground up.

"From my talk this morning with Mike [Curtiz], I was left with the impression that you and he both wanted me to continue with the more serious treatment, using whatever parts of the Epstein script coincided with this intention. I was proceeding to plan out the scenes in this next part along those lines when I received your letter, which puts an entirely different complexion on the assignment.

"If you are in favor of the approach taken by the Epsteins, it would seem to me best that they do the patching on the few places you don't like.

"As for speeding up the script, ever since I was called on the assignment I've been working as hard as I can—first on the construction of the story, then on the first half of the screenplay. I would continue to work hard, but I can't turn out a third of the screenplay in three days—not the kind of screenplay I thought you and Mike wanted."

While outwardly firm when dealing with the studio bosses, Koch knew he was fighting a losing battle against the screenwriter's worst enemy: time. Koch had been asked to help the producer with a problem script, and he slowly began to realize that blame for delays might fall on him.

"I began to think of the camera as a monster devouring my pages faster than I could write them," Koch recalled.

Throughout the difficult process of writing the script, Wallis and his writers also struggled against stumbling blocks of a different sort: censorship. The creative tampering foisted upon Warner Bros. and the other Hollywood studios had a tremendous impact on filmmaking throughout the most fruitful years of the studio system, yet the consequences of creative restrictions were even greater during the war years.

During the most productive decades of the studio system, the film companies were governed by the heavy hand of the Production Code, a policy established by the industry's own Motion Picture Producers and Distributors Association of America, under the leadership of Will Hays (the association was known throughout Hollywood as "The Hays Office").

Created in the early 1930s to counter attempts by community and religious organizations to impose their own form of censorship on the movie industry, the Production Code responded to public outcry about "horrors" displayed in films, such as growing levels of screen violence and casual sexual attitudes. The Hays Office had hoped that by forming an internal watchdog organization and an internal Production Code to guide filmmakers, it would eliminate community pressure on moviemaking. The plan didn't work completely, but the strict enforcement of the Production Code beginning in 1934 did stave off the most drastic pressure from religious groups and others who sought federal intervention in the motion picture industry.

However, federal involvement in filmmaking did come to Hollywood during World War II. "Censorship" in its literal sense was not the government's goal; rather, federal agencies hoped to merely "influence" the content of the studios' wartime products with an injection of themes and issues important to the military effort. While the studios were only too happy to help with the war effort, they didn't want direct government interference in their film planning and production. Nevertheless, the Hollywood studios were reluctantly teamed with the government for the duration of the war, "cooperating" in ways that would be unheard of today. Throughout those years, Warner Bros. faced a barrage of efforts by the government to influence its films, and *Casablanca* was no exception.

But federal involvement played only an indirect role in Warner Bros.'s wartime production; the omnipotent presence of censorship remained the long and influential arm of the Hays Office. At the height of the studio era, the only force more powerful than the studio moguls was the film industry's self-imposed censorship staff, under the direction of Joseph Breen. The administrator of the film industry's much-maligned Production Code led a staff of moral arbiters who held sway over every script produced in Hollywood.

Dealings with the Production Code office always offered opportunities for give and take between censors and producers, but problems gaining approval for the *Casablanca* script were compounded by the constant revisions to the material. When the Breen readers reviewed the script drafts, they approved the project in principle; the modest love story set in war-torn North Africa raised no hackles among the film industry censors, in spite of the relationship between

Casablanca

04

Rick and Ilsa that delicately tiptoed the boundaries of the propriety of the day.

The Production Code officials found minor problems here and there, and provided a host of suggestions: unsure whether or not Rick knew that Ilsa was married while they had an affair in Paris, they asked for the change of a phrase or two to clarify Rick's innocence. The censors permitted Ilsa's titillating line "I was married, even when I knew you in Paris," to remain in the film because, the censors determined, she thought her husband was dead when she was in love with Rick—although when astonished audiences in 1943 first heard that line, they assumed that Rick and Ilsa had an extramarital affair.

The censors also suggested several filmmaking "techniques" to further sanitize the production.

"The present material seems to contain a suggestion of a sex affair which would be unacceptable if it comes through in the finished picture," said the censors of one scene. "We believe this could possibly be corrected by replacing the fade on page 135 with a dissolve, and shooting the succeeding scene without any sign of a bed or couch, or anything whatever suggestive of a sex affair.

"If shot in this way, we believe the finished scene would be acceptable under the provisions of the Production Code. However, great care will be needed to avoid anything suggestive of a sex affair. Otherwise it could not be approved."

The Breen staff also objected to the idea of Rick shooting Major Strasser in the back. Although Nazis were mowed down with great regularity in many wartime films of the era, the censors felt that the film industry's standards for "decently" dispatching a villain should be maintained, and that Strasser should be shot while armed and in direct confrontation with Rick. (In fact, the idea that Bogart would kill an unarmed man—even a Nazi—by emptying a clipful of Luger rounds into his back didn't sit well with the studio either, and certainly not with Bogart. Some film historians later recalled the shoot-the-Nazi-in-the-back issue as a source of dispute during production, but the idea of Rick killing Strasser in cold blood never survived in a script draft that actually made it to the set.)

In part because of the Breen staff, and also for more acceptable reasons of plot resolution, the shooting would be changed to the showdown so familiar in the final film—face-to-face. But even this more "palatable" gunfight, as Curtiz would discover during the waning days of production, would cause trouble between the director and his producer.

However, these issues of Nazi-killing and a seemingly wicked romance between hero and heroine were small fry compared to the Breen staff's principal objection with the script. The censors squawked loud and long over a plot thread woven through the script that they insisted be changed: the characterization of Louis Renault, the prefect of police.

In early drafts, the Epsteins, no doubt to build the script's comic charms, flooded the plot with wildly suggestive comments about Renault's sexual prowess, in particular his swapping sex for exit visas.

"The present material contains certain elements which seems to be unacceptable from the standpoint of the Production Code," Breen wrote to Warner on May 21. "Specifically, we cannot approve the present suggestion that Capt. Renault makes a practice of seducing the women to whom he grants visas. Any such inference of illicit sex could not be approved in the finished picture."

It was no wonder that Breen reacted so harshly; the Epsteins wrote spicy material the likes of which would not be heard in American movie theaters for another quarter of a century. The early drafts included a number of references to "visa problems" involving beautiful women, and less than subtle references to solving the problem on the couch in Renault's office.

The specific line that sent the censors screaming appeared early in the script, when an aide tells Renault that more "visa difficulties" have come up, and the police chief discovers that the "problem" is actually two gorgeous women, both waiting in his anteroom.

"Which one?" Renault asks himself, and then, clearly recalling the sexual vigor of youth and multiple liaisons, sighs, "Ten years ago there would have been no problem. Oh, well, tell the dark one to wait in my private office and we'll go into the visa matter thoroughly."

If that eyepopper wasn't enough, Renault then tells his aide, "And it wouldn't hurt to have the other one leave her address and phone number."

As far as the censors were concerned, the issue was indisputable: Renault's philandering had to be cut—or at the very least toned down considerably—otherwise the entire script would be stamped unacceptable. Ultimately, however, resolution of the Renault problem was not the product of unilateral slashing by the censors, but rather through diplomatic negotiations between the Breen office and Warner Bros.

In addition to the cut-and-dried dictates of the rules for "acceptable" motion pictures as spelled out in the text of the Production Code, the industry censors allowed themselves far more leeway in their decision-making when they developed the concept of "compensating moral values."

The concept of compensating moral values meant that a film character could commit acts specifically forbidden by the Production Code—including, as the Code described them, "crime, wrongdoing, evil or sin"—as long as the character ultimately paid a high price for his or her actions. Or, as *Citizen Kane* co-writer Herman Mankiewicz bluntly put it, "The villain can lay anybody he wants, have as much fun as he wants cheating and stealing, getting rich and whipping the servants. But you have to shoot him in the end."

Although the words "compensating moral values" don't appear in the film industry's much-maligned Production Code, the Breen office successfully instituted the concept as a driving force behind its ability to dictate morals in films.

Similarly, characters were occasionally given leeway to commit all sorts of interesting indiscretions, such as Renault's womanizing, as long as their actions were justified by some later act of high morality, or if they achieved a higher social plane. Wallis and his staff not only made the case that Louis Renault's amorous adventures were important to the plot, but they proved that the self-admitted "poor corrupt official" could indeed become a moral man who helps save the day in the end.

Thus, Warner Bros. and the Breen office struck a bargain that would allow Renault a certain amount of sexual bribery, as long as he clearly redeemed himself politically and morally by the close of the film. The Breen office also wanted additional changes in Renault's dialogue as part of the bargain, requiring, as Breen put it in a follow-up letter to Warner, "that the several references to this particular phase of the gentleman's character will be materially toned down."

These changes included a number of outright deletions, among them, sadly, the entire scene about Renault's sexual prowess and "ten years ago there would have been no problem." (Viewers can only imagine how Rains would have delivered *that* line.) Also cut were other blatant references to sex; for example, in the script for a scene that was trimmed from the final print, the line, "the girl will be released in the morning" was changed to "the girl will be released later."

Wallis also agreed to a number of word changes here and there requested by the Breen office; some alterations were so subtle in their difference in meaning that the rationale for the change was mystifying bordering on ludicrous. For example, before the studio deleted the conversation between Renault and Strasser about war and women ("You enjoy war. I enjoy women. We are both very good at our jobs."), the censors requested that Renault's response to Strasser's "the German viewpoint is a much healthier one" be changed from "At least your work keeps you outdoors" to "At least your work gets you plenty of fresh air."

Or when Annina (the Bulgarian refugee who asks Rick if Renault will keep his word about providing visas if she "does a bad thing") tells Rick that she has brought her husband to the café for a meeting with Renault: Rick's original response was "Captain Renault is branching out." Instead, the line was rewritten to read, "Captain Renault is getting broad-minded."

The Breen staff even insisted on a minor script change that actually improved a line of dialogue, and as edited the phrase would become one of the film's favorite quotables. In an early scene, after Rick dumps Yvonne, his erstwhile girlfriend, Renault cracks, "How extravagant you are, throwing away women like that. Someday they may be rationed." As part of the Breen-Warner agreement, the line was changed to "Someday they may be scarce."

Yet in spite of the censor's penchant for pickiness, other more blatant references to sex-for-visas and adult situations were allowed to remain in the script. Apparently the Breen office was satisfied with the dialogue changes and outright script deletions concerning Renault—his "compensating moral values" displayed in emerging script drafts helped as well—because in the film as released and approved by the Breen censors, Renault clearly swaps visas for female companionship. The subject of sex-for-visas becomes one of the more interesting sidelights of the film, especially when such a meaty concept is characterized by a masterful scene stealer like Claude Rains.

The final script retained several direct comments about Renault's indiscretions, including a blatant reference to the subject in his meeting with Strasser (rewritten without the "you enjoy war/I enjoy women" exchange). Instead, the conversation ends with a police aide telling Renault that "another visa problem has come up." Strasser smirks while Renault straightens his uniform and says, "Show her in."

Beyond Renault's sexual indiscretions, another more serious passage was also permitted to remain in the script as a result of the compromises between the Breen and Wallis offices. When a drunk Rick confronts Ilsa on her first night in French Morocco, he tells her, "I heard a story once—as a matter of fact, I've heard a lot of stories in my time. They went along with the sound of a tinny piano playing in the parlor downstairs. 'Mister, I met a man once when I was a kid,' it always begins." Rick's reference to an unmentionable social horror was allowed to remain, although the censors originally insisted on its outright deletion.

The Breen office would eventually approve the entire script—in some cases not a moment too soon; the last of the approvals arrived in mid-June, only days before some scenes would be filmed. But the result of the give-and-take over the Production Code standards and the script would not only satisfy the industry's censors, but as Wallis would later discover, the whole dispute would have a gloriously happy ending, courtesy of Joe Breen himself.

Strangely enough, the most important debate over censorship that could have affected the script concerned a problem that never developed: the possibility that Ilsa might remain with Rick. Had the resolution of the ending shifted in that direction, no power at Warner Bros. could have stopped the Breen censors from taking action against the studio.

The Breen staff never had the opportunity to pass judgment on what could have been the main plot point in *Casablanca*: Ilsa leaving Laszlo and choosing to stay in French Morocco. Several actors associated with the making of the film recall that throughout the production schedule, the ending of the film and fate of the main characters was in doubt—a story repeated so often it has become entrenched in Hollywood lore as

May 19, 1942

Mr. J. L. Warner,
Warner Brothers,
Burbank, Calif.,

Dear Mr. Warner:

We have read Part I of the incomplete script
for your proposed picture CASABLANCA. While of course
we cannot give you a final opinion until we receive the
balance of the script, we are happy to report that, with
the exceptions noted below, the present material seems
to meet the requirements of the Production Code.

Going through the material so far submitted, we
call your attention to the following:

Pages 5 and 6: The following lines seem unacceptably sex suggestive, and should be changed:

Page 5: "Of course, a beautiful young girl
for M'sieur Renault, the Prefect
of Police".

Page 6: "The girl will be released in the
morning".

Page 14: Please submit all lyrics to be used
throughout this production.

Also the following lines seem unacceptably sex
suggestive:

"It used to take a Villa at Cannes, or the very
least, a string of pearls - Now all I ask is an exit visa".

Page 28: The following dialogue seems unacceptable:

"How extravagant you are - throwing away women
like that. Some day they may be rationed."

Page 82: With regard to this South American
singer, in scene 96, you will receive a separate letter
from Mr. Addison Durland, our Latin-American adviser.

We will be happy to read the balance of the
script, and to report further, whenever you have it ready.

Cordially yours,

Joseph I. Breen

fact. Some at Warner Bros. actually remember that two endings were
written: one that featured Ilsa leaving on the Lisbon plane with Laszlo;
the other with Ilsa and Rick reunited and Laszlo bravely flying off.

In fact, the ending of *Casablanca* had never been in doubt—not in *Everybody Comes to Rick's,* nor in any version of the script as adapted for the film. From first draft to last, Ilsa *always* departed with Laszlo while Rick remained bravely behind to face his destiny. No other resolution was ever considered by Wallis or any of the writers—indeed, no other conclusion was possible.

But had Warner Bros. considered the idea of reuniting Rick and Ilsa permanently, even the most clever negotiators at the studio would have been unable to sway the censors in 1940s Hollywood to permit a wife to leave her husband for another man (no doubt it had been a difficult pill for the Breen censors to swallow that Ilsa and Rick are reunited at all—if only temporarily). Given the restrictive morals and self-imposed film industry censorship of the day, any other ending for *Casablanca* remains the stuff of Hollywood fairy tales.

Later, after *Casablanca* was ready for release, censorship in a more powerful form—the U.S. government—blocked the film's distribution to the actual site of its story. While President Roosevelt had promised no direct censorship of American motion pictures, that policy only applied to production and distribution at home. From the earliest days of World War II, the federal government involved itself in motion picture production, and aggressively monitored films bound for theaters overseas to ensure not only that "proper" Allied values were lauded, but also that fragile overseas relations were not jeopardized by a film's content.

Responsibility for censorship of films bound for export fell to the Office of War Information, an agency formed in June 1942 that combined a host of other government departments into a massive agency that dealt with building a sense of public spirit in the war effort. Also known as OWI, the Office of War Information created a mission for itself to increase public understanding of the war, both at home and abroad; motion pictures quickly became a prime candidate for its policies. Years after Adolf Hitler understood the potent propaganda power of film, OWI recognized that perhaps the most important vehicle to carry the American message to the Allied nations of the world was the bright light of the motion picture screen.

The OWI worked with the Hollywood studios to instill the belief that every motion picture was important to help build support at home for the war effort. The responsibilities of OWI's Bureau of Motion Pictures soon expanded to include gauging the impact of American films abroad.

The Bureau of Motion Pictures wanted to flood theaters with issues critical to the Allied cause at every possible opportunity, and involved itself in script review—sometimes suggesting original story ideas, or encouraging changes or additions to existing material that, in its view, would strengthen a film's contribution to the war effort.

The bureau also published a manual for producers in which the studios were urged to consider seven points as they planned their projects: first and most important of these questions was, Will this picture help win the war?

But the manual went on to encourage producers to ask themselves an assortment of questions about their scripts. Among them: Did the motion picture deal with a specific war information problem by clarifying, dramatizing, or interpreting it? Or, if the film was "escapist," the manual's guidelines asked, Did the film harm the war effort by creating a false picture of America or the Allies? Did a film merely use the war as the basis for a profitable picture, contribute nothing of real significance to the war effort, and possibly lessen the effect of other pictures of more

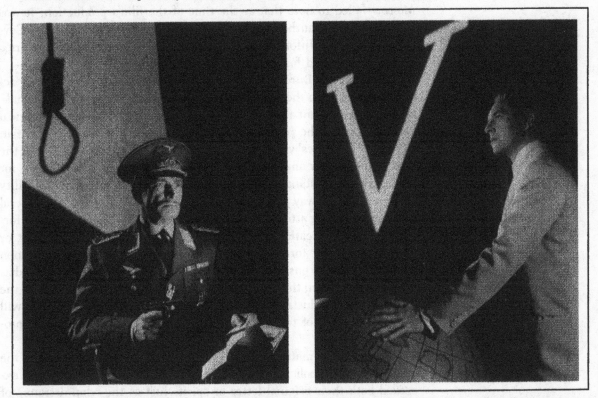

importance? Did the project contribute something new to the understanding of the world conflict and the various forces involved? Did the picture reflect conditions as they are and fill a need current at that time, or was it outdated?

These questions, the bureau suggested, could be brought to the screen by focusing on such themes as "Why We Fight," "The Enemy," "The Home Front," "The Fighting Forces," and "The United Nations." For Warner Bros., the last subject later proved to be a particularly agonizing issue, because the Soviet Union and its Communist regime was one of the thirty Allied nations fighting against the Axis. Referring delicately to the needs of wartime cooperation, the manual tactfully

Warners used the less-than-subtle approach to create imagery of wartime good and evil for these photographs of Conrad Veidt and Paul Henreid.

acknowledged that "Yes, we Americans reject communism." However, at the same time, the manual stressed, "We do not reject our Russian ally."

As a result, both Warners and the federal government thought the war interests were well-served by producing *Mission to Moscow* in 1943, a taut Michael Curtiz–directed dramatization of the book by Joseph Davies, former U.S. ambassador to the Soviet Union. However, the endeavor blew skyhigh after the war when the House Subcommittee on Un-American Activities pointed directly at *Mission to Moscow* as a prime example of the Communist infiltration of Hollywood. The red-crazed congressmen who in 1947 hounded Warner Bros. for creating *Mission to Moscow* failed to note that at the time of the film's production, it was hailed by federal authorities as "a magnificent contribution to the Government's War Information Program"—such was the bitter price Warners later paid for supporting the war effort.

Although the Bureau of Motion Pictures couldn't deny that its actions intruded into the normal business and creative process of filmmaking, the government felt the tampering was justified, given the critical need to sustain the public's enthusiasm for the war effort. While in retrospect the Allies' victory seems predestined, in the spring of 1942 the final outcome was anything but inevitable. Given the critical need for public opinion to stand solidly behind the Allied mission, and the ability of the studios to sway public opinion, it seems admirable that the federal government didn't attempt to exert more direct control over such a formidable communications tool. No direct orders about film content or themes were ever forced upon Hollywood, and the Bureau of Motion Pictures strived to ensure that American films were never interpreted as mind manipulation; the final guideline in the government manual for the motion picture industry asked, "Does the picture tell the truth, and will the young people of today have reason to say they were misled by propaganda?"

However, no matter how noble the government's intentions, the interpretation of policies governing war-related themes in films far exceeded both their original letter or spirit. Just as the administrators of the film industry's Production Code expanded their authority by creating new policies that were not specifically mentioned in the code (such as "compensating moral values"), the government's enforcement of rules about film content soon swelled beyond the original intent of the guidelines. Agencies within the Office of War Information that were created to provide advice and consultation were soon generating larger-scale decisions about content and themes—especially for films set for export. More than a few films suffered as a result. Warner Bros. would soon discover that government concerns about *Casablanca* would involve quibbling over such seemingly insignificant issues as the development of the main character during the course of the picture.

To Warner Bros., the actions of OWI were, at the very least, yet another traffic jam that slowed film production at a time when American theaters desperately needed new product; at worst, the OWI could rise up as a no-appeal government blockade that stifled filmmaking and distribution. Several Warner films scheduled for export were edited to delete "offensive" material, and some were actually banned outright from specific regions of the globe for the duration of the conflict.

Warners' *Passage to Marseille*, for example, contains a scene in the film's closing moments in which Bogart, aboard a freighter, machine guns the crew of a downed Nazi aircraft after the Germans had tried to sink the ship. The Office of War Information strenuously objected to the scene as a less-than-heroic act, and demanded that the scene be cut before an export license was granted. The studio countered that the actions by Bogart's character were justified by the Nazi attack on the ship.

The government position held fast. While the domestic version of *Passage to Marseille* includes the killings, Warners was forced to remove the offending footage before the federal government would permit the export of the film.

Admittedly, the image of an American gunning down unarmed Nazis wasn't exactly a shining example of Allied fair play, even at the height of the war, and the scene was deleted from *Passage to Marseille* with virtually no impact on the plot. However, this form of federal interference in the workings of the motion picture industry shows the great lengths the U.S. government was taking to shape American policy overseas; now, even such seemingly minor editorial adjustments of a film would never be tolerated—either in war or peace.

Casablanca, too, became a victim of intervention by the government. As a film containing war-related themes set in a front-line locale, the film was welcomed by the Office of War Information—at least for domestic distribution. As far as foreign distribution was concerned, however, the film proved troublesome to government regulators for two reasons: the character of Rick, and the conflicting views about the French government described in the film. First the Office of War Information complained about Rick's apolitical nature—saying that he remained cynical "for too long"—while ignoring the fact that his long transformation from cynic to patriot was crucial to the climax of the film.

The government censors had greater concerns about the picture's portrayal of the Vichy regime. In early 1943, when the picture was ready for release overseas, the U.S. government's view of the Nazi-collaborating regime was not as firmly shaped as it might have seemed; incredibly, the OWI believed that *Casablanca* might actually spur more harm than good for the American cause in regions where the divisions between Vichy and Free French were still a hotbed of political and military conflict.

Thus, "based on the advice of several Frenchmen within our organization who feel that it is bound to create resentment," the OWI banned the export of the film to North Africa—a strange ruling about a film that would be remembered by Americans and French alike as one of the most inspiring—hardly resentment-inducing—motion pictures of the war. Even stranger was the fact that the decision to ban the film from North Africa came not from an unsympathetic government bureaucrat, but rather from a writer with a long history of creating stories for the screen about the underdog fighting the establishment. Robert Riskin, who headed the OWI's Overseas Branch, wrote several of Frank Capra's most powerful films, including *It Happened One Night, You Can't Take It with You,* and *Mr. Deeds Goes to Town*—all of which, one would think, should have given Riskin more sympathy for a picture about the plight of the oppressed struggling against the authorities.

Fortunately, the OWI ruling didn't apply to screening the feature for American troops stationed in North Africa. Still, at a time when the picture's powerful messages could have been used to generate feelings of goodwill and international cooperation in a key military sector, the opportunity was lost, thanks to well-intentioned but befuddled government involvement in film distribution.

In spite of these misguided efforts to censor, government interest in films during the war nurtured a strong sense of cooperation at Warner Bros. to support the Allied cause. This cooperation was often found in surprising forms: for example, just before filming of *Casablanca* began, several offices at Warners devoted extraordinary time and attention to determining the nationalities of characters in the production, with the idea to link sympathetic characters with Allied or neutral countries, and at the same time, associate villains or less-than-sympathetic characters with the Axis powers. This procedure was commonplace when developing films during the war, but because of its vast international and political scope, it was especially important for *Casablanca*.

Worrying about such details was not as strange as it might seem. Then as now, an individual character can create a tremendous impression on an audience: during the wartime filming of a production featuring an international cast, Warners considered it crucial to associate certain character types with specific nationalities; good foreign relations—both political and financial—could be affected by the identification of a single character in a film. (Decades later, an offshoot of this notion of identifying heroes and villains would be employed by advertising agencies for automobile companies, who used a modified version of the same technique when developing, of all things, sponsorship packages for police programs on television. Advertisers would pay television production companies to use a particular brand of car in the program, as long as: (1) the heroes drove the sponsor's brand, and (2) the criminals drove cars built by the competition.)

With *Casablanca*, some assignments of nationality were simple: for example, the "Dark European" pickpocket played by Curt Bois was presumed to be Italian, rather than a citizen of Spain, Portugal, or an Allied nation, because it was more appropriate to link a thief with one of the Axis powers. On the other hand, the character of Señor Ferrari played by Sydney Greenstreet was assumed to be a Spaniard (apparently the studio assumed that Spaniards wouldn't be concerned about being linked to a character who identified himself as "the leader of all illegal activities in Casablanca," but they *would* mind being associated with a common pickpocket).

In the same vein, the café singer played by Corinna Mura was described as "South American"—out of respect to Warners' valued markets south of the border—but strangely without linking her to a specific country (the name of Mura's character, although not mentioned in the film or official cast list, was "Señorita Androya"). Wallis ordered that if Mura's character was introduced by name in the film, that she be identified as "South American."

This process of linking characters to nationalities was not always easy. For example, Peter Lorre's character, Ugarte, the murderer of the two German couriers: Should his nationality be identified in the film, and if so, should he be described as Spanish or Italian? The process was complicated by trying to determine if Ugarte would be considered a villain because he was a murderer, or a somewhat more sympathetic character because his victims were Nazis—not an easy task when reading an unfinished script. Wallis soon sorted out the various issues, and decided that Ugarte should be Italian if the need arose to to identify him—however, the producer requested, if the name "Ugarte" was determined to be Spanish, then the character's name would have to be changed. As the script soon developed, virtually all of the identification of characters by nationality was eliminated from the dialogue; only scattered references remained, such as Berger, Laszlo's underground contact played by John Qualen, identifying himself as Norwegian.

The task of analyzing these issues fell to the Research Department at Warner Bros., headed by Carl Schaefer. Schaefer, a researcher with a superb command of detail who could grasp the importance of every item worth checking in a rough script, was renowned at Warners for combining straightforward analysis with his own imaginative ideas about filmmaking. For example, in the interests of maintaining friendly U.S.-Soviet relations, Schaefer suggested that when Rick is kissed by his Russian bartender Sascha, Bogart's rebuff be done "in good humor."

By the third week of May, while writing proceeded (if not progressed), the Epsteins and Koch had still not resolved enough crucial plot points to satisfy the studio that production could proceed—even if Wallis took a huge risk and proceeded with a partial script.

The principal problems, everyone agreed, were the romance between Ilsa and Rick, and the still-to-be resolved issue of the ending. The relationship between the two star-crossed lovers needed strengthening and clarifying; the ending lacked power and audience appeal.

The Epsteins and Koch *were* making progress with the script overall, but the concerns about the romance were legitimate. The chemistry between Ilsa and Rick hadn't solidified, and it certainly wasn't improving. Early script drafts featured stilted conversations and flat emotions between the two—far from the emotional conflict and deep romance that would eventually find its way into the final script.

Included among the deleted passages were such conversations as: "What is there about champagne?" Ilsa asks Rick during the flashback to Paris.

"The difference between bubbles or flatness—between life or death," Rick replies. "The difference between having you or having nothing."

Or when Ilsa, once again in Rick's arms, says just before kissing him, "We're still terrible people."

And the capper—perhaps the worst wartime romantic come-on ever deleted from a script: Ilsa says to Rick as the Germans near Paris, "Hitler or no Hitler, kiss me."

With so many problems creating a powerful romance for his two talented stars, it was evident that Wallis, the Epsteins, and Koch needed help. To bail out the floundering romance, the producer called on one of the best writers at the studio.

By 1942, Casey Robinson was not only one of the top writers at Warner Bros., but he had also established a close working relationship with Wallis. Robinson developed something of a specialty for himself by writing screen adaptations of books, such as *King's Row*, so his involvement in reworking *Casablanca* seemed a natural extension of his proven talents. Except in this case, Robinson would not be writing a script from scratch; Wallis asked him to look at the most difficult plot points—the romance and the ending—and analyze the problems, first in a memo, and later in actual draft material.

"My impression about *Casablanca* is that the melodrama is well done, the humor excellent, but the love story deficient," Robinson wrote to Wallis on May 20.

Robinson proposed several new approaches to the romance; it was he who suggested that Rick and Ilsa meet at the café for the second time late at night, after the flashback scene.

"It is Rick's bitterness, his brutality (which spring from his wounded pride) which stop Ilsa from telling him and make her angry enough and disillusioned enough to go home," Robinson said. "In other words, her disillusionment in him and what he has become instead of the old Rick she remembers, is for the moment enough to turn her away from him and send her home."

Robinson proposed a variety of other plot devices, including increasing the tension between Rick and Ilsa, in particular when the two ex-lovers confront each other about the letters of transit, which Robinson called "visas."

"Ilsa comes for the visas," Robinson summarized. "She tries to be hard-boiled. She can't be. She breaks down completely. But completely. She tells Rick that she loves him and will do anything he wants. She will go anywhere, stay here, anything. She is absolutely helpless in the great passionate love she has for him. She will leave Victor. Rick can get him out of Casablanca. She knows that she's doing wrong, she even says so. She knows that in a way it is a violation of all the high idealism and honor of her nature. She knows she is being wicked but she can't help herself. This is a great scene for a woman to play.

"At the end of the scene, she says that she will go home to her husband and tell him. With an enigmatic look on his face, Rick tells her not to do it. Better that she come with her husband to his place for the letters without telling her husband first, for otherwise he might not come. Better, anyway, that they tell him together.

"Now you're really set up for a swell twist when Rick sends her away on the plane with Victor. For now, in doing so, he is not just solving a love triangle. He is forcing the girl to live up to the idealism of her nature, forcing her to carry on with the work that in these days is far more important than the love of two little people. It is something they will both be glad for when the pain is over."

With new inspiration, Wallis assigned Robinson temporarily to work on the script. With the addition of Robinson to the writing corps, Wallis tied up four of the studio's most talented and expensive writers in work on his production. The Epsteins, Koch, and Robinson worked for the most part independently of each other writing and rewriting material for Wallis and Curtiz; the producer and director then somehow synthesized all of the material into a unified whole.

The writing and revisions dragged on for weeks, and except for the last few days of shooting, would continue through most of the production schedule. No filmmaking expertise was needed to realize that the daily shooting was gobbling up acceptable script pages faster than revisions were being produced to complete the remaining scenes. Once filming began, it became obvious to all involved that good fortune, prayer, and fast fingers on typewriter keys would determine which would come first: completed script pages or the dawn over a new day of shooting.

"On Sundays," Wallis recalled, "Mike Curtiz and the writers came out to my farm in the San Fernando Valley, and we spread the pages out and tried to combine them into a satisfactory draft."

Although revisions continued, Wallis realized he could not wait any longer to decide the production's start date. The company finally ran out of time: "With about half a script," the producer recalled, "it was advisable to postpone production until May 25"—the same day Casey Robinson was officially assigned to the production. The studio administrators had already informed all departments on the lot that *Casablanca* was assigned Production Number 410 and designated an "all-star" production under the direction of Michael Curtiz.

Bogart on the set of Sahara, the film that almost cost him his role in Casablanca.

Casablanca

118

The wheels of the Warner studio machine were turning, and script or no script, *Casablanca* would face the cameras on May 25.

The Hollywood studios of the 1940s, especially the biggest of the "majors," such as MGM, Paramount, and Warner Bros., were justifiably proud of their finely honed production methods, which seemed to hum along with unerring perfection. True, the system worked and worked well nearly all of the time, but there were certainly exceptions to the rule; more pictures went before the camera without completed scripts than nervous studio chiefs and anxious producers wanted to admit. While all of the major studios were capable of producing a full-length motion picture every week to ten days, occasionally some of the cogs in the machinery slipped. And more often than not, the script rested at the source of the problem.

Other high-profile films of the period started production without complete scripts: production of RKO's *Love Affair*, for example, ground to a halt in 1939 while director Leo McCarey and his writers rewrote the script on the set. George Stevens's multimillion dollar adventure epic *Gunga Din* required substantial revisions on-location while a cast of thousands waited for new material. The script for Hollywood's biggest production of them all, *Gone With the Wind*, was constantly revised during the film's year-long production schedule, and a "final" version of the script didn't actually exist until producer David O. Selznick produced one by default as he edited his picture.

But with *Casablanca*, Wallis's problems with the script presented concerns far more serious than mere production delays. With America in the first months of war, and with resources—both manufactured and human—stretched to their limits, the pressures on the production clearly strained the studio's patience. With the endless demands of film production and distribution acting as the prime motivator in Hollywood in the 1940s, the studio needed Wallis to produce a picture on schedule, or it would find a better use of everyone's time.

At the very least, continuing script problems could have forced indefinite postponement of the production, and reassignment of all involved to other projects; under those circumstances, reacquiring the same talented off-screen crew and the one-of-a-kind cast would have been impossible. At worst, further delays could have compelled Wallis to cut his losses and cancel the project entirely.

As difficult as it may seem today to imagine *Casablanca* without Bogart, Bergman, Henreid, Rains, or the adroit and colorful supporting actors, the loss of key cast members was by no means out of the question as a price Wallis might have been forced to pay for production delays. Incredibly enough, at the top of the list of potential casualties of the potential production delays was Humphrey Bogart. After all the machinations, career twists and turns, and star grooming by the studio, Bogart almost lost the biggest role of his career because of the studio's urgent obligation to fix a simple scheduling conflict, and Warners' need for another acting superstar of the day.

In 1941 the studio desperately sought Cary Grant, who then worked under joint contract with Columbia and RKO, to appear in the starring role in the Warner Bros. screen adaptation of the Broadway smash hit *Arsenic and Old Lace*. As payment for a swap of Grant, Columbia production chief Harry Cohn demanded the services of Bogart to play Sergeant Joe Gunn, the hard-as-nails tank sergeant in his desert war drama *Sahara*—a trade that would be Bogart's first picture for a studio other than Warner Bros. since he appeared in *Stand-In* for William Wyler at United Artists in 1937.

Warners agreed to the swap, "but Columbia kept switching the dates on *Sahara*," recalled Wallis. For weeks, Warners was forced to gamble that Bogart would be available, with the distinct possibility remaining that the production might lose its star to a production at another studio.

Eventually, logistics were worked out to the satisfaction of all concerned. Columbia rescheduled the *Sahara* production until later in 1942 with Bogart in the lead role, and Grant, under the direction of Frank Capra, starred in the wildly farcical production of *Arsenic and Old Lace*. As a result, Bogart remained in *Casablanca*.

At the time, the loss of Bogart from *Casablanca* might have seemed a mere inconvenience, requiring his replacement with a lesser talent from the studio roster. Viewed in retrospect, however, the Grant-Bogart swap nearly cost fans of classic Hollywood one of their most treasured performances.

s e v e n

The Curtiz Show

$\mathcal{M}$onday, May 25—a balmy spring day in Los Angeles, and the race between script and production began. With Wallis's writing quartet of Epstein, Epstein, Koch, and Robinson working at full tilt, the filming of *Casablanca* kicked off—without a completed script.

Director Michael Curtiz was ready to go, except for the minor complication of starting the production with the use of only one hand. According to Warner publicity, Curtiz's right hand was heavily bandaged. The release reported that "Snowy Baker hit Curtiz with a polo mallet— accidentally."

By the first day of shooting, most, but not all, of the supporting cast was signed aboard. Wallis and company were still making decisions about some of the production's lesser, but still choice, roles. The casting would continue for several weeks into the production, with some roles filled only when the need to shoot made their casting an absolute must.

By the time Wallis signed S. Z. Sakall, the bubbly Hungarian character actor known throughout the movie business as "Cuddles," on June

15 to play the brief but significant role of Carl the waiter, the picture was already three weeks into production. Sakall appeared in his first scene only two days later. Even by the prevailing standard of the studio era, Wallis was cutting it close.

Others actors began to report to the production. Madeleine LeBeau, a nineteen-year-old French émigré newly arrived from Europe who in cheesecake publicity photos looked astonishingly like Barbara Stanwyck, was signed to play Yvonne, Rick's cast-off girlfriend. (LeBeau, fresh from the ravages of war-torn France, would find residence in Los Angeles at an address that years later would be known for terror of a different sort. On the call list of cast and crew, LeBeau listed her residence as 10050 Cielo Drive, Beverly Hills. Nearly three decades later, the sprawling ranch house on a canyon road would be forever linked to Hollywood's greatest real-life horror: There, in August 1969, Sharon Tate and four others were murdered by the Manson family.)

Bogart with two of his colorful supporting players, Leonid Kinskey (left) and S. Z. Sakall.

Besides Sakall, several stalwart character-acting veterans also joined the company, among them: Curt Bois, a wide-eyed, nervous-looking character actor who specialized in playing a "Dark European"—precisely the term used to describe the pickpocket character in *Casablanca* who

warned his victims of "vultures, vultures everywhere" as he fleeced them; Dan Seymour, claimant of the dubious distinction of being the fattest actor in Hollywood, provided the ideal blockade against café gate-crashers as Abdul the doorman; and Leonid Kinskey, a pointy-faced Russian who, as Sascha the bartender, lit up his scenes with agitated emotion.

As Annina and Jan, the desperate Bulgarian couple who gambled in Rick's casino to win money for their visas so Annina wouldn't have to pay Renault with her virtue, Wallis cast Joy Page, a Hollywood newcomer who would later appear infrequently in such films as *The Bullfighter and the Lady* and *Conquest of Cochise,* and Helmut Dantine, another Viennese transplant who later in the war would specialize in roles as Nazi officers.

Also signed to the cast was Marcel Dalio to play the brief role of Emil the roulette croupier. Dalio was yet another artistic refugee in Hollywood escaping the Axis wrath, but his background differed from the others in the cast. When he came to America, Dalio left behind a promising career as a rising star in French motion pictures. Under the direction of Jean Renoir, Dalio appeared in *La Grande Illusion* and later *La Règle du Jeu (The Rules of the Game),* a world-acclaimed masterpiece often cited as among the best films ever made.

Marcel Dalio (center) was a protégé of Jean Renoir who found character work in Hollywood for the duration of the war.

After the war, Dalio continued a notable career in both starring and character roles on both sides of the Atlantic. But, for the duration of the conflict, Dalio was, like many others, just another bit player seeking temporary refuge in Hollywood.

While the studio was willing to go to extremes to find the ideal performers for the top slots in a production, they were just as anxious to slash costs in the lower tiers of players. Concerns about studio finances weighed heavily on the casting sections of the *Casablanca* budget; just before filming began, Warner executive assistant Steve Trilling told Mike Curtiz to proceed cautiously in choosing his extras and actors for the lesser roles.

"Mr. Wallis suggested, on account of the heavy cost of the cast, that we be very careful not to go overboard on bits and small parts—and not to carry anybody," Trilling told Curtiz in a May 25 memo after conferring with Wallis.

Trilling's comments were followed by a detailed analysis of every proposed small part in the script, along with the studio administration's recommendations for how to cast or cut each one. For example, Trilling deleted a small part for a Moroccan named "Muezzin" who was featured in early drafts, simply because retaining the minor role wasn't worth the cost of carrying an additional bit player.

Other parts and the performers to play them were approved or denied based entirely on how long their services would be required; Curt Bois had been approved to play the "Dark European" pickpocket, providing the part could be completed in a week's time. "If longer," Trilling said tersely, "recast."

Bois remained in his role; others weren't so lucky. Trilling ordered the replacement of Martin Kosleck, originally slated to play Heinze, the aide to Major Strasser, when, in the studio's view, the costs of carrying him on the production's books exceeded his value to the picture. Kosleck, a regular in other Warner wartime productions—he played Nazi propaganda minister Josef Goebbels in three pictures, including *Confessions of a Nazi Spy*—was replaced by Richard Ryen, a bit player who was originally assigned to appear as one of the anonymous Nazi officers in Strasser's command.

Other bits and small parts were analyzed with the same clinical efficiency. Marcel Dalio, for example, was approved for the role of Emil the croupier but because of his $500-a-week salary, "he should be finished in as few days as possible," Trilling ordered. Some parts, such as several of the military officers, were to be played by extras, per studio instructions (extras cost less than actors who normally played small parts). However, Trilling also requested that the extras selected be "very good types."

One extra valued for his specialized performances was hired for the cast and, with the role, found a place in film history. Gino Corrado, an extra who made a career for himself primarily playing bit parts as waiters and other service occupations, was cast to appear on the staff of Rick's Café Américaine (Corrado is the waiter who takes Strasser's order for champagne and caviar). Two years before, Corrado played another waiter —this time in *Citizen Kane* (early in the film, Corrado asks Gus Schilling, manager of the nightclub owned by Kane's second wife, if she wants "another double"). Thus, Corrado will be remembered in movie lore for playing the same role in two of Hollywood's most beloved films.

With such stars as Bogart, Bergman, Rains, and Henreid, and a remarkable supporting cast of Greenstreet, Veidt, Lorre, et al., *Casablanca* had been assured screen immortality—if for no other reason than the talent and personality of its performers. But the real-life experience that the cast would bring to the company was far more important than their acting skills; like their screen characters, many in the cast were themselves refugees of war, or faced other harrowing wartime experiences.

Paul Henreid was forced to leave Austria by the encroaching Nazi advance. Conrad Veidt, in addition to his own bitter experiences in Germany, helped smuggle his Jewish in-laws out of Germany through the Alps into Switzerland. Michael Curtiz escaped the Hungarian revolt in 1919, and some in his family, who remained in Europe at the outbreak of World War II, barely escaped the Nazi invasion. Robert Aisner, the technical adviser hired for the production, had been a French army officer and served time in concentration camps early in the war before escaping and making his way to America.

When Ingrid Bergman's husband, Dr. Peter Lindstrom, joined his wife in the United States, he had been forced to duplicate in part the "tortuous refugee trail to America" that became part of the *Casablanca* script. With the principal shipping lanes shut down by the war, Lindstrom departed for America via Lisbon, for a six-week trip by freighter.

Curt Bois, a successful stage and film performer in Germany before coming to America, escaped Europe during the early days of the Nazi rise, as had Peter Lorre, Madeleine LeBeau, and Marcel Dalio. Lorre, as a stage performer, had taunted the Hitler brownshirts in satirical sketches on the stages of Berlin—a deadly risk for a performer at a time when performers who publicly opposed the Nazis were often found bludgeoned in a back alley, or simply disappeared.

Later the company would discover that several bit players were also recent refugees from the war; Warner publicity reported an incident on the set early in production that if true, must have further energized the production that was already emotionally charged by the overseas conflict. During filming of the Paris street scenes, while shooting Bogart and

Bergman listening to the dreadful news of the French defeat, an extra sitting behind the stars lowered her head onto her folded arms and her shoulders shook with uncontrollable sobs.

Curtiz cut the take. "That is not what I wanted," he supposedly shouted. "I told you people that I wanted you to look grim, defiant—to talk fiercely to each other. This is not a moment for breaking down into tears."

A little bearded man, also an extra, tapped Curtiz on the shoulder. "I am very sorry, sir," the man said quietly, "but that is my wife. Please pardon her. You see, our home was Paris. And we went through that awful day."

Two days before filming began, Jack Warner gave Michael Curtiz a final "pep talk" via memo—actually more of a friendly warning to add further pressure to the director's already ample load of concerns.

"These are turbulent days, and I know you will finish *Casablanca* in top seven weeks," Warner wrote in his peculiar, broken style. "I am depending on you to be the old Curtiz I know you to be, and I am positive you are going to make one great picture."

The "Old Curtiz" certainly didn't need the aggravation of a minor scolding from the top boss before committing a single gaff during his new production. Squabbles with the top brass and lofty stars notwithstanding, the studio's leading director needed no apologies to justify his work habits—and his track record of profitable hits proved it. However, the gentle warning to Curtiz just before the start of the all-star production not only provided Warner with a less-than-subtle method of putting the director on notice, but also demonstrated the studio chief's deep concerns during one of the most critical moments in the studio's history.

Warner Bros. had experienced tougher moments financially, particularly during the darkest days of the depression, which coincided with the huge financial burden of converting the studio to the filming of motion pictures with sound. But in May 1942, substantive problems brought on by World War II loomed large: cost containment, impending shortages of virtually all supplies and equipment needed to produce motion pictures, drafted actors, and government restrictions on all aspects of nonmilitary manufacturing cast a growing shadow over the studio.

But all financial and logistical issues paled before the grim realities of the war abroad and the terrifying possibility that the West Coast, especially industry-saturated California, might actually be attacked by Axis forces. As unlikely as it may seem today that a Japanese armada would cross thousands of miles of ocean to invade the American mainland, in the uncertain early months of World War II, with American forces decimated in the Pacific and solid military victories in the European theater still months away, feelings ran high that Americans might soon be fighting World War II in their own backyards.

While actual invasion by troops may have been unlikely, a West

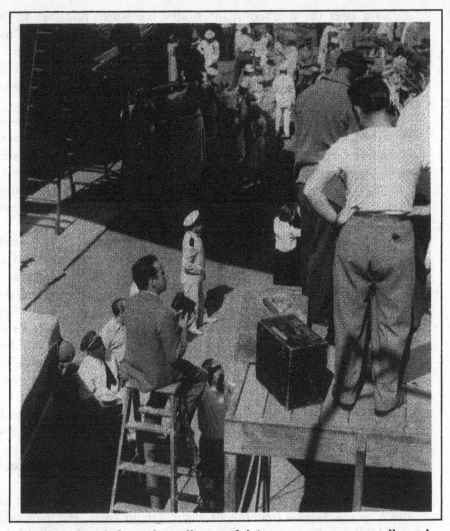

Coast air attack from the still-powerful Japanese navy, especially with memories of Pearl Harbor still fresh in the minds of all Americans, seemed a genuine threat. Air-raid alerts wailed regularly throughout Southern California, and more than a few false alarms jangled nerves all along the West Coast. Then, too, a brief artillery salvo fired by a lone Japanese submarine spurred panic headlines in newspapers across the state and added substantially to war fears.

"Anyone who was in California will recall the apprehension," Warner remembered of the early weeks of the war. "The feeling persisted that an attack was imminent either by land or sea or air, or all three, and crude bomb shelters were thrown up overnight. We had one at the studio, and I vaguely remember sitting in this rough underground haven playing checkers with [producers] Jesse Lasky, Mervyn LeRoy, and others, and expecting to have the game broken up any moment by bombs."

Soon after the war began, the studios recognized that they might have to dig in and face real bombs and bullets; executives from all of the picture companies gulped hard and considered a plan to pool studio space and other filmmaking resources in case the unthinkable attack occurred, "so if one producer is stopped by bombing," the *Hollywood Reporter* wrote, "work will immediately be shifted to another studio."

Most of the large film studios developed ingenious plans to camouflage their operations. Studio painters, construction crews, and nursery departments were prepared to create elaborate artistic schemes that overnight could shroud an entire complex. By combining paint, greenery, and netting, the crews could produce a clever re-creation of the natural landscape, so a studio could "disappear" from view by air—practically on a moment's notice.

Although the studios themselves were never forced to resort to such drastic camouflage measures, their plans were used with great effectiveness to disguise aircraft plants and other key military production plants in Los Angeles, by transforming the roofs of industrial buildings and the surrounding grounds into miniature rural settings complete with rolling hillsides, trees, and scattered buildings. Had reconnaissance planes or bombers flown over these disguised facilities, the difference in size between the tiny but carefully crafted scenery and an authentic rustic environment would have been impossible to detect.

Jack Warner remembered that he helped ease the tension at his studio by ordering workmen to paint a sign on a studio roof that said, "Lockheed—That-A-Way," along with an arrow pointing toward the massive aircraft plant a few miles away in Burbank. (Robert Gross, president of Lockheed, reportedly wanted his own sign pointing back toward the studio that read, "Warner Bros.—that-a-way.")

But no one on the Warner lot could rule out the possibility that an attack on Los Angeles from the air might actually come, and the studio would fall directly in the line of fire. Nestled against the foothills of the San Fernando Valley, the studio's location placed it in a near-direct line with the Pacific Ocean, the Douglas aircraft plant in Santa Monica, and the Lockheed aircraft assembly facility in Burbank. A near miss—or an intentional attack invited by the studio's uncomfortably close resemblance to a large industrial factory or airplane hangars—must have seemed a very real possibility indeed.

As the American military forces regrouped and began to tally victories, the fears about invasion eased in Southern California. However, all of the Hollywood studios faced scores of more cut-and-dried problems caused by the war.

Not the least of the war-influenced obstacles to filmmaking was the shortage of virtually every raw material critical to the business of making movies. Lumber, paint, cement, cloth, bricks, tools, gasoline, light bulbs, and countless other construction items—all were either strictly rationed or usually in short supply. Even such mundane articles as the metal cans in which film reels were packed and shipped were vulnerable to shortage. One of the first changes announced by the motion picture industry to accommodate wartime shortages was the shift from tin cans to cardboard or fiberboard boxes for shipment of prints from film laboratories.

Provisions taken for granted in peacetime were in particularly short supply. Items made of metal were especially difficult to obtain; nails were the worst. A commodity so commonplace that its availability was taken for granted before the war, nails were among the first products to appear on Warner's endangered list. To those outside the industry, nails might not seem the most important item in a studio's inventory, but Warners used hundreds of thousands of nails every year; without nails, set construction would have been impossible.

Had the shortage of such an innocuous item not been so critical to work at the studio, the studio's approach to coping with the nail problem might have seemed amusing, but in 1942, no one at Warners was laughing about nails. Studio craftsmen were barraged with "save nails—save jobs" messages, both in studio workshops and in the company's employee newspaper; the studio spent $1,000 to design and construct a nail-sorting machine so carpenters' aprons filled with mixed nails could be re-sorted rather than sold for scrap.

"If you want to keep on working, save nails," growled the *Warner Club News*. "The demand for steel for implements of war has become so great that it is almost impossible to secure nails and is becoming more so every day. Nails are a vital necessity to this studio. Without them, we cannot build sets, without sets it would be almost impossible to make pictures."

The company's emphasis on saving nails must have been particularly gratifying for Harry Warner. Trained as a boy to be a shoemaker—he hated it—Warner never lost one habit of the profession: the executive was noted at the studio for always being on the lookout for loose nails. On many occasions, the eldest Warner was spotted walking on the studio grounds, stooping quickly to pick up a nail or two, and cobbler-style, popping them into his mouth.

During the war's early months, the studios discovered that in addition to shortages of traditional supplies, other needs were now difficult to fill. As new war pictures went into production, the studios discovered that only scant supplies of stock footage of the Pacific theater was available, and newsreel and recent documentary footage of war scenes in Pacific island settings could be obtained only at premium prices. One of the first productions affected by this shortage was Warner's *Air Force* (the picture, directed by Howard Hawks, did quite well under the circumstances).

With the talk at Warners dominated by shortages, in the early days of the war many began to wonder what was the greater threat to production: an air raid or the specter of running out of raw materials to use to make movies. (A case could also be made that shortages were *good* for the studio. As long as shortages didn't threaten production, but only forced everyone at the studio to economize, the wartime restrictions may have actually helped boost the studio's profits.) To counter fears, Jack Warner met with all of his department heads only a few days after the war started, and reviewed methods to keep shortages under control.

Warner committed the studio to reducing set construction to a minimum, with limits on "big expensive sets" except under special circumstances, such as a large-scale war-related feature. (For *Casablanca*, with its North African setting, this emphasis on frugal sets worked well. Some existing outdoor streets on the studio's backlot were reused for the production with only limited modifications, including "Arab backstreet" sets also seen in *Desert Song*. Rather than build a railroad station specifically for the one scene of Rick's emotional departure from Paris, the Curtiz company used the studio's standing railway station set hot on the heels of *Now, Voyager*.)

Eventually, supply channels for raw materials settled somewhat, and Warner productions were never stymied by shortages. In fact, sets for *Casablanca* designed by art director Carl Jules Weyl and decorated by set dresser George James Hopkins were remarkably well executed and extraordinarily detailed under any circumstances—let alone during wartime shortages. Little new construction from scratch was required for the sets, with the exception of the interiors of Rick's Café. Virtually all of the other construction elements—wall panels, flooring, window frames, and other components of set design—were taken from existing studio stores, or scavenged from recent productions.

The sets appear crafted but not lavish. As Wallis would discover during shooting, a lush, mysterious look to the café scenes could be accomplished far better with lighting and movement than with fancy props. Nevertheless, when viewed in photographs taken before shooting began (*see page 136*), the sets look remarkably like real-life locations, with no scrimping on items that were out of camera range, such as floor tiles or furniture and paintings deep in backgrounds.

When dressing the sets with props, furniture, and fixtures, few new items needed to be purchased for the production; props were either rented or came out of the studio's carefully tended stock of furniture, desks, and other supplies needed to make Rick's Café appear like an authentic bar and restaurant. The customers' chairs in the café—woven from bamboo and rattan with a distinctive horizontal double loop on the back—were rented from a local prop supplier to the movie industry. (The same group of chairs appeared in restaurant scenes in a number of films, including *White Christmas* and *Cornered*. In *Funny Face*, the chairs are stacked in a pile on the patio of a Paris café during a Fred Astaire dance number.)

Fortunately, Hollywood never encountered a critical shortage of the sole irreplaceable commodity in moviemaking: raw film stock. As early as January 1942, motion picture industry analysts reported that film would be available to ensure normal production for the foreseeable future, much to the relief of studios already leery about other shortages; later in the war, supplies tightened slightly, but only enough to encourage conservation, and not to threaten filmmaking.

However, conserving film was a priority early in the war. Throughout the war, the movie industry's own Film Conservation Committee worked to reduce the use of film as much as possible, and recommended—without requiring—a number of measures to cut consumption, such as a maximum of three takes for each camera setup (the same committee created a tentative proposal to eliminate on-screen production credits from wartime productions—a plan that was overwhelmingly vetoed by directors in a test vote). Jack Warner, ever preoccupied with cost-cutting, was only too happy to encourage his directors to reduce their number of takes as much as possible.

As if the specter of material shortages, the draft, and federal intervention weren't enough to worry the studios, the early days of the war also brought an edict from military authorities that threatened to substantially alter the production methods of the studios, and could have crippled the industry's ability to make movies.

A month after the United States was attacked, U.S. Army officials issued sweeping orders that temporarily restricted virtually all filming away from the studio. The army ordered the elimination of location shooting along the West Coast; at one point, the studios were notified that location shooting was all but forbidden not only in coastal locations, but in all of Southern California; if film crews wanted to shoot on location, the army ordered, they would need to move beyond the restricted area, possibly as far as Arizona, New Mexico, or Nevada.

Prohibited were short location jaunts anywhere within Los Angeles, including street scenes, building exteriors, or most chase scenes (some location shootings were eventually permitted in Los Angeles, but in a city made jittery by air-raid warnings, production companies were ordered to stop using sirens during chase scenes involving police cars or fire trucks). Shots aboard trains weren't prohibited—if the trains were regularly scheduled and the filming didn't hamper normal railroad operations. But because the armed forces had requisitioned all available rolling stock, no railroad cars were available for special shooting sessions.

The army's list of locations denied to the studios extended to virtually every landmark in Southern California. The orders stopped filming near the entrances to railroad tunnels or near railroad bridges (as a protection against possible sabotage, most tunnels and bridges were already under armed guard along the entire Pacific coast). No camera crews were allowed near dams or army reservations, coastal harbors from San Diego to Seattle, or manufacturing plants. The army was even concerned about filming in desolate country near Los Angeles for westerns.

Restrictions on airplanes were even worse—an edict that would soon occupy the time of Al Alleborn, the unit manager on *Casablanca*. Because private planes were grounded, air shots were impossible, as was photographing any airport.

Other rules about airplanes were even more drastic—but fortunately didn't last long. "It is permissible to photograph an airplane, but it must not be done at any recognized airport and it must be a stationary shot," wrote the *Hollywood Reporter*. "It is forbidden to even taxi the plane. If it is necessary to have the motor of the plane running, the propeller must be removed first, so that it will be physically impossible to get the ship off the ground. If a plane is to be used, it must be dismantled and taken to the spot where the shot is to be taken. At that spot, it will be reassembled under the eyes of armed soldiers, who will step back when the shot is taken but will stay within easy gun range."

While these policies about aircraft may seem somewhat extreme, the army could justify its other rules about location shooting with more reasonable explanations: first of course, the military wanted to keep new footage of key locations out of the hands of the enemy; while a military attack on Southern California may have been unlikely, espionage and sabotage were always real possibilities. The military intelligence officers quite rightly believed that handing over pictures of strategic locations in Southern California via movie screens simply eased the Axis' reconnaissance job. Also, by preventing friendly camera crews from working in the field, Army Intelligence and local police knew that anyone who *was* filming key locations was probably up to no good.

Practical explanations justified the other military orders, especially attempts to curb location shooting on the streets of Los Angeles. Then as now, filming away from the studio attracted huge crowds, and draft-decimated police forces were unable to handle the requirements of crowd control.

Fortunately for all of the studios, the army remained realistic about a crucial aspect of filmmaking: night photography. Under military area rules, night exteriors on the studio lots were still permitted, and sets were allowed to be flood-lit—of course, with strict adherence to civil defense rules during blackouts—and the army did prohibit floodlights from being pointed skyward. However, most studios voluntarily reduced night shooting during the earliest days of the war, only to begin again when attack concerns eased. (The voluntary cutback of night production was a sound civil defense move, but it also served a public relations purpose. A night shooting didn't help a studio's standing in the community if the only light in an otherwise blacked-out neighborhood had been the bright-white corona of a night shooting on the lot.)

For Warners, with its prewar emphasis on action movies, westerns, and other productions that required extensive location shooting, the army's restrictions could have proved a near-disaster. Restrictions on off-lot shooting could have meant that the studio might have needed to duplicate location sites within studio walls, thus magnifying the problem of material shortages by forcing unanticipated set construction.

However, as with other shortages and restrictions that loomed large in December 1941, limitations on location filming soon sorted themselves out to the satisfaction of most everyone at the studios. The motion picture industry discovered that their location needs could usually be met by working closely with the military. The army had no interest in restricting the film industry right out of business; rather, the military authorities were near-manic in their desire to keep track of every out-of-the-ordinary occurrence in Southern California (and as production manager Al Alleborn would later discover on *Casablanca*, a little compromise and a lot of patient effort when working with the military command usually yielded happy results). Also, while production crews were hampered by not being able to shoot film at will in militarily sensitive areas, any picture that required such footage was likely to be war-oriented and could be completed with the generous cooperation of the military branch involved.

Restrictions aside, even the seemingly routine day-to-day business of filmmaking at Warner Bros. during the war years—and only minutes from the hub of the Southern California defense industry—was disrupted by the defense effort. Outdoor filming at most of the studios was hampered to a degree by the escalation of aircraft construction, which required a vastly increased number of noisy flights near the back lots during testing. Over the hills from Warners in West Los Angeles near the Douglas aircraft plant, MGM and 20th Century-Fox suffered more from noise problems than the other studios farther to the east in Hollywood. In the San Fernando Valley, Warner Bros. and Universal were both bothered by aircraft noise, but Warners, with its back lot less than one minute's flight time from Lockheed, was the principal victim.

Aircraft noise had been a minor annoyance since the dawn of the sound era—although far fewer planes flew in Southern California in the 1930s and 1940s than do today—but the problem was amplified during the war because military aircraft produce considerably more noise than their civilian cousins. As wartime aircraft production neared its peak, noise from Lockheed aircraft flights near Warner Bros. forced sound technicians to watch the skies as well as their equipment to ensure that a take wouldn't be disrupted by the approach of a roaring warbird. During the outdoor scenes of the black market and city streets for *Casablanca*, soundman Francis Scheid and other production aides had to listen carefully between takes to ensure that Curtiz would have enough time to shoot a scene without disruption from above.

There was only one consolation about the problem of aircraft noise: "Present day planes," said a Warner sound technician, "move awful fast."

Neither war, nor budget, nor shortages, nor lack of script would prevent *Casablanca* from meeting its date before the cameras. On May 25 in La Belle Aurore Café sets on Stage 12-A, director of photography Arthur Edeson rolled the first shot of Production 410—the scenes of Humphrey Bogart, Ingrid Bergman, and Dooley Wilson drinking champagne to "take the sting out of being occupied" while waiting for the arrival of German troops.

Hollywood legend recalls that difficulties with the script forced Curtiz to shoot *Casablanca* in script order scene by scene—a misconception bolstered by the flawed recollections of several actors that were often repeated in other "historical" accounts of the film's production.

Actually, some scenes were indeed photographed in rough chronological order. But the majority of the production was filmed in the sequence that best suited the logistics of the production and the frantic writing and polishing of the script.

In the first week of shooting, for example, including the first day's shots in La Belle Aurore Café, Curtiz photographed sixty-one different setups. Among them:

· Several versions of Bogart and Bergman dancing on the Paris nightclub set.
· Shots of Bogart and Bergman in her Paris apartment (scenes in which she says to Rick, "A franc for your thoughts").
· A variety of takes in Rick's Paris apartment (when Bogart asks the classic questions of Bergman, "Who are you really? What were you before? What did you do? What did you think?").
· Crowds of anxious Parisians listening to loudspeaker announcements of war news.
· Several shots in Rick's Café Américaine, including Rick ejecting the pompous Deutsches Bank executive from the gambling room, conversations with Rick and Ugarte about the letters of transit, patter between Ferrari and Rick about selling the café (when Rick tells Ferrari that he "doesn't buy or sell human beings"), and scenes of Rick rejecting his erstwhile girlfriend Yvonne, and throwing her out of the café.

The schedule for the first week seemed frenetic, and Curtiz seemed to be roaring through material at his usual breakneck pace, but it wasn't fast enough. Scarcely a week into shooting, the company was already falling behind schedule—"actually two days behind schedule," reported production manager Al Alleborn, "because Mike is only averaging a page and a half of dialogue a day."

The first day of
shooting on Stage 12-a;
production 410 begins,
with Rick, Ilsa, and
Sam "taking the sting
out of being occupied."

Behind the
Scenes

135

The problems lay not in Curtiz's pace nor, amazingly enough, with the script. While Wallis bore his burdens in the form of written words, Curtiz faced a weighty obstacle of his own: the absence of two of his principal stars.

As production began on *Casablanca*, Claude Rains was still completing his assignment on *Now, Voyager* under the direction of Irving Rapper, as was Paul Henreid. But Henreid was home with the flu, and his illness delayed his completion of scenes with Bette Davis. A logjam of work was forming behind Henreid—on not one production, but two.

With Henreid and Rains out, Curtiz was forced into a frantic juggling act, not only shooting scenes around the two actors but also trying to use the highest-priced performers first.

At the same time, Warners was trying to *avoid* using some of the high-priced talent on weekly salary, so their performances could be grouped into the shortest shooting period. "We do not want to start expensive cast in order to keep working," said Alleborn of filming on the café set. "It works out better shooting as we are, remaining in the set and maybe finishing the stage in its entirety before we start this coming week

Preparing for a camera pan (note the camera pointing left), Curtiz lines up his shot of Bogart and Bergman reading the grim war news. The Warner construction crews crafted a near-perfect re-creation of a Montmartre café out of a backlot street for this brief scene in which Rick and Ilsa learn of the French defeat. Although this set appears on-screen for only a few seconds, it is accurate to the smallest detail— right down to the French war bulletins posted in windows that never appear on the screen.

with Paul Henreid, and then go ahead and pick up other members of the cast. These people all have guarantees, and we are watching this closely in order not to run over."

Filming around expensive contract talent was an old trick during the studio system, and especially important on the *Casablanca* production. By Hollywood standards, the picture wasn't particularly expensive—early in the shooting, the budget estimates for direct costs totaled $638,222—a mere pittance by today's standards and not wildly expensive even by 1942 measures.

But with few expensive sets and minimal location shooting, acting talent comprised a substantial portion of the total budget—some $217,603 or about one-third of the cost of the picture (the single costliest category in the budget, as with most productions, was the 35 percent budget surcharge for general studio overhead, a figure estimated at $223,822; add another $15,956 to account for the studio's depreciation charges, for a preliminary estimated total cost of $878,000).

In Hollywood's most cost-conscious days, where box-office power-houses like Bogart earned six-figure salaries per year, as opposed to today's ten-figure deals per picture, squeezing every penny out of the budget was a high priority.

On *Casablanca*, however, the tactic of shaving the budget by shooting around actors failed—at least as far as Sydney Greenstreet's role in the project was concerned. Originally signed to appear for only two weeks, Greenstreet, because his scenes intertwined with Henreid's, remained assigned to the production nearly twice as long as expected—at a salary of more than $3,500 per week, this was a minor disaster by the studio's standards.

Cost-cutting tactics and an absence of performers quickly hampered Curtiz's ability to shoot scenes on schedule; the company was forced to film around actors in virtually every scene of the picture during its first month in production.

Now, Voyager delayed Rains's arrival on the set for only a few days; the character actor reported June 4. Veidt joined the company on June 6 (he was scheduled to begin work on June 5 but could not be used because of a persistent fever blister). But Henreid's absence created larger difficulties.

At first it seemed that Henreid's illness would postpone his first appearance only briefly. "I understand this morning," said Alleborn on Wednesday, June 3, "Henreid will be available to start in the picture on Monday."

Henreid's delay on *Now, Voyager* was a nightmare come true for Wallis; early in the production he had decided to gamble that the actor would be ready. "I decided to wait for Henreid," he recalled. And wait he did.

The "few days" of Henreid's absence stretched into weeks; by June

Casablanca

Bogart works on his dance steps with the assistance of extra Barry Norton, while Bergman observes.

10, word came to the *Casablanca* set that *Now, Voyager*, "the Rapper Show" as it was called in the daily progress reports, was falling behind. With Henreid recovered from his illness but other production snags on *Now, Voyager* postponing his arrival on the *Casablanca* set, his appearance in the new Wallis production was in jeopardy. "We can shoot around this man for a few days yet," said Alleborn to studio manager T. C. Wright, but "there is a possibility of a re-cast from the discussion I heard."

Fortunately for Henreid's place in film history, Curtiz had plenty of material to shoot without the Austrian actor, and the scene-juggling continued until the last week of June. Finally, Rapper released Henreid from *Now, Voyager;* Henreid's first scene for *Casablanca*—his arrival with Ilsa at Rick's Café—was shot on June 25, exactly one month into production.

"You Know How Mike Is"

Curtiz, the consummate studio pro, found plenty to occupy cast and crew, even without the services of Henreid and Greenstreet. Bogart and Bergman were available, and in the first month of production, the director used them to their fullest—shooting most of their interactions, the romance, and their confrontations—along with plot-developing scenes featuring Rains, Wilson, and the other supporting actors.

But other than scenes played between Bogart and Bergman alone, or atmospheric material at the café, there was little of substance that Curtiz could film until his cast filled out considerably. As usual, the director took the brunt of the blame, even though the issue of cast members' absence was out of his control.

"I saw last night's dailies," crabbed Wallis at Curtiz after seeing the previous day's film at the end of the second week of filming, "and again, it is just a lot of odds and bits and reactions of people in the café to Sam's song, all of which could have been done some other time as pickup shots.

"I don't feel yet that we have gotten into the picture," Wallis said, "and while I know you have been under a handicap because you didn't have your actors, you now have Rains and I would like to get into some solid material and really get some work done."

With an incomplete cast and script turmoil still bubbling, Curtiz certainly took his share of unfair criticism. His long-standing habits on set didn't help.

"One of Mike's peculiar habits was leaving out scenes that were in the script—for no better reason than he didn't like them," Wallis recalled years later. "I had to watch the daily work very carefully to see that he didn't make arbitrary cuts."

The headstrong director followed his own instincts, even though he knew that his producer and longtime colleague would recall his previous shenanigans on the set.

The Wallis-Curtz honeymoon survived precisely two days into the production—until the director filmed takes of the blissful Rick and Ilsa, the spring breeze blowing their hair, motoring through the French countryside (the car, of course, was stagebound, the environs of Paris a back projection, the wind provided by an off-camera fan).

Curtiz shot the scene as he wanted it: without the lengthy dialogue as written—a point that didn't go unnoticed by Wallis.

"I want you to reshoot the scene of Bogart and the girl in the automobile, and this time I want you to do it with the script dialogue," Wallis ordered Curtiz after the producer saw the dailies. "You shot it as a silent scene.

"I don't know why you changed this. Do you have any reason for dropping this dialogue?

"For the balance of the picture," Wallis snapped, "I will greatly appreciate it if you will call me on the telephone when you drop dialogue out of a scene, or make changes. It will be far simpler, and considerably less expensive, for us to discuss these things before you do them than to go back and retake the scenes later."

Despite Wallis's orders, Curtiz ultimately got what he wanted. The scene of Rick and Ilsa driving makes only the briefest of appearances in the film, as part of a montage of scenes of romance between Rick and Ilsa; the dialogue, which strangely Wallis recalled years later as "vital to an understanding of their love affair," never appeared in the film.

Meanwhile, shooting continued with the cast that was available. On June 3, Curtiz shot Bogart and Wilson standing in the rain at the Gare de Lyon railway station in Paris, with Rick "getting his guts kicked out" after he receives the letter from Ilsa that tells him she can't leave Paris. The railway station, at the time a standing set at Warner Bros., would also be seen in slightly modified form in *Now, Voyager*.

Rather than build a new train station specifically for *Casablanca*, the two companies used the same set, with modifications to transform an

American railroad platform into a Parisian station made practically overnight. With wartime conservation in mind, many other large-scale props
were shared by more than one production. The beacon that marked the
airport was packed immediately after the Curtiz production was completed and rushed to Tampa, Florida, for use in Howard Hawks's filming
of *Air Force*.

Considering the problems of missing stars, script revisions, wartime
shortages, and mandatory raw material restrictions, production continued at a surprisingly steady pace. "This company is moving along much
better," said Alleborn to studio manager T. C. Wright on June 9. "I have
hopes of them picking up as they go along." A few days later, Alleborn
said, "[Cinematographer Art] Edeson and Mike are having their little
arguments now and then, but nothing serious. You know how Mike is."

The lingering obstacle to progress remained, of course, the script.
"We are very anxious to get script that is final on this picture," Alleborn
wrote in more than a dozen different daily reports. Pages continued to
emerge from the writers' building, but it was never enough to plan out
the schedule for the entire course of production.

While writers toiled and filming continued, Wallis turned his concerns to the visual direction of the picture. With thoughts of the dark
moodiness of *Algiers* still fresh, Wallis sought the same cinematic quality
for *Casablanca*.

*Curtiz (on dolly in
shirtsleeves, holding the
bar with his right arm)
directed Strasser's air-
port arrival at the Los
Angeles Metropolitan
Airport in the San
Fernando Valley,
nearby the Warner
studios in Burbank.*

"I am anxious to get real blacks and whites with the walls and the background in shadow, and dim, sketchy lighting," Wallis told Edeson several times during the early stages of production. "I want to again ask that you get as much contrast as possible in your lighting in the picture, especially in the scenes in Rick's Café."

With fancy costumes glittering on dozens of extras, waves of characters walking or dancing through the café, lush sets designed by art director Carl Weyl, and clouds of cigarette smoke swirling through every scene, it would have seemed that the café was already awash in atmosphere without extra attention devoted to lighting. But Edeson and gaffer William Conger boosted the mood of the café considerably by directing lights through plants, people, and carved wooden screens to throw dramatic shadows across the set. In addition, lights shining through ceiling fans added additional movement to the lighting on the set.

Edeson also lit scenes using a variety of on-set prop lamps designed to cast attractive shadows. Early in the film, for example, while Ugarte is saying to Rick, "You despise me, don't you," a shaded lamp behind Bogart casts an intricate stained glass–like pattern on the ceiling over their heads. To heighten the tone of wartime tension, the crew also panned a mammoth searchlight across the front of the café. (Ostensibly the light came from the navigation beam in the airport tower, but the effect took liberties with reality for the sake of the wartime drama; authentic landing lights are directed outward at incoming planes, not toward the ground.)

To meet Wallis's other lighting requests, Edeson lit his scenes upward from the floor or across from sidelights, casting shadows of people high on walls in locations that would be physically impossible in real life. Viewers can note shadows of window frames, ceiling fans, or carved filigree thrown behind almost every scene shot in the café—most of which in a real restaurant could have no explicable source. For example, during the "Knock on Wood" musical number early in the film, shadows of musicians are cast high up on the café's walls from lights positioned on the floor.

Creating additional lighting and shadows to meet the persistent demands of the producer spawned myriad problems of continuity—sharp-eyed viewers can note marked differences in light and shadows during some scenes shot after lighting was changed between takes or on different shooting days.

For instance, when Ugarte begs Rick to hide him from the police, a deep shadow of a heavily ornamented wooden window frame in a pattern of eight-pointed stars is cast across Bogart's back and on the wall behind Peter Lorre. In the close-up of Lorre inserted into the same scene, the shadows abruptly change to a much softer square pattern. As Ugarte is grabbed by the gendarmes, the star shadows return. After Ugarte's abrupt departure, when Rick says, "I stick my neck out for no one," the shadows have disappeared entirely.

But taking such liberties with reality, even for a seemingly insignificant detail like lighting, is the nature of the movie business. The results of Edeson's efforts were immensely effective in building a mysterious aura throughout the production, and added considerably to the "sketchy, interesting," mood Wallis sought. Edeson, a studio veteran, had not been Wallis's first choice to film *Casablanca*; the producer had hoped to pull legendary cinematographer James Wong Howe from other assignments to serve on the *Casablanca* team, but his services were still required elsewhere long after production on *Casablanca* began shooting. Nevertheless, Edeson proved he was more than capable of the task of filming the complex project; for this work on *Casablanca*, Edeson received an Academy Award nomination for best black-and-white cinematography, the third of his career.

At Wallis's request, cinematographer Art Edeson adjusted the lighting of the café scenes from the soft tones early in the production, to the "sketchy, interesting lighting" the producer wanted.

Throughout the early days of production, Wallis also kept a close eye on a production detail of even greater importance: the costumes.

With Orry-Kelly, the studio's lead designer, creating the fashions for *Casablanca,* the production could be assured of top-notch high-fashion outfits—all produced, of course, with the imposed restrictions of wartime conservation—along with a host of military and police uniforms. The uniforms were adorned with hundreds of medals fabricated in the Warner craft shop or found in thrift shops by Herbert "Limey" Plews, the propman assigned to the production. The Iron Cross worn by Veidt, Warner publicity reported, was the real thing, purchased in a pawnshop on Main Street in downtown Los Angeles for thirty cents.

One luxurious prop was manufactured within the bounds of wartime restrictions: the ring used by resistance fighter John Qualen to identify himself to Laszlo. The ring was created by H. B. Crouch, a Welsh jeweler who owned a shop on Wilshire Boulevard in Los Angeles. In the film, Qualen merely flips up a dark gem on the ring to reveal the Free French Cross of Lorraine underneath. But true to the standards of Hollywood ballyhoo, the ring supposedly also had other more sinister features; it was, Warner publicity reported, "a combination ID signal, poison cabinet, and microfilm encyclopedia."

Studio publicity reported that Orry-Kelly's designs were carefully crafted within the new wartime government regulations covering the new material used in costume garments—elegant though they appear to be. (The film's sets were restricted by the same guidelines.) Bergman's gloves, for example, "were tailored in strict accordance with priority rulings and without wasted pins, unnecessary zippers or real silk," the publicists reported.

As an alternative to silk, some of Bergman's outfits were tailored using cotton, a material in plentiful supply even during the war. "Many cottons are made now that photographically rival fine wools and silks in quality and beauty," Orry-Kelly said. "The African coast setting of *Casablanca* makes the use of lighter material both proper and beautiful."

Wallis was preoccupied about a fashion question of a different sort: the appropriateness of garbing his players in glittery formal wear while the world faced the tough days of war.

"Somehow or other these evening costumes seem to rub me the wrong way," the producer said about an array of dazzling formal wear designed by Orry-Kelly for Bergman. "We should think seriously about whether this girl should ever appear in an evening outfit.

"After all," Wallis said, "these two people are trying to escape from the country. The Gestapo is after them. They are refugees making their way from country to country, and they are not going to Rick's for social purposes. It seems a little incongruous to me for her to dress up in evening clothes as though she carried a wardrobe. I think it would be better for Henreid to wear a plain sport outfit, or a Palm Beach

suit, and if she wore just a plain little street suit."

Curtiz agreed, and Henreid and Bergman cast off their formal attire for dress more appropriate to desert travelers although Bergman does appear in more glittery formal wear during her scenes with Bogart set in Paris "of happier days." Henreid wore two suits: a double-breasted suit in the café scenes, and a single-breasted outfit for daytime wear and his airport departure—both lightweight cream-colored outfits perfectly suited to the North African desert. Bergman's dresses and traveling

Ingrid Bergman models one of Orry-Kelly's gowns for the scenes in Paris "of happier days."

clothes, a selection of summer-weight fashions, and a short-sleeve evening suit were designed with the same hot weather serviceability in mind. Together, Bergman and Henreid appear as precisely what they were: two refugees on the run, Hollywood-style.

Wallis may have decided wisely about the propriety of formal wear for his two desperate refugees, but he missed the mark in his requests for Bogart's attire—requests that Curtiz wisely chose to ignore.

"Please be careful about the kind of hats you have Bogart wear," Wallis told Curtiz before filming began. "As far as I am concerned, I would just as soon see him go through the whole picture without wearing a hat.

"We might give him one in the railroad station in Paris, and perhaps a Panama hat [worn in the scene outside the Blue Parrot]. Otherwise, I would play him without a hat."

Instead, Curtiz shot Bogart wearing a hat in every scene played outdoors, except in the romance montage while driving a convertible and riding in a boat on the Seine with Bergman at his side, and when chatting about his past with Renault on the patio of the café.

Orry-Kelly dressed Bogart in a trenchcoat for the Paris railroad station scene and the airport sequence; although he had worn a trench-coat and snap-brim hat—the outfit that would become his trademark—occasionally in other films, studio publicity prior to *Casablanca* reported that Bogart's on-screen "uniform" was a brown-striped suit and blue double-breasted overcoat—hardly the image of the actor burned into film legend.

Had Wallis's fashion advice for Bogart prevailed, and if Orry-Kelly had bowed to studio convention, film fans would have been deprived of one of the classic images of film history: a fog-shrouded Bogart, in trench coat with collar upturned, and a snap-brim fedora pulled low—the ultimate vision of the 1940s Hollywood screen hero.

With lighting, costumes, and set design under control, and only a stubborn script slowing the process, production of the Curtiz Show continued at a surprisingly steady pace. Frankly, the ups and downs associated with the production were not uncommon; only the near-microscopic examination that *Casablanca* receives has showcased problems that were quite similar to those faced by lesser pictures of the day.

Despite the extraordinary on-set pressures and occasional outburst from Curtiz—reported with mild amusement in Alleborn's "you know how Mike is" comments in the daily reports—the director guided the production with his usual skill, pace, and aplomb. Bergman recalled Curtiz as "an excellent director. He was very sweet and nice to me." Henreid concurred with Bergman's assessment of their director. "Curtiz has an instinctual visual sense," Henreid recalled. "It's quite different from the way actors visualize. Every now and again he would stop the camera and say, 'There's something wrong here, I don't know what it is.' By and by he'd realize what it was and we'd begin the scene again."

One of the studio system's principal strengths was its ability to bring together "stock companies" of performers and technicians who often worked together, thus bringing a sense of creative continuity to their work. Several of the principals and many of the bit players had appeared in Warner productions before, and even the most potent screen performers involved in the filming knew how to complement—or upstage—their colleagues.

"Sparring with Humphrey is getting to be a habit," said Sydney Greenstreet in a studio press release, after appearing with Bogart in *The Maltese Falcon* and *Across the Pacific* (and again, later, in *Passage to Marseille*). "We know each other's tricks so well that neither of us is in

"Sparring with Humphrey is getting to be a habit," said Greenstreet of their appearances together. "We know each other's tricks so well that neither of us is in a position to do any scene-stealing."

a position to do any scene-stealing. I don't know whether I can out-point him—but I'll certainly outweigh him!"

Bogart accepted his assignment to *Casablanca* with the same spirit of professionalism that had marked all of his work at the studio. He was neither overly excited nor disappointed about being cast as Richard Blaine, and he proceeded through the production with his usual level of wry camaraderie with his associates. Candid photos taken on the set show Bogart during breaks chatting amiably with colleagues, comparing notes with Bergman, or immersed in chess games with Curtiz, Rains, or Henreid.

Curiously, the studio publicists didn't put many words of praise about the picture into the mouth of the star; in fact, one of the few statements from Bogart during the production showcased the actor's criticism of his own character losing Ilsa: "It just doesn't ring true," a studio release reported Bogart saying about Ilsa's departure with Laszlo. "Miss Bergman is the kind of lady that no man would give up willingly, even to the tune of a lot of high-standing philosophy. But that was the story and I had to let her slide right out of my arms."

Bogart, Ingrid Bergman said, "was an excellent companion because he always worked very hard and was very concerned about our scenes. When you see the picture now you realize what an enormous talent he had with that rough, tough way, yet he brings out so much love." Yet Bergman also remembered that Bogart "was very much by himself. I kissed him, but I didn't know him. He was polite naturally, but I always felt there was a distance; he was behind a wall."

In spite of Bergman's memories of Bogart's "distance," some on the set thought that Bogart might have been infatuated with the actress.

"I think Bogart was in love with Ingrid," said Bob Williams, Bogart's publicist. "I had a feeling he was kind of smitten with her."

Considering the turmoil in Bogart's personal life in 1942, it would not have been surprising if, as Bergman thought, he seemed distant or, as others believed, he was infatuated with his co-star. Bogart was mired in the roughest days of his marriage to Mayo Methot, the most tumultuous of his four marriages that often found both husband and wife dishing out punches. Methot, who Bogart quite accurately called "Sluggy," actually stabbed her husband in one altercation—fortunately resulting in only a flesh wound.

Soon after *Casablanca,* Bogart met a lanky new actress on the lot, Lauren Bacall, and their blissful marriage lasted the rest of his life. But during production, with his turmoil-filled relationship with Methot on the skids, it would have been easy for Bogart's confidants to notice that the actor seemed drawn to the gentle and attentive Bergman in the quiet harbor of the studio—while outwardly staying "behind a wall" as perceived by his co-star.

Real-life personal feelings notwithstanding, however, on-screen Bergman and Bogart most certainly projected a powerful relationship as, under the careful guidance of Curtiz, they created one of the great romances of screen history. "Bogart was a natural actor and had no complications with getting into the mood," Bergman said. "He was always in the mood."

When Bergman started work on *Casablanca*, she was unfamiliar with Bogart's screen personality. She prepared for her on-screen relationship with several viewings of *The Maltese Falcon*, which was playing in Hollywood during its original release. "I felt I got to know him a little better through that picture," she said.

Bergman would recall her assignment to *Casablanca* with fondness for her director and co-stars, but with some troubled memories of the day-to-day progress on the set. Of all the actors involved in the production, Bergman, with her pivotal character torn between two leading men, and much of the interplay between principals still to be resolved by the writers, felt the most substantial impact from the lack of a completed script. No wonder that Bergman felt unsettled.

"We were shooting off the cuff," Bergman remembered. "Every day they were handing out dialogue and we were trying to make some sense of it. Every morning we said, 'Well, who are we? What are we doing here?' And Michael Curtiz would say, 'We're not quite sure, but let's get through this scene today and we'll let you know tomorrow.' "

Three decades after the filming, Bergman remembered that the issue of her character leaving with Laszlo or staying with Rick was yet to be resolved during the rewrites—not surprising, since her script contained gaping holes where an ending was supposed to be. Although the writers and Wallis had always known that Ilsa would leave Rick, with dialogue changes arriving daily, the actors could easily assume that the ending might change as well.

"I said to the writers, 'Now which of these two men do I end up with?' And they said, 'We haven't decided yet so we're going to shoot it both ways.' 'But that is impossible,' I said. 'You must tell me because after all, there is a little bit of difference in acting toward a man that you love and another man for whom you may just feel pity or affection.'

" 'Well,' they said, 'don't give too much of anything. Play it in between, you know, so that we can decide in the end.' Well, there was nothing for me to do but go ahead and try to play it in between." No wonder Bergman said, "No one knew where the picture was going, which didn't help any of us with our characterizations."

Several factors no doubt contributed to the apprehension of all the performers: First, the revisions added nearly every day to each actor's script brought new reminders to everyone involved in the Curtiz Show that the script was still rough (the different color pages—scattering of white, yellow, and pink—provided a visual demonstration of just how disorganized the draft remained).

Also, Wallis unintentionally added to the actors' concerns by holding back dialogue from his performers as long as he could to ensure that they would see a script that was as close to complete as possible. Just before production began—and with no expectation that rewrites would continue throughout shooting—Wallis informed the studio departments that for budget planning, any further changes in a large section of the script would affect primarily the dialogue and not the plot itself.

Drafts of the temporary script, Wallis said on May 21, *will not go to members of the cast, as I do not want them to see this portion of the script in rough form,* which meant that the cast was trying to work with a script that was not only rough but also contained gaping holes—four days before shooting began. Thus, it was not surprising that Bergman remembered that during production "we were all a bit on edge."

However, the artistic uncertainty that Bergman felt may have helped her better play Ilsa as torn between two men. She played the role perfectly, expressing distance and intimacy at just the right moments.

With the emergence of *Casablanca* as a screen legend, the frequent recounting of incidents during production has created a trove of stories—some true, most merely amusing legends—about the people and incidents associated with the picture. A few of these yarns, although nearly impossible to verify, are simply too entertaining to be ignored. So without corroboration—but without apology either—here is a selection of the tales from the production:

· Curtiz, ever mangling the English language, reportedly spouted a fresh crop of malaprops during the production. Curtizisms supposedly flew thick and fast during production; for example, Warner recalled that Curtiz described the story line of *Casablanca*, "Well, Jack, the scenario isn't the exact truth, but we have the facts to prove it."

Or, while Curtiz directed extras on the café set, he reported said, "Now we will hear mutters from the natives and visitors in the café. And in the background I will have the low throbbing music of the native tom-thumbs."

Or, when Curtiz directed Bergman, he told her, "Don't play it hard. Act easy-go-lucky."

Or, Paul Henreid recalled that, while filming the bazaar scenes, Curtiz wanted a "poodle" for the shot. The prop man, mystified by the request, nevertheless complied, and soon a large black poodle was brought to the set.

"What do I want with a dog?" Curtiz asked.

"You said you wanted a poodle."

"I wanted a poodle in the street," Curtiz shouted. "A poodle, a poodle of water!"

"You mean a puddle!"

"Right. A poodle, a puddle—that's what I want, not a goddamn dog!"

· When Curtiz filmed Rains as Renault entering the café to arrest Laszlo, the crew supposedly shot nine takes of Rains coming through the door, but Curtiz was not happy with the results. Rains, growing impatient, asked, "My dear Mike, what do you want?"

"I want you to come in faster," Curtiz told Rains.

Rains huddled with prop man Limey Plews, and then declared he was ready to perform. On the next take, Rains roared through the door, riding a studio messenger's bicycle. (A great story, and the reference to a bicycle may or may not be true, but the large number of shots mentioned in the story isn't close to accurate; according to Art Edeson's camera reports, Curtiz got the shot of Rains entering the café in a breezy three takes.)

· Peter Lorre, ever the on-set jester, was up to his usual tricks of assaulting cast and crew with a nonstop barrage of practical jokes. Although assigned to the production for only a few weeks, Lorre created near-constant mayhem that helped soften the edge of the daily grind of filming.

Peter Lorre played his arrest for maximum effect—and nearly caused an off-camera incident in the process.

· Lorre, Paul Henreid recalled, continually erased the chalk marks on the stage floor that cinematographer Arthur Edeson used to painstakingly position the actors and camera for each shot. "Lorre would wait until the stand-ins had left," Henreid said, "then he'd sneak onto the set while the actors were being called, erase the original chalk marks, and put in new ones a short distance away. Unsuspecting, we actors would step up to the new marks and Edeson would look into the his camera, then shake his head angrily. "That's all wrong! Are you on the marks?" Eventually everyone except Edeson knew what Lorre was doing. Moving camera marks on the set, or other production-disrupting pranks, were viewed with extreme disfavor at every studio, but Lorre, a favorite on the lot, somehow managed to pull off his prank without incurring the wrath of Warner or Wallis.

· Also during the production of *Casablanca*, Lorre supposedly staged the prank to end all pranks—this one at Curtiz's expense. With the director's frequent sexual encounters the worst kept "secret" on the lot, Lorre, the legend goes, persuaded the sound staff to plant a hidden microphone in the director's favorite studio tryst nest and run a loudspeaker back to the set. Fortunately for Lorre, the story goes, Curtiz never found out that his amplified groans of pleasure entertained the entire cast and crew.

· Another joke backfired on Lorre. Studio publicity reported that after filming Ugarte's arrest, Lorre, still invigorated after being dragged through the scene by several burly bit players dressed as French police, grabbed a woman he thought was an extra on the production, and yelled. The woman, thinking she was being attacked by a hysterical actor escaping from real policemen, nearly fainted. "It turned out," said a studio release, "that the woman was a guest on the set—Mrs. Charles Mac-Dougal and husband, an Iowa theater man."

By the final day of June, with only three weeks remaining of scheduled shooting, Wallis and company began to breathe easier—for the moment. Curtiz had shot footage covering more than eighty minutes of a film planned for roughly 110 minutes, and the director hadn't lost additional time since the early days of production. The Curtiz Show remained only two days behind—an admirable accomplishment given the continuing snags with actors and script. "This picture is going along smoothly," wrote Alleborn on June 29. "Everything is in order."

Alleborn continued to exude confidence in his progress reports, and he had a right to be confident. Wallis and Curtiz may have shouldered the burden of keeping the picture afloat, but Alleborn, one of the studio's veteran production managers with, by 1942, more than twenty-five years in the picture business, successfully dealt with the mind-boggling minutiae required to maintain a film about war during a real war. For example, during the highest period of military alert in the nation's history, Alleborn needed to obtain permission from the Fourth Interceptor Command, which governed the air space around Los Angeles, to move a plane from Lancaster, California, to the Los Angeles Metropolitan Airport in the San Fernando Valley for the scenes of Major Strasser's arrival.

Even more difficult during a time of near-nightly blackouts, Alleborn also needed permission to light up the airport for shooting second-unit night scenes of the Lisbon plane firing up its engines and taxiing down the runway. Eventually and amazingly, Alleborn worked out the details for both problems.

But the strain of the production was beginning to show. By June's end, the script, incredibly enough, was still not finished; more than a month after the cameras began rolling, a satisfactory final draft had not appeared.

On July 1, Wallis and Curtiz looked at all the footage shot up to that point. "Now I think we will get script up to the end of the picture so we can lay it out with a sensible schedule," Alleborn said hopefully. His report sounded optimistic, but he had said the same thing on June 30, on June 24, and on many other days. The reports would soon begin to change.

The delays weren't for lack of trying. Koch and the Epsteins were working at fever pitch, and Robinson contributed substantial rewrites to solidify the romance and the relationship. But their work wasn't enough. By July 6, script revisions were barely keeping up with the next day's shooting. That day Alleborn reported, "I am anxious to get script from Mr. Wallis *for shooting tomorrow* on Stage 8," which meant that the company would be filming dialogue completed so hastily that the film's production manager, actors and most of the production team saw the revised pages for the first time only hours before shooting.

From then on, delays would come thick and fast; because Rains and Henreid were absent early in production, all of their scenes were crowded together into the final weeks of shooting. It was these scenes that were still mired in rewrites.

By early July, the production slowed. Curtiz began to lose almost half a day of schedule for every two days completed. On July 6, the production was 2½ days behind schedule; by July 8, 3½ days behind; by July 11, 4 days behind; and on and on. Optimistic reports couldn't conceal the fact that the company was coming close to the day when the completed script would be used up, and production would be forced to shut down.

The problem, of course, was not that *Casablanca* might be left incomplete or be canceled once production began; one way or another, Wallis would ensure that the film was completed within a reasonable time schedule. Rather, the near-overwhelming difficulty with the script could have forced a rushed completion, an unsatisfactory ending, and a fast shuffle for the film into obscurity. That we remember *Casablanca* as a classic film today, given the circumstances of its completion, is a near miracle; considering the ordeal endured by the cast and crew during the first half of 1942, it's a wonder the film is remembered at all.

What problems plagued the script that four writers and an entire production staff couldn't fix? By July 6, as production entered its sixth week, the script still required polishing of dialogue here and there, and the refinement of a character or two (especially Renault, after the long Breen office ordeal cut away much of his best material). However, the biggest issue remained the ending. No one could find the solution to the puzzle that plagued everyone from the earliest readings of *Everybody Comes to Rick's* in December 1941: How could the movie conclude with Ilsa giving up Rick forever and still leave audiences satisfied with the result? That question continued to occupy the minds of all involved in the script, but the writers were quickly running out of time to look for an answer.

Still, there was progress. Wallis and the writers wisely shifted the ending from the café to the airport. But clearly, Rick's "I drink myself dizzy" excuses from earlier drafts, followed by Victor begging Ilsa to leave with him, weren't the stuff of a socko finish. Much of substance needed to be injected into the closing scenes: a sense of noble purpose, a clear articulation of the idea that the problems of individuals may pale when compared to the grim reality of a world in flames, but every person has the opportunity to fight evil and make the world a better place.

The distance of decades and countless viewings of *Casablanca* so firmly ingrains the ending's simplicity in the minds of audiences that today we may have little sympathy for the plight of Messrs. Epstein, Epstein, Koch, and Robinson in the panicked final weeks of filming. But in 1942, without our benefit of hindsight, all the writers, and the rest of the company, were stumped.

Then the first breakthrough came. "I think we have successfully licked the big scene between Ilsa and Rick at the airport by bringing Laszlo in at the finish of it," Wallis gleefully wrote to Curtiz on July 6. "It was practically impossible to write a convincing scene between the two people in which Rick could sell Ilsa on the idea of leaving without him. No arguments that Rick could put up would be sufficient to sway her from her decision to remain. That, I think, is why we always had so much trouble in trying to write such a scene.

"However, by bringing Laszlo in for the additional few lines, it makes it impossible for Ilsa to protest further, and in this way, the scene can be finished convincingly."

Perhaps not a perfect solution, but it was a fresh start. The final resolution of "the big scene between Ilsa and Rick" would require another ten days of polishing, and a final draft that would reach Stage 1 and the airport hanger set literally hours before the cameras rolled.

n i n e

Fights and Finishes

The week that began July 13 marked the turning point for *Casablanca*. By that date, most of the principal photography was complete. Daytime location shots of Major Strasser's arrival were done on July 10 in the broiling sun at the Metropolitan Airport in Los Angeles. Footage covering more than a hundred minutes of script was in the can, and Alleborn received permission to begin striking sets and returning rental property.

The biggest obstacle—the airport departure scenes—remained to be shot, except now they could no longer be avoided; Curtiz had depleted his cache of other scenes to film. On Friday, July 17, the company would shoot the film's climax scene at the airport, whether a satisfactory ending was ready or not.

Those final days, Koch recalled, "were a nightmare of which I remember only fragments. I felt like a weary traveler who had arrived at a destination but with only the foggiest notion where or how he had got there."

Epstein, too, recalled the same frantic days.

"Warner Bros. had seventy-five writers at the studio, and all seventy-five of them were trying to come up with an ending," Epstein remembered. "Everybody in the studio was trying to come up with an ending. They were panic-stricken."

By July 13 the reason why some recalled the film as being shot in chronological order would become clear: Because of the last-minute completion of script pages, Curtiz filmed some of the final scenes one right after the other. On Tuesday, Curtiz shot Rick and Renault plotting the capture of Laszlo with the letters of transit in his possession. On Wednesday, the company filmed Strasser receiving his warning phone call from Renault about Laszlo's escape, as well as scenes of Strasser roaring to the airport to intercept him. The production was rushing headlong toward its conclusion, but as the week began, it was still, as Rick would tell Ilsa in an earlier scene, "a story without an ending."

On July 14, the end was in sight. A new round of script changes for the closing scenes—likely the product of Wallis's Sunday script surgery sessions—was distributed to the company.

The tone of the July 14 material was more polished than earlier drafts, and the haziness that enshrouded the potential impact of the scene was finally beginning to clear.

"I'll be all right, Ilsa," Rick says, as he convinces her that she must leave with Victor. "You've done that for me. You've given me back my . . . myself. And we'll always have that to remember. A few moments that were ours. But if we're honest, we know that's all we've a right to."

Ilsa protests. "You're just saying that, Richard, to make me go . . ."

"Maybe I am," he replies. "But what difference does it make? What good are words now? Inside of us we both know you belong to Victor. You decided that once. This time it's my turn. Maybe you'll hate me for it now, but you'll be thankful for the rest of your life."

Better than previous drafts, but still not good enough. Now the success of *Casablanca*—eight months of work, nearly a million dollars in studio expense, and the work of hundreds of actors and off-camera talent—boiled down to perfecting scenes 259 through 262: a mere three pages of script, fewer than thirty sentences of dialogue, or four minutes of film.

Good fortune arrived on July 16, the day before the airport scenes were shot, when a new and final draft of the ending was distributed to cast and crew.

Finally, the beloved airport departure scene emerged, combining what would become, under Curtiz's capable direction, a magical blending of romance, commitment to a higher ideal, and a perfectly constructed rationale for why a woman should leave the man she loves in a bittersweet wartime parting.

"The Changes for New Ending" dated July 16 vary only a word or two from the scenes as shot, and begin with Ilsa realizing that she and Laszlo will leave on the Lisbon plane while Rick stays behind.

"No, Richard, no!" Ilsa cries. "What's happened to you? Last night we said—"

"Last night we said a good many things," Rick says, "You said I was to do the thinking for both of us. Well, I've done a lot of it since then and it all adds up to one thing. You're getting on that plane with Victor where you belong."

"But Richard," Ilsa says, protesting, "no, I, I—"

"Now you've got to listen to me," Rick explains. "Do you have any idea what you'd have to look forward to if you stay here? Nine chances out of ten we'd both land in a concentration camp. Isn't that true, Louis?"

"I'm afraid Major Strasser would insist," Renault says, as he finishes signing the letters of transit.

"You're only saying this to make me go," says Ilsa.

"I'm saying it because it's true," Rick says. "Inside of us we both know you belong with Victor. You're part of his work. The thing that keeps him going. If that plane leaves the ground and you're not with him, you'll regret it."

"No," Ilsa says, but weakening.

"Maybe not today, maybe not tomorrow, but soon, and for the rest of your life."

"But what about us?" Ilsa says, near tears.

"We'll always have Paris," says Rick. "We didn't have it—we'd lost it—until you came to Casablanca. We got it back last night."

"And I said that I would never leave you," says Ilsa, convinced.

"And you never will," Rick concludes. "But I've got a job to do, too. Where I'm going you can't follow—what I've got to do, you can be no part of. I'm no good at being noble, Ilsa, but it doesn't take much to see that the problems of three little people don't amount to a hill of beans in this crazy world. Someday you'll understand that. Not now. Here's looking at you kid."

Finally, with less than a day to spare, the job was done. Although a few words in this draft would be altered on the set, the significance of the scene was clear. The script doctors, at last, saved their patient; shooting would continue, with precisely the sort of ending that all involved in the production had sought for eight months.

The Epsteins, Koch, and Robinson created a powerful and unforgettable conclusion, but the airport parting of Rick and Ilsa marked only one of several cinematic miracles created during weeks of near-panic effort by the seven writers associated with the production.

First and foremost, and in spite of great temptation to do otherwise during dozens of rewrites, the Epsteins, Koch, and Robinson wisely retained virtually all of the original plot lines that had first attracted Wallis to the Burnett-Alison story. Knowing decades later the frustrations endured by the writers, their faith in the original plot and early drafts seems amazing; with so many obstacles throughout the production, they could have sought an easy solution or tried new directions, created additional characters, or used more convenient settings and situations.

Fortunately, no one wavered, and all of the important elements from the earliest drafts remain: the story of intrigue and black-market workings set against a wartime backdrop, the letters of transit, the ill-fated love affair between Rick and Ilsa, and the surprising and ultimately satisfying conclusion with the two reunited lovers separating for the greater good of mankind.

The writers combined material from the original stage play with all of the new charms created for the screen adaptation: the slaps at Nazis, the wit and repartee between Rick and Renault, and the buildup of the powerful romance—all somehow intertwined with the deadly serious business of struggles against Axis power and the agony of wartime refugees. While the plight of refugees was indeed important in the film version of the Burnett-Alison plot, the Warner Bros. writers wisely trimmed the significance of the Bulgarian refugees Jan and Annina and instead made them only a minor part of the story.

These elements were enlivened with line after line of marvelously crafted dialogue—most of which was written for the earliest drafts by the Epsteins. Out of context, some of the material may seem trite or clichéd, but with such a capable scene maker as Curtiz at the helm directing in his traditional lightning-fast style, and backed by Max Steiner's all-engulfing score, the film succeeds where lesser efforts containing the same lines might have been hooted off the screen.

Material retained from the early drafts includes such memorable lines as Renault's comments when he describes Rick to Ilsa before she realizes that the café owner is her former lover:

"If I were a woman," Renault says, "and I [tapping his chest] were not around, I would be in love with Rick."

Or, when Yvonne is spurned by Rick:

"Where were you last night?" Yvonne asks.

"That's so long ago, I don't remember," Rick replies, not looking up from his paperwork.

"Will I see you tonight?" she begs.

"I never plan that far ahead," he says, closing the subject.

Or, in the deadly serious confrontation when Strasser asks Laszlo to reveal the names of underground leaders for the honor of serving the

Third Reich. "I was in a concentration camp for a year," Laszlo tells Strasser. "That's honor enough for a lifetime."

Or, during the emotional scenes in the dark café with Sam and a drunken Rick, doubtless the finest screen moment of Humphrey Bogart's career.

"If it's December 1941 in Casablanca," Rick says. "What time is it in New York?"

"Huh? My watch stopped?"

"I'll bet they're asleep in New York," Rick says, longing for home. "I bet they're asleep all over America."

The scene closes with perhaps the most famous of all lines in the movie: the conversation—so often misquoted—between Rick and Sam about the song "As Time Goes By."

"Of all the gin joints in all the towns in all the world, she walks into mine," Rick says about Ilsa. "What's that you're playing?" he asks Sam, at the piano.

"Oh, just a little something of my own," Sam replies.

Bogart's finest moment on-screen: "Of all the gin joints in all the towns in all the world, she walks into mine."

"Well, stop it. You know what I want to hear."

"No, I don't."

"You played it for her. You can play it for me."

"Well, I don't think I can remember it."

"If she can stand it, I can. Play it!"

Or finally, in the closing scene of the film, when Renault gives the unforgettable order, "Round up the usual suspects." The line had been included in early drafts by the Epsteins for Renault's conversation with Strasser at the beginning of the film when the Nazi arrives in French Morocco. Later, the line was also inserted into the film's closing scenes, when seemingly the entire studio was struggling to smooth out the ending.

Julius Epstein recalled that he and his brother, Philip, were discussing the problem of the ending while driving to the studio along Sunset Boulevard in Bel-Air—in particular wondering how Bogart could escape arrest after killing Strasser. As the brothers approached the corner of Beverly Glen, Epstein said, "We turned to each other and yelled, 'Round up the usual suspects!'"

The Epsteins were also responsible for including—but not writing—the most romantic phrase of the film: "Here's looking at you, kid." Rick's loving salute to Ilsa from their Paris days was included in the earliest script drafts. The phrase originated as an old toast from the days of glass-bottomed mugs ("here's looking at you" meaning "looking at you" through the bottom of the mug). Thus, the Epsteins turned a chug-a-lug cheer into one of the endearing romantic lines in film history.

While the Epsteins can lay claim to Renault's "round up the usual suspects" as well as including "here's looking at you, kid," as Rick's romantic endearment to Ilsa, identifying the specific writer responsible for the last-second final draft of the airport sequence unfortunately becomes an impossible task, even with the aid of the Warner files. Although clearly all the writers, Curtiz, Wallis, and their staffs were involved in the final script sessions, it is nevertheless ironic that credit for writing the scene noted as perhaps the most memorable single moment in film history will remain forever a mystery.

In addition to their work crafting quotable dialogue, the Epsteins, Koch, and Robinson also created some brilliant solutions to lingering problems; besides the concluding airport scenes, the most inspired of these script fixes was having Ilsa ask Rick "to do the thinking for both of us, for all of us"—a convenience that allowed Rick to cook up his elaborate escape plan for Laszlo, along with the idea that Ilsa would leave with her husband as well. The scene not only provides a gateway to the logical solution of the story, but also creates a setting for a huge buildup of suspense and the emergence of Rick from his cynical shell as the defeated idealist.

Knowing the story behind the writing of *Casablanca*, it would be convenient to think of the script as a serendipitous near-miracle that was completed only because an assemblage of fleet-fingered scribes devoted so much time to the project that their success was inevitable. However, the haste of writing cannot disguise the fact that those involved—both writers and editors—were supremely competent studio craftsmen with decades of experience in bringing stories to the screen.

The seemingly endless assignment of writing and rewriting was not undertaken simply to make the script "better." Rather, the mission was far more specific: to finely hone each character with precisely the right characterization and shadings of personality that could be meshed seamlessly into the story line. The writers merged these characters with the broad range of plot points that were already established in the earliest versions of the script—sometimes accomplishing their task with only a few words or several sentences to flesh out a character. In some instances, this mission required weeks of work that produced only a few lines of dialogue—the price Wallis paid to achieve the desired results.

Indeed, many of the most important story lines are explored with the briefest of conversations; even the climax of the picture—the emotional conversation between Rick and Ilsa during the airport departure—accounted for only three pages of script. Creating a personality with only a line or two was far more important than accomplishing the same job with pages of dialogue. If the final result took the most talented writers at the studio day after day of concentrated polishing, then the product was well worth the effort.

One of these triumphs of plot polishing was the creation of the relationship between Victor Laszlo and Ilsa Lund. With only a modicum of dialogue exchanged between husband and wife, the writers established a bond that balanced Victor's love for his wife, and Ilsa's deep respect and near worship—but not love—for her husband. The audience knows that Ilsa's heart belongs with Rick, but she still manages to accept Laszlo's affections and conceal her true feelings without lying to her husband.

The writers accomplished this seemingly formidable task with the sparest of dialogue—barely four pages in all—in the film's two private conversations between Victor and Ilsa. In the Blue Parrot Café, after Victor tries unsuccessfully to convince Ilsa to leave without him, and he says, "I love you very much, Ilsa." In response, she looks at him, smiling tenderly and, without lying, says, "Your secret will be safe with me."

Later, at their hotel, after Victor realizes that Ilsa and Rick had been in love in Paris, he again tells her, "I love you very much, my dear." Again, she avoids lying and says, "Yes, yes I know."

Next comes a brilliant stroke of screenwriting that provides Ilsa with the perfect excuse to, if not deceive her husband, then to painlessly conceal the truth from him. Knowing that Victor suspects her Paris affair, but still hoping to avoid hurting him, Ilsa hesitantly says, "Victor, whatever I do, will you believe that I, that I—"

"You don't even have to say it," Victors stops her. "I'll believe."

Then, as Victor prepares to leave for his meeting with the underground, Ilsa runs to him. Just when viewers think she is finally going to lie about her feelings, she says instead, "Victor, be careful."

On paper, these lines seem somewhat cold and unfeeling, but as captured on screen, with Bergman's gentle performance as directed by Curtiz, and with a massive swell of Steiner's music behind it, the conversation creates a powerful portrayal of Ilsa's deep respect for her husband, while at the same time she tries to reconcile her near-overwhelming love for Rick.

But of all the literary gems that eventually found their way into the script, the most important was the creation of Richard Blaine as the cynical hero with the mysterious past. The script is packed with references to Rick and his background that are intentionally incomplete—adding immensely to Rick's allure by providing hints about his personality but without giving the audience more than a hint of his past.

Rick, as Ferrari says, is a "difficult customer. One never knows what he'll do or why." Rick is supposedly apathetic and apolitical, yet he once ran guns to Ethiopia, fought in the Civil War on the Loyalist side, and ejects an official of the warmongering Deutsches Bank from the café's gambling room as easily as if he were a common thief. Carl the waiter tells diners at the café that Rick is a saloon owner who never drinks with patrons. When Renault asks Rick why he doesn't return to America, wondering if perhaps he stole the church funds, ran off with a senator's wife, or killed a man, Rick answers, "It was a combination of all three." Renault presses Rick, and asks him why he came to Casablanca. Rick replies, "For the waters." When Renault points out that there are no waters in Casablanca because the city is in the desert, Rick says, "I was misinformed."

Ugarte, the black market criminal, also knows only hints of Rick's past. After Rick ejects the Nazi banker from his gambling room, Ugarte says, "You know, Rick, watching you just now with the Deutsches Bank, one would think you'd been doing this all your life."

"Well, what makes you think I haven't?" Rick asks.

"Oh, nothing. But when you first came to Casablanca, I thought—"

"You thought what?"

"What right do I have to think?"

Even the Nazis can shed little light on Rick's past; all Strasser can say is that Blaine "cannot return to his country. The reason is a little vague."

These comments and Rick's eventual emergence as a romantic, patriotic personality add an intriguing sense of mystery to the character as embodied by Humphrey Bogart; the man of the world with a "cynical shell," as Louis Renault says of Rick, but "at heart a sentimentalist." Rick is a character so hardened by fate that he hides his true feelings from even his closest friends; but when he has the opportunity to rekindle his lost love even for a moment, he risks his life for the opportunity.

Of the seven writers assigned off-and-on to the production, Julius and Philip Epstein contributed most to the creation of this mysterious aura for Rick's character, primarily in references in early drafts of the script (although Rick's actions would become better defined in later polishings with help from both Koch and Robinson). While the Epsteins intended to create at least a minor air of mystery around Rick, the eventual shaping of the character was a near-accident that emerged almost as a convenience; incredibly, the Epsteins were concerned that the material left unsaid about Rick would shortchange the audience.

"After reading the scene in which Claude Rains's character asks Bogart, 'I've often speculated why you don't return to America,' Wallis said, 'Yeah, why can't he go back to America? The audience will want to know,' " Julius Epstein recalled.

"We sat around and came up with a lot of excuses, and they were all so . . . weak," Epstein said. "As an explanation, I finally suggested 'unpaid parking tickets.'

"Finally we told Wallis to leave the explanation as it is. The lack of explanation may be weak, but it will be better for the viewers to use their own imaginations than to pinpoint the reason and have the audience disappointed in it. It worked out that way, I think."

Indeed, it did "work out." Whether intentional or not, the personality as originally established by the Epsteins, plus all of the other contributions, helped solidify a character of vital importance—not just for Bogart but for the continuing refinement of the American screen hero.

This hard-boiled figure—self-confident and stand-alone, with an unknown past and a personal code, who could be moved by powerful emotion or a higher purpose—was a character type that Bogart would recreate again and again through other screen incarnations in some of the most memorable roles of his career: He started with Sam Spade in *The Maltese Falcon*, reached full flower with Richard Blaine in *Casablanca*, and continued to flourish as Harry Morgan in *To Have and Have Not*, detective Philip Marlowe in *The Big Sleep*, and many other roles that formed a body of work that would elevate Bogart to become one of the most popular screen legends in cinema history.

Perhaps the greatest appeal of the postwar screen hero is the information left *unsaid* about his personality, with only shadows and textures revealed about a slice of his life—no past, no future, only the present— that leaves the audience guessing about his true motivation and personality. This screen image would inspire generations of Hollywood's top actors who understood the appeal of a screen hero who answered the beat of a different drummer: Clint Eastwood, Kirk Douglas, Burt Lancaster, Robert Mitchum, Steve McQueen, Harrison Ford, and hundreds of others.

Whether portraying a steel-nerved detective working the back streets of a nameless city, a cyborg in a science fiction thriller, the "Man with No Name" in a spaghetti western, or any one of a thousand other screen characters, many of the most popular picture heroes would find inspiration in the roles created by Humphrey Bogart—in particular by his portrayal of Richard Blaine, the cynical saloon owner in the white dinner jacket who turned against the world because of a romance lost, but who found renewed meaning for his life when that love returned—if only for a moment.

In part because of this milestone status of Rick's character, and also because *Casablanca*'s legacy continues to flourish, some critics continue to explore "faults" in the plot of the film, as if picking at story flaws might have relevance in measuring the impact of the motion picture. For example, some critics have wondered why possession of the "letters of transit" would protect Laszlo, an important enemy of the Third Reich, even if the visas, as Ugarte said, "cannot be rescinded, not even questioned." Or, why were German couriers carrying papers signed by General De Gaulle, the archenemy of Vichy France? Or, if Laszlo was so important to the underground movement, couldn't his friends simply hire or hijack a boat and smuggle Laszlo aboard for the brief journey to neutral Portugal?

Or, how could the script ignore what would have been the Nazis' simplest answer to the Victor Laszlo problem: merely assassinate him as they had so many other insurgents—a possibility that Laszlo himself breezily explains away by telling Strasser that "any violation of neutrality would reflect on Captain Renault" (the writers did add a convenient plot point that kept Laszlo alive: the fact that the Nazis hoped to get the names of other resistance leaders from Laszlo, even if they had to use "persuasive methods").

The writers themselves realized that the basic plot was not without its flaws. Julius Epstein has called the plot "slick shit" practically from the day the film was released, and of the script remarked, "There wasn't a single word of truth in it." And Koch recalled, "When the picture opened, I wondered what all the excitement was about. I was still blind to the virtues of the film and saw only what I considered its faults."

But one can also ask those who toil over this criticism why they concern themselves with such issues. The points either included or ignored in the script are mere quibblings and add little to understanding why the picture remains as powerful and entertaining today as it was the night it premiered.

What *is* important in *Casablanca* is the swirl of intrigue, the potent drama, the powerful romance, and the bittersweet parting of star-crossed lovers trapped in the anguish of a world at war as they go on to missions of greater purpose. The writers of the film and some latter-day critics may wonder how *Casablanca* became one of the genuine classics of American cinema, but audiences who first saw the picture in 1942, and the generations of viewers since who have seen it on a movie screen or television, have always understood.

July 17 marked the forty-fifth shooting day on the *Casablanca* set. A 9:00 A.M. casting call brought the beginning of the most important—and the most explosive—day of the production.

"During the day the company had several delays caused by arguments with Curtiz the director, and Bogart the actor," Alleborn reported. "I had to go and get Wallis and bring him over to the set to straighten out the situation. At one time they sat around for a long time and argued, finally deciding on how to do the scene."

What had occurred on this pivotal day of the production? Over the years, legend recalls that Bogart and Curtiz fought over how Rick should handle the shooting of Strasser; Curtiz, according to many versions of the story, still wanted Bogart to shoot Strasser in the back, and the actor strenuously objected. The actor and director, the story goes, argued so heatedly that Wallis was forced to referee and negotiate a new scene on the spot.

This story of the argument has been passed down with such frequency through so many accounts of the filming of *Casablanca* that it is usually accepted as fact. And a marvelous tale it would be—if it were true. In fact, the murder of Strasser in cold blood had been eliminated from the script weeks before, and his shootout with Rick would not be filmed for three more days. The actual cause for the artistic explosion on the airport set occurred over entirely different issues.

For July 17, Alleborn and Curtiz scheduled eleven different setups as part of the day's shooting, including the principal takes of Rick and Ilsa's parting at the airport (scheduling was, of course, delayed until the last minute because of the late arrival of the final script).

With the first takes of the day, shooting proceeded smoothly: first, Curtiz filmed a long shot across the hangar of bit player Jean De Briac as he read the weather report in his phone call to the radio tower. Then the crew completed several shots needed for special effect "glass shots" that would be used in postproduction.

The strain began to show just before lunch, with the filming of the arrival at the airport of Bogart, Bergman, Henreid, and Rains (driving his car but held at gunpoint).

The shot, which lasts only only a few seconds on the screen, required a complex setup: The scene begins with a medium shot of De Briac reading the weather report; as he completes his dialogue, the camera picks up Rains's car through a window. The camera then dollies across the set and follows the automobile around to the front of the hangar. Rains was supposed to drive the car to a fixed mark on the set, with all of the passengers piling out, hitting their individual marks, and then delivering several lines of dialogue. All the while, Curtiz's ever-active camera, operated by Edeson, would be rolled around the set to track the action.

It was, Henreid would recall, "a tricky shot." Every element had to work perfectly: the car, the passengers' emergence from the car, and their dialogue—all in sync with the camera moving across the stage to pick up the action. The brief sequence includes a moment of cinematic choreography; to move his mark quickly and to avoid drowning out his own lines, Rains doesn't close the car door; instead, he shuts it halfway while on the move. Bergman, behind him, grabs the door in motion, and quietly swings it shut while Rains moves into the foreground.

The arrival at the airport required a complex orchestration of car, people, and camera moves.

WARNER BROS. PICTURES, Inc.
FOREIGN DEPT.

KEY LETTER __A__

TITLE _Casablanca_   PRODUCTION NO. _410_   DATE _7-17-42_

FILM NO. 545 — SCRIPT SCENE 258 — SET: Airport & Hangar
- 1st: 1 2 3 4 5 6 7 8 9
- 2nd: O
- 10 11 12 13 14 15 16 17 18

1 CAMERAS L. S. Intg. Officer Talks
REMARKS: in phone, gets weather report – plane & people in tg.

FILM NO. 548 — SCRIPT SCENE 259 — SET: "
- 1st: 1 2 3 4 5 6 7 8 9
- 2nd: X O
- 10 11 12 13 14 15 16 17 18

1 CAMERAS Dolly CE Rick, Ilsa &
REMARKS: Renault

FILM NO. 545A — SCRIPT SCENE 258 — SET: "
- 1st: 1 2 3 4 5 6 7 8 9
- 2nd: O
- 10 11 12 13 14 15 16 17 18

Wild Shot
1 CAMERAS Glass Shot
REMARKS:

FILM NO. 549 — SCRIPT SCENE 259 — SET: "
- 1st: 1 2 3 4 5 6 7 8 9
- 2nd: X OX OX X X X X X
- 10 11 12 13 14 15 16 17 18

Hold only no print
1 CAMERAS Lg CU Rick & Ilsa
REMARKS: during 548

FILM NO. 546 — SCRIPT SCENE 258 — SET: "
- 1st: 1 2 3 4 5 6 7 8 9
- 2nd: O
- 10 11 12 13 14 15 16 17 18

1 CAMERAS L.S. alternate to 545
REMARKS:

FILM NO. 550 — SCRIPT SCENE 259 — SET: "
- 1st: 1 2 3 4 5 6 7 8 9
- 2nd: X X O
- 10 11 12 13 14 15 16 17 18

1 CAMERAS alternate to 549
REMARKS:

FILM NO. 546A — SCRIPT SCENE 258 — SET: "
- 1st: 1 2 3 4 5 6 7 8 9
- 2nd: O
- 10 11 12 13 14 15 16 17 18

Wild Shot
1 CAMERAS Glass Shot
REMARKS: alternate to 545A

FILM NO. 551 — SCRIPT SCENE 263B — SET: "
- 1st: 1 2 3 4 5 6 7 8 9
- 2nd: OX X X O
- 10 11 12 13 14 15 16 17 18

1 CAMERAS Dolly M Rick & Ilsa
REMARKS: to CU to Lg CU

FILM NO. 547 — SCRIPT SCENE 259 — SET: "
- 1st: 1 2 3 4 5 6 7 8 9
- 2nd: X X X X OX OX OX O
- 10 11 12 13 14 15 16 17 18

1 CAMERAS Dolly LS Car drives
REMARKS: in Renault across street to plane. Luggage – hello & Man ex.

FILM NO. 552 — SCRIPT SCENE 263C — SET: "
- 1st: 1 2 3 4 5 6 7 8 9
- 2nd: X O
- 10 11 12 13 14 15 16 17 18

1 CAMERAS Pick up on 551 –
REMARKS: Lg CU Rick & Ilsa

INSTRUCTIONS: American Print put a circle around the take O
Foreign Print put a square around the take □
Hold Print put on OX under the takes.
On N. G. Takes put a cross over the take X

Time after time, the shot failed. For one reason or another, each take went awry—Rains missed the car's stop point, passengers exited clumsily, doors were slammed at the wrong moment, or dialogue was garbled—and each new take required time-consuming reset of the car, camera, and players. The crew struggled through eight lengthy takes and new setups of the scene before Curtiz was satisfied.

But even with the completion of the shot, the strain grew. The struggle through weeks of uncertainty about the script, and last-minute changes that often brought new versions of material to the set minutes before shooting, would soon disrupt filming of the most important shot of the picture. As Alleborn would later point out, "There were also numerous delays, due to the cast not knowing the dialogue, which was a rewritten scene that came out the night before."

The emotion-charged parting of Rick and Ilsa took seventeen takes from different angles before Curtiz was satisfied.

The breaking point came after lunch. Frustrations from the morning's shooting spilled over to the afternoon with the filming of the climax of the movie: Rick's parting words to Ilsa, as rewritten for the final time the day before. But what legend recalled as a debate over killing a Nazi was in reality an argument over the delivery of romantic dialogue.

Years later, Wallis recalled that disputes erupted occasionally on the set. "Mike and Bogey argued so frequently," Wallis remembered, "that I had to come on the set to control the quarrels." Even studio publicity releases noted "creative differences" between Bogart and Curtiz over how Rick should handle his rekindled romance with Ilsa.

But the July 17 battles were by far the worst of the production. Bogart and Curtiz couldn't agree over how Rick should deliver his farewell lines, and after Curtiz shot two takes of the emotionally charged scene, Bogart, fed up with the last-second revisions that again altered the nature of his character, called a halt. The argument, discussion, and negotiations over the reading of the scene took two hours to resolve, forcing the entire company to wait while Bogart and Curtiz hashed out their differences with Wallis acting as referee.

Filming continued. Curtiz shot seventeen grueling takes of Bogart and Bergman in their parting moments before production was stopped for a second time when arguments again disrupted the set. Cast and crew waited again while Curtiz and Bogart worked out their differences—this time in slightly less than an hour.

By the time shooting wrapped a few minutes before six, in spite of arguments, hours of delay, and complex setups, Curtiz completed some thirty-five takes for a grand total of one minute and forty-six seconds of "OK takes." Curtiz shot various versions of Bogart and Bergman a total of twenty-two times; the scenes that inspired so much argument, dozens of strenuous takes, and acrimony between star and director yielded precisely thirty-nine seconds of usable film.

All of the arguing may have eventually placated both director and star, but it didn't satisfy the producer. After the hours of aggravation on the set, Wallis didn't like what he saw on the screen. Following his review of the rushes of the Rick-Ilsa parting, he ordered retakes and new closeups of much of the scene; the new footage was shot four days later.

Wallis and Curtiz would clash once more during the filming, and this time the argument indeed concerned Strasser's death. Strangely enough, after decades of reminiscences recalling Curtiz and Bogart fighting over the shooting scene, it was instead Curtiz and Wallis who played out a minor drama over the closing shots of the film.

Curtiz, ever up to his old tricks, was still trying to inject old ideas into the new material. Despite the arrival of revised script for the airport scenes in which Rick and Strasser shoot it out in a fair fight, the director

The airport hangar set, as seen during a break in the filming on July 21, 1942, in the only existing photograph that shows the set from this angle. The stage has been set up for filming after Strasser's death (note the telephone handset already lying on the ground). During this break in production, Bogart (the slightly blurred trench-coated figure) talks to several crew members, including Curtiz (far left).

didn't think the Nazi deserved the opportunity. Curtiz filmed the shoot-out but added an additional line to Bogart's dialogue.

"We cannot use Bogart's line, 'All right, Major, you're asking for it,' because of the censorship reasons which I explained to you," Wallis patiently told Curtiz on July 22, two days after the company first filmed Strasser's death at Rick's hand. "This would make Strasser's shot one of self-defense.

"Therefore, we will want to pick up the line as it was in the script—'I was willing to shoot Renault, and I am willing to shoot you.' "

For once Curtiz couldn't slip his own ideas past his producer. The dialogue was reshot, and the Wallis version was used in the film.

t e n

"This Production Finished as of Yesterday"

The filming of the airport scenes on Stage 1—with on-set arguments, eleventh-hour arrivals of dialogue, and directorial script manipulations—marked a turning point in the production. The shooting had passed its toughest obstacles; as the most difficult filming was completed, the production rolled toward its conclusion.

With sighs of relief all around, Curtiz wrapped up the last of the airport sequences on July 22—the most arduous five shooting days of the picture. The day before, the Curtiz Show passed its planned completion date; the production was by this time officially over schedule.

The next day, a Warner second unit directed by Ross Lederman filmed the on-location night shots of the "Lisbon plane"—a two-engine Lockheed Electra—at the Los Angeles Metropolitan Airport. The night shooting had indeed been arranged; in the midst of world war, Alleborn's influence with the Fourth Interceptor Command had prevailed.

From then on, Curtiz merely mopped up an assortment of shots—mostly takes involving Henreid that were rescheduled from earlier in the production, scenes with Bergman in the open-air black market, conversations with Greenstreet in the Blue Parrot, and several night shots with Henreid in the streets.

The only on-set conflict worth noting in the final days of production involved a squabble over security guards, who were sneaking inside the air-conditioned stage to escape the blistering heat of the San Fernando Valley—and thus leaving a take vulnerable to interruption. For Alleborn, with more than two months of scheduling, rescheduling, and production juggling behind him, a personnel problem so easy to correct must have seemed a welcome distraction.

With the completion of the bulk of the picture, Curtiz began to finish work with his principal actors. Rains and Veidt both wrapped up their final takes with the conclusion of the airport scenes; Greenstreet departed on July 25, having been held over some ten days past his agreed-upon assignment, which meant he ended up earning one of the largest total salaries assigned to the production.

On Saturday, August 1, Curtiz filmed Bogart's last takes—the outdoor market scenes of Rick apologizing to Ilsa for his drunken behavior in the café. On August 3, Bergman and Henreid completed a work day that lasted only forty minutes—their final on the production—with a single shot walking together on the black market street. By 4:00 P.M., with the filming of several shots of refugees herded into buildings, out of

Bogart completed his last day on Casablanca *by first posing with Bergman and a feathered friend from the set, and then filming scenes in the black market, including Rick's apology to Ilsa.*

wagons, and watching in desperation as the Lisbon plane flew overhead, Curtiz wrapped principal photography of *Casablanca*—eleven days over schedule. "This production," a relieved Alleborn wrote on August 4, "finished as of yesterday."

Although on-set production concluded in early August, the behind-the-scenes work on the picture had only just begun. Wallis chose editor Owen Marks to work with him to assemble the nearly two and a half miles of film into a rough print that could be previewed to the public, and then edited and reedited until a final print met the producer's satisfaction.

For a producer working in the heyday of the Hollywood studio system, the screening room and the editing booth were his definitive domain, his seat the judge's bench from which final verdicts were issued on the content, timing, and pace of each scene. In the cutting room, working without the distraction of temperamental actors and headstrong directors, while studying rough prints and dictating notes, a studio producer could hone the film to a fine edge. Some directors—especially "renegades" like John Ford and Howard Hawks—may have dreaded producers "tampering" with work created so painstakingly on the set, but more often than not, an experienced producer could add immeasurably to a production during editing, often transforming a lackadaisically paced production into a crisp and entertaining final work. It was as much in the screening room as on the set where the fast-paced, punchy Warner Bros. style was created.

Wallis's notes from these projection and editing sessions are filled with cuts and deletions, each designed to tighten the action to clarify a scene. While many of Wallis's edits deleted long sequences or entire scenes, many more involved only the briefest bits of film, some as short as a foot long—only two-thirds of a second.

Long after Marks pieced together a roughly completed print, Wallis generated dozens of new orders for trims, deletions, and additions; his notes are filled with such comments as "trim just a few frames on the two closeups . . . lose the long shot of the waiter bringing the bottle and glasses . . . let Bergman's closeup run a couple of feet longer . . . you can lose probably five or six feet off the beginning of the shot of Bogart and the girl in the automobile . . . hold on Rick a little longer after Ilsa leaves him outside the black market . . . shorten the cut after Laszlo and Ilsa sit . . . add a foot to Laszlo's line at the airport 'this time our side will win,' " and on and on.

Wallis continued to edit the rough print after in-studio screenings and previews to the public in Huntington Park and other Southern California theaters. Audiences recommended cuts of some material in the first sections of the picture, and the producer agreed; in addition to ceaseless tightening of virtually every scene to speed the action along, Wallis eliminated a number of entire takes that seemed to slow the plot.

August 5, 1942

CUTTING NOTES

"CASABLANCA"

Trim just a few frames on the two closeups of the refugees who turn around when the Police whistle blows.

Take out the this gang group of soldiers before the cut of the leading the refugees into the patrol wagon.

When you come back to Curt Bois at the table, pick him up on the later speech, "Unfortunately".

Take out the scene of Jan and Annina in front of the Police Prefect when you cut away from Bois. Just go to the shot of the refugees coming out of the truck and back.

From the Free French insert, in the hand of the man who was shot, make a direct cut instead of a dissolve.

Trim a little on Rains' line, "And I am prepared to refuse it".

See if you can cut Carl when he comes into the gambling place.. Take him right to the table...the man with the dialogue about Amsterdam and the woman who asks about having Rick drink. Then cut to the man approaching Rick; have him okay the check, then go to the door.

Trim just a little before he says, "Tonight I will sell these for more".

After Ferrari comes into the Cafe, finish the "Knock Wood" song as quickly as possible. Try and drop eight or twelve bars in there somewhere.

Take out two of the last four shots from Ugarti.

Trim on Strasser, "You were not always so carefully neutral". Pick him right up on the speech.

Stay on Henreid for the full introduction, "Miss Ilsa Lund". Then cut sharply to her, just as she's nodding.

Trim just a feet before she speaks that line, "What a lovely uniform".

Trim on Bergman's closeup, "with Mademoiselle". Don't have her looking down when you cut to her.

Lose the long shot of the waiter bringing the bottle and glasses. Cut to Bergman right on her line, "Ask the piano player to come over".

Take out that long look of Bergman looking around before he says, "Where is Rick?".

Pick her up with the full footage looking at Sam, as long as you can let that run after she turns back.

Wallis's cutting notes from a review of an early version of the film. Note several of the lines that Wallis wanted trimmed "a little" (such as Rains's line, "And I am prepared to refuse it," and Bergman's comment, "What a lovely uniform") were eventually cut entirely.

Deleted were several shots of the refugee roundups early in the picture, including a spectacular take of stuntman George Suzanne dressed as a refugee crashing through a window. Also clipped were several early scenes of Jan and Annina, as well as a few superfluous conversations between the principal characters in Rick's café.

Preview audiences encouraged more explanation of the plot early in the film, especially concerning the importance of the letters of transit. As originally cut, the preview audience first learn about the letters of transit about eleven minutes into the film, when Peter Lorre explains their significance to Bogart, in the scene when Ugarte asks Rick to hide the documents "for a little while." The "roundup of the usual suspects" at the beginning of the film was carried out solely to hunt down the killer of the two German couriers, without explanation of the documents they carried.

To solve this problem, Wallis decided to build up the letters of transit by explaining their importance in the first shot of the picture, and ordered the shooting of an additional scene. On August 22, Curtiz directed bit player Jean Del Val as a police officer who reads a teletyped message explaining the death of the German couriers and the importance of the documents they carried. Thus, filming was finally complete; the last shot filmed became the first scene of the movie.

Also completed in the postproduction work was the fine-tuning of several special effects by Lawrence Butler and Willard Van Enger, including models of the Nazi aircraft and the Lisbon plane, and several "glass shots"—scenes filmed on the set through a glass plate that includes a painting of part of the scene that didn't exist on the actual set. Used so a larger, more expensive construction was not needed, glass shots were employed in *Casablanca* primarily during the outdoor black market scenes to hide the Burbank skyline over the tops of the sets and to disguise the interior of Stage 1 during the filming of the airport scenes.

The postproduction staff also created the introductory scenes of the film following the credits, which feature a revolving globe, an animated map, and a montage of wartime scenes, all accompanied by a dramatic narration and explanation of the "tortuous refugee trail" that included Casablanca as an "embarkation" point to neutral Portugal. Lou Marcelle, an announcer at Warner-owned KFWB radio, narrated the montage. Marcelle's voice was already familiar to theatergoers of the day for his work in Warner previews of coming attractions (his brief audio contributions to *Casablanca* would be remembered for his curious pronunciation of visas as "veezays").

The montage of wartime documentary footage was created by Don Siegel and James Leicester. Siegel and Leicester would also help create the other war documentary visual montage of the Germans marching toward Paris in Rick's flashback scene. Siegel, who quickly worked his way up through the studio system, soon became a talented director of an extraordinary variety of films, including such studio-era classics as *The*

Big Steal and *Invasion of the Body Snatchers,* and the first of Clint Eastwood's American blockbuster hits, *Two Mules for Sister Sara* and *Dirty Harry.*

While postproduction progressed, Wallis remained unhappy with the film's closing lines. At one point while writing the script, the film simply ended with Rick's line, "It doesn't make a bit of difference, Louis, you still owe me 5,000 francs." Another incarnation of the closing line was, "Louis, I might have known you'd mix your patriotism with a little larceny." Other drafts shaped the final scene into a conclusion that was close to, but not quite, as seen in the film.

After so many other writers contributed draft after draft of the difficult final scene, it was Wallis who offered the final adaptation of the film's closing line as Rick and Renault walk across the airport tarmac together. On August 21, Wallis requested that Bogart record a "wild" track of one additional bit of dialogue, to be looped into the existing final shot after Renault says that their bet over Laszlo's escape should "just about pay their expenses" to a Free French garrison at Brazzaville.

"Our expenses?" Rick says. "Louis, I think this is the beginning of a beautiful friendship."

"It was marvelous," Robinson said of Wallis's new version of the line. "It was inspired."

Earlier in the production, Wallis requested the assignment of one of the studio's most important "invisible stars," an artist who himself never appeared in a Warner picture but whose creative contributions were critical in some of the studio's finest productions.

Composer Max Steiner was, in the words of Hal Wallis, "A tiny, fast-talking, hypersensitive gnome with great wit and a strong streak of schmaltz." Corny characterizations aside, Wallis eagerly admitted that Steiner's role as composer of musical soundtracks was as crucial to a film's good fortune as the performance of any on-screen talent: "Steiner," Wallis said, "was as much a part of Warner pictures as our stock company."

From the earliest days of Warner Bros., music played a crucial role in the studio's pictures, and Warners was renowned as a pioneering company in the use of music in movies. Well before the arrival of the sound era in 1927, silent films produced by Warner Bros. featured spectacular musical accompaniments, often played by full orchestras.

Curiously, the Warners first explored the use of sound-on-film technology for its potential to convey music in a motion picture. Harry Warner believed that the principal advantage of sound was not to bring the spoken word to movies but rather to merge music more effectively into a production.

"Who the hell wants to hear actors talk?" a short-sighted Harry asked Jack in 1925. "The music—that's the big plus about this."

As a result, even the studio's earliest efforts at producing sound films included music; *Don Juan*, starring John Barrymore in 1926, was the first film with a fully-synchronized musical score; a year later, Al Jolson's first spoken scenes in the milestone sound movie *The Jazz Singer* included singing numbers.

During the depression, the studio's musicals, including *42nd Street*, *Gold Diggers of 1933*, and *Footlight Parade*—with wildly imaginative dance productions directed by Broadway transplant Busby Berkeley—lifted the spirits of film audiences across the United States. The studio eventually shifted its interests away from musicals, but Warner never forgot the importance of music in its other projects. "Films are fantasy," Jack Warner often said, "and fantasy needs music."

As Warner converted his moviemaking from silent pictures to sound, he set up one of Hollywood's most formidable music departments, eventually hiring Leo Forbstein, former conductor of the orchestra at Grauman's Metropolitan Theater in Hollywood, to direct it. Forbstein assembled a talented music department—including Hugo Friedhofer, Erich Wolfgang Korngold, and Adolf Deutsch—that was considered as the best assemblage of film composers in Hollywood. Eventually Steiner would join them.

Steiner was yet another Austrian transplant associated with the *Casablanca* production. Born in Vienna and a pupil of composer Gustav Mahler, Steiner demonstrated his musical talent at an early age, having written his first operetta at age sixteen. After coming to the United States, he wound up on Broadway, conducting and orchestrating scores for the likes of George Gershwin, Jerome Kern, and Victor Herbert.

When musicians began to establish careers in Hollywood with the dawn of the sound era—and simultaneously Broadway theater business began to decline because of the depression—Steiner traveled west. He joined the RKO music department staff as an orchestrator but nearly left the film business before writing a single original composition for the screen. Frustrated by the creative limitations of orchestration—essentially preparing the individual musical parts based on another composer's work—he arranged to leave Hollywood for other musical pursuits. But when RKO needed a score for Wesley Ruggles's *Cimarron*, all of the studio's frontline composers were tied up with other projects, so Steiner was given a major motion picture for his first assignment. His composition for *Cimarron*, a rousing twenty-five-minute score, was soon noted as one of the landmark examples of music for the screen.

Steiner became renowned as one of the pioneers of the composition of music for film, and he set a standard for innovative works that transcend mere musical accompaniment for a film score. Steiner's music not only complemented the action, it wove its way into the plot, recounting its own musical version of the story that enhanced, sometimes surpassed, the film's plot.

Steiner reveled in soaring themes, virtually nonstop music behind the dialogue (if he had his way), and "Mickey Mousing"—the subtle film composer's art of linking a bit of music to a specific on-screen action or character reference. ("Mickey Mouses" are dotted throughout *Casablanca*; for example, in the closing moments of the film, when Rains pours a glass of Vichy water, then changes his mind and throws away the bottle—the "plunk" of violin strings as the bottle hits the trash can is a "Mickey Mouse.") Steiner also contributed to the technical as well as artistic aspects of his craft; he was noted for his role in the development of the "click track," a metronome synchronized to the film that helps a composer determine the cues for music at a precise location in a scene.

Over the course of his career, Steiner composed scores for nearly three hundred feature films, including such potent scores as *King Kong, Now, Voyager, Dark Victory,* and one of the masterpieces of cinema music more than three hours of music for *Gone With the Wind.* By the summer of 1942, Steiner was fifty-four, had won an Academy Award for his score for *The Informer,* and only months before completed the soundtrack for *Now, Voyager,* which would earn him his second Oscar the next year (he would later win a third Academy Award for *Since You Went Away*, and was nominated for fifteen others).

Looking back at Steiner's career at Warner Bros. during the 1940s, the consistent quality of his work seems all the more astounding because during those years he often created as many as a dozen scores per year, and produced even more during particularly frenetic periods. His work required a frantic schedule of analyzing stories and character, composing, and recording, none of which could start until most of the filming was completed, and all of which needed to be completed on the shortest possible time schedule—often as little as two weeks.

After Steiner saw a film in its roughly final form, the music department would create cue sheets that described the action on screen and how music should be placed around it.

"While the cue sheets are being made, I begin working on themes for the different characters and scenes, but without regard for the required timing," Steiner said. "During this period, I also digest what I have seen, and try to plan the music for this picture. There may be a scene that is played a shade too slowly, which I might be able to quicken with a little animated music; or to a scene that is too fast, I may be able to give it a little more feeling by using slower music.

"After my themes are set and my timing is complete, I begin to work. I run the picture reel by reel again to refresh my memory. Then I put my stopwatch on the piano and try to compose the music that is necessary for the picture within the limits allowed by this timing. Once all my themes are set, I am apt to discard them and compose others, because, frequently, after I have worked on a picture for a little while, my feeling toward it changes."

Although Steiner thrived professionally within the studio system, the vocal and opinionated composer thought little of the Hollywood machine, in particular the top brass. "They're amazing people," Steiner said of the studio bosses of the 1940s. "They seem to think that if they pay you well, they own you."

The indefatigable Steiner—who often worked across the span of several days without sleep to finish a production on a tight deadline—once recalled a time when he was so ill with the flu that even he could not report to work.

"After several days in bed, Forbstein phoned and asked if I could come in the following morning and conduct a recording session," Steiner told a reporter. "I explained that I was flat on my back, under sedation, and so weak I couldn't get up to go to the bathroom. All he could say was 'Max, we gotta have you there.'

"My doctor was with me, and I put him on the phone, and he told Leo how sick I was. Afterwards, the doctor handed the phone to me, and I said to Leo, 'It would cost me my life to get there at nine tomorrow morning.'

"There was a long pause," Steiner recalled, "and then Leo asked, 'Well, how about one o'clock?' "

Other crafty studio executives knew how to tempt Steiner's fiery nature. When David Selznick, Steiner's onetime boss at RKO, hired the composer to write the score for *Gone With the Wind*, the assignment came so late in the film's production that little more than a month was available for both composition and recording of the music. Steiner repeatedly told Selznick that the assignment was impossible. So without informing Steiner, Selznick hired Herbert Stothart, who had composed parts of the score for *The Wizard of Oz*, to serve as back-up composer on the project.

"Stothart had a few drinks on Saturday night, and did a lot of loose talking about how *he* was going to have to fix up Max's work," Selznick wrote to financier John Hay Whitney in the closing days of production on *Gone With the Wind*. "Within 10 minutes, it was back to Max, and he was in a rage. Max really went to town, and the result is that by tomorrow we will have considerably more than half the picture scored."

Casablanca

―――――――――

180

However, as far as *Casablanca* was concerned, Steiner had no love for his new assignment, primarily because he was forced to use another composer's song as one of the principal themes of the score. Chief among the tunes imposed on Steiner was "As Time Goes By," a moderately successful ballad written by Herman Hupfield in 1931 for the musical revue *Everybody's Welcome*. The song, a favorite of Murray Burnett, had been included in *Everybody Comes to Rick's*, and it was carried over to the film version.

Even though Wallis specifically requested Steiner to write the soundtrack, the producer knew that his favorite composer would resist the assignment. "Even before Steiner started work, he told me he hated 'As Time Goes By,' " Wallis said.

Wallis also insisted that Steiner use another standard, "Perfidia," the Warner-owned tune that was used as standard nightclub background music in several of the studio's productions, including *The Mask of Dimitrios* and *Dark Passage* (in *Casablanca*, while Rick and Ilsa dance during the Paris flashback scenes, "Perfidia" plays in the background).

Wallis also chose several popular tunes of the 1930s and 1940s to spice up the atmosphere in the café. *Casablanca* is peppered with hit numbers performed in the background of the café scenes: In the first shots of Rick's Café Américaine, Sam sings "It Had to Be You" as the camera pans across the nightclub, the scene interspersed with vignettes of black market negotiations and sales of exit visas. When Ilsa asks Sam to "play some of the old songs," the pianist plays the gentle ballad "Avalon."

As Yvonne, Rick's rejected girlfriend, arrives at the café with a German soldier for a date, the orchestra performs "You Must Have Been a Beautiful Baby." Later, when Laszlo and Ilsa return to Rick's café for the second time, Sam is "playing" another instrumental version of "It Had to Be You." (Dooley Wilson, a drummer, did not play the piano. He skillfully pantomimed his keyboard performance, working hard to mimic the actions of studio musician Elliott Carpenter, who recorded all of the piano sequences.)

Wallis also commissioned two new tunes for Sam's musical numbers: "Knock on Wood" and "Dat's What Noah Done"—both written by M. K. Jerome and Jack Scholl. Planned as an elaborate musical number to showcase Sam and the band similar to "Knock on Wood," "Dat's What Noah Done" didn't survive Wallis's cutting—it originally followed Ugarte's arrest as Rick tries to calm his frightened customers. But "Knock on Wood" remains, and Sam sings it with gusto along with bits of silliness by the band while Rick hides the letters of transit in his piano.

Steiner's efforts at composition would be further complicated by the need to include three patriotic songs in various passages of the score. Key elements of the plot included Nazi Germany's national anthem, "Deutschland über Alles"; the German nationalist song, "Die Wacht am Rhein" (Watch on the Rhine); and "La Marseillaise," the rousing French national anthem. "Die Wacht am Rhein" and "Le Marseillaise" are

Casablanca's most rousing moment: the clash of "La Marseillaise" and "Die Wacht am Rhein"—masterfully orchestrated by Steiner.

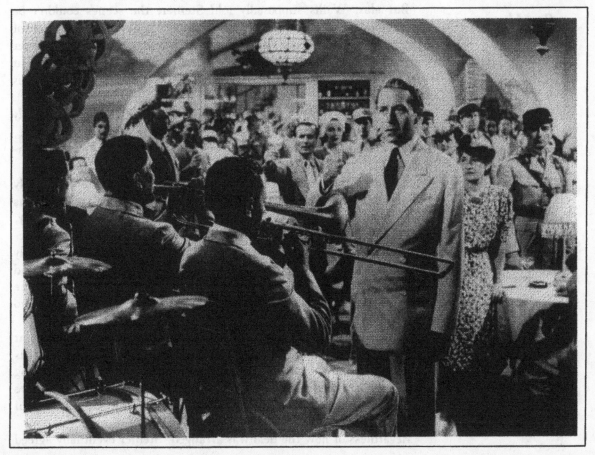

performed in conflict during *Casablanca*'s most electrifying scene, when a chorus of German soldiers led by Strasser are drowned out by Laszlo and the patrons of the café in a tearful singing of the French national anthem—all backed by a rousing arrangement for full orchestra.

Steiner would add a note of patriotic fervor to the opening credits by weaving "La Marseillaise" into the music playing behind the film's opening credits. Not coincidentally, "La Marseillaise" roars to a crescendo at the precise moment when the composer's name appears on screen in the opening credits.

To placate Steiner, Wallis resorted to some old-fashioned fast talking —or so the composer said. In an interview soon after *Casablanca* was released Steiner recalled that Wallis permitted the composer to write a love song to serve as an alternative to "As Time Goes By."

Of course, Steiner said, the addition of a new song would require that those scenes including "As Time Goes By" would have to be reshot, because Steiner came into the project in late July when filming was nearly complete. (Wallis hadn't requested Steiner's assignment to the project until July 11, when all but the troublesome ending scenes had already been filmed.)

But alas, Wallis supposedly told Steiner, the scenes couldn't be filmed again, because Ingrid Bergman already cut her hair for the role of Maria in *For Whom the Bell Tolls* (when telling this story, Steiner conveniently neglected to remember that the makeup department at Warners could do wonders with wigs). Needless to say, "As Time Goes By" stayed in the picture.

"Steiner had to use 'As Time Goes By' and like it," wrote *PM Daily* columnist Mark Schubart. "He still doesn't think it's much of a tune, but now admits that it must have something to attract so much attention."

An incredible story, whether real or imagined, but a completely unlikely tale given the pressure of the production schedule, and concerns about the budget, unless Wallis simply lied to the composer. Most likely, Steiner "misrecalled" his agreement with Wallis, for few studio producers would have been willing to reshoot dozens of scenes in a film simply to placate a composer—even for an artist as formidable as Steiner—and certainly not when reshooting would have involved bringing back one star on loan-out (Bergman) and a second (Bogart) already assigned to other work.

Also, there is no mention in the Warner memos of any arrangement involving Steiner using a song other than "As Time Goes By," nor is there even a hint of reshooting scenes for any reason other than undoing mistakes in previous takes. An old studio hand like Steiner would have known this; in all likelihood, his tale was simply the stuff of wishful thinking.

Regardless of how the deal was arranged, Steiner eventually agreed to compose the score. And in spite of the musical obstacles, and his own dissatisfaction with material written by others that he was required to use, Steiner produced one of his most memorable compositions—a soundtrack packed with his own musical themes, all skillfully meshed in variations of the other pieces foisted upon him.

For the opening credits, Steiner gave *Casablanca* an exotic and dramatic "intrigue theme," bolstered by jungle drums, a gong crash, and a "snake charmer" passage played on oboe. The "snake charmer" concept would pop up again as the audience's introduction to Señor Ferrari's café, the Blue Parrot (Steiner would compose and record the themes for the Blue Parrot scenes as if the music were being played in the café, even though no musicians are visible in the Blue Parrot).

Steiner created brief musical vignettes to flesh out several key points in the film. A lilting "romance" theme is heard only briefly at the beginning of the Paris flashback scenes, but it provides an ideal backing for Rick and Ilsa's lighthearted affair. Steiner also wrote a sparkling "high ideals" theme to use with Laszlo's character and other scenes associated with patriotism—first when Ilsa and Laszlo are talking in their hotel room before he leaves for the meeting of the underground and later during the airport scene, as Rick lies to Laszlo about Ilsa's love.

Even those popular melodies that Steiner didn't compose were melded into the score with grace and skill; *Casablanca*'s music is as much a masterwork of arrangement as it is a showpiece of original composition. Devotees of film music will note time and again the smooth transitions in the composition—from original Steiner material, to previously written melodies, and back to Steiner's own score (the masterful arrangement is especially apparent in an eight-minute "suite" included in a compilation of his work available on compact disc).

Whatever negative opinions Steiner may have harbored about "As Time Goes By" must have been forgotten when the composer took pen in hand, because he used Hupfield's melody literally dozens of times throughout the score, and also in seemingly endless variation. The melody is orchestrated with beauty and tenderness usually played on strings, including several passages used as a background theme for Ilsa.

Steiner also used "As Time Goes By" as a musical motif to symbolize virtue, in opposition to the Nazi themes of evil. During the climactic airport scenes, variations of "As Time Goes By" on violins are played in sharp conflict with "Deutschland über Alles" as orchestrated in harsh scoring for trumpet and brass. Under Steiner's skillful guidance, the two themes clash to marvelous effect in several scenes, including the agonizing moment after Strasser's death when Renault orders his men to "round up the usual suspects."

Surprisingly, Steiner's musical score for *Casablanca* was ignored in the 1944 Academy Awards, lost in the shuffle among fifteen other nominees for best music scoring of a dramatic or comedy picture. Nevertheless, his compositions for the film contributed yet another element of *Casablanca* that would be cited as one of the most important ingredients in its success.

By late August, all of the disparate pieces of cinematic technology that would comprise *Casablanca* were assembled: Steiner's score, montage sequences, special effects, and credits, all merged into a rough cut that was becoming a tight film as edited by Marks and trimmed even further by Wallis.

The picture's preview in Warner's Huntington Park theater drew only moderate enthusiasm; "the audience seemed to like it, though they didn't rave," remembered Wallis.

In spite of lukewarm reactions, Warners knew its new release was at very least a prospect for box-office success. By late August, the studio was beginning to understand just how big it would be.

The first indication of the movie's popularity came from the most unlikely of sources: the staff of the Production Code administration. All of the struggles over the script at the Breen office were forgotten when the industry censors became the first viewers other than studio staff members or preview audiences to see *Casablanca*.

"Joe Breen called me yesterday after he and his staff had seen *Casablanca*," Wallis wrote to Warner publicity chief S. Charles Einfield. "'I have never heard him rave about a picture as he did about this one. He told me he thought it not only one of the most outstanding pictures to come off the lot in some time, but one of the best he had seen in some years.

"I thought," concluded Wallis, "perhaps this enthusiasm might inspire you to plan a campaign for *Casablanca* as a really big picture."

As events unfolded, Wallis need not have worried how to position *Casablanca*. Late in September, after yet another round of Wallis cuts and trims, the picture went into the can, ready to distribute, with a release date set for June 1943. But, to paraphrase Rick, destiny had taken a hand—both in the selection of the release date of the film and in its emergence as one of the treasures of cinema.

eleven

The Beginning of a
Beautiful Friendship

W arner Bros. originally intended to release *Casablanca* during the 1943 summer season—more than a year after the cameras first rolled. Instead, by the summer of 1943, the film was already firmly entrenched in U.S. theaters, seen by thousands of troops on the war front, and well on its way to winning the Academy Award for the Best Picture.

Today, *Casablanca*'s reputation as an unfading film classic is undisputed, but it began that journey toward immortality with the aid of two of the most staggering coincidences that ever assisted a motion picture's rise to success.

By the fall of 1942, Allied forces, once reeling from near-knockout blows from Axis attack, were prepared for their first substantive forays into enemy territory. Although the actual location of the American push was a closely guarded secret, as November approached the press began to speculate about some of the likeliest spots for an Allied landing. At the top of the list of probable sites, with its strategic position along the

Atlantic and easy access to the Mediterranean, was Casablanca.

In the early days of November, the near-unbelievable coincidence that Warner Bros. possessed a film ready to distribute with a theme focused on the precise location of the focal point of World War II was not lost on studio executives.

"I thought you might be interested in the attached front page from the *San Francisco Chronicle*, with mention of Casablanca coming into more and more prominence in the war picture," Hal Wallis wrote to Jack Warner on November 6. "This writer feels that Casablanca is apt to be more of a hot spot than Dakar."

Indeed, the *Chronicle* was correct. By the time Warner was reading Wallis's memo, an armada carrying joint U.S. and British forces had already begun their November 7 invasion of French Morocco and Algeria, establishing the final foothold necessary to retake Axis-held territory in Africa.

By November 1942, although U.S. forces had already inflicted substantial damage on Japanese forces during the war in the Pacific, the invasion of North Africa marked the first substantial push by the United States against the Nazis. The effect on the American home front was electric—as stunning as the bombing raid on Tokyo led by Gen. Jimmy Doolittle had been seven months earlier. The city of Casablanca roared into the headlines of every newspaper, magazine, and radio program in the United States.

For Warner Bros., the moment to release its like-named picture would never be more opportune. Within days of the announcement of the North Africa invasion, the studio decided to reschedule the release and pushed up the premiere to the first convenient date that could be arranged.

With the attention of the entire globe focused on Casablanca, Wallis and Warner were supremely confident of their aptly named property. But incredibly, they still felt uncertain about the ending, and explored several ways to change the close of the film. First, the studio considered tagging on a documentary-style closing scene, including footage of the actual North African invasion. Fortunately, those plans fell through.

"It's impossible to change this picture and make sense with the story we told originally," Jack Warner told his New York executives on November 10. "The story we want to tell of the Allies landing would have to be a complete new picture and would not fit in the present film.

"It's such a great picture as it is, it would be a misrepresentation if we were to come in now with a small tag scene about American troops landing.

"The entire industry envies us with a picture having the title *Casablanca* ready to release," Warner said. "We should take advantage of this great scoop."

Casablanca

———————

186

As an alternative to the documentary ending Wallis suggested an addition of a brief closing shot with Bogart and Rains as Free French soldiers on board ship on their way to fight the Nazis. On November 11, the producer told studio manager T. C. Wright that he wanted to shoot a night sequence in fog on the standing freighter set on Stage 7. Wallis even planned to bring Rains back from travels in Pennsylvania to shoot the footage, with Curtiz directing at night until the work was completed.

Again, changes were canceled, in part due to the enthusiasm of David Selznick, who, because of his contract star Ingrid Bergman's involvement in *Casablanca*, had more than a passing interest in the film's success. The same day Wallis set plans into motion to shoot a new ending, Selznick screened the yet-unchanged version of the film.

"Saw *Casablanca* last night. Think it a swell movie and an all-around fine job of picture making," Selznick telegrammed to Wallis. "Told Jack [Warner] as forcibly as I could that I thought it would be a terrible mistake to change the ending, and also that I thought the picture ought to be rushed out."

Despite input from Selznick, Wallis was not yet convinced to leave the ending alone. Ultimately, however, business considerations prevented further tinkering. Although additional closing footage would have distracted substantially from the magnificent conclusion already in the can, a more practical reason figured as well: the addition of a new ending would delay the release. "The longer we wait," Warner pointed out, "the less important the title will be."

Finally, after another round of screenings, the studio chief had the last word, and the early lukewarm previews were forgotten.

"Regarding *Casablanca*, we will definitely not touch the picture," Warner wrote to his New York office. "Previewed it again last night and audience reaction was beyond belief. From main title to the end was applause and anxiety. Hundreds said do not touch the picture.

"My personal opinion is if the picture is touched now it will become a patched job. Therefore, ship your negatives and positives".

The premiere of *Casablanca* was set for November 26—Thanksgiving Day—1942, at the Hollywood Theater in New York, only nineteen days after the Allied landing in North Africa and scarcely two weeks shy of one year from the day that Steven Karnot received the manuscript of *Everybody Comes to Rick's*.

Casablanca premiered at a star-studded event held in association with Free French organizations, who took full advantage of the Hollywood hoopla to tout their cause to the American public on the streets of New York. Sponsored by France Forever and the Fighting French Relief Committee, the prefilm festivities included a flag-laden parade of aviators recently returned from the fighting fronts, Foreign Legionnaires, and veterans of the North African battles. For the first time, the new Free French Flag—the tricolor emblazoned with the cross of Lorraine—flew over midtown Manhattan.

But the prescreening ballyhoo paled by comparison to the critical and audience acclaim the movie itself received following its world premiere.

"Against the electric background of a sleek café in a North African port, through which swirls a backwash of connivers, crooks and fleeing European refugees, the Warner Brothers are telling a rich, suave, exciting and moving tale in their new film, *Casablanca*," wrote the *New York Times*. "Yes, indeed, the Warners here have a picture which makes the spine tingle and the heart take a leap.

"In short," the *Times* reported, "we will say that *Casablanca* is one of the year's most exciting and trenchant films."

The other critics agreed with the *Times*'s appraisal. The *New York Morning Telegraph* called *Casablanca* "a crackling, timely melodrama with a superb all-star cast." The *New York Journal-American* said, "Warners score again with *Casablanca* . . . it has everything." The *New York Mirror* reported, "Warners has the scoop of the film year . . . a moving modern drama and blistering romance . . . today's headlines translated into arresting drama." *PM Daily* called *Casablanca* "a movie of distinct enjoyment," while the *New York Herald Tribune* described the film as "A smashing and moving melodrama . . . a superior show."

Film industry trade papers—always a bellwether of exhibitor interest in a picture, as well as potential box-office success—spouted equally enthusiastic reviews. *Film Daily* shouted, "*Casablanca*! A magic word, that. A word that will open theater doors wide and keep them open." *Film Daily* summarized the picture by calling it a "smashing melodrama of timely import that should click heavily at box offices everywhere."

Said the *Hollywood Reporter*, "Here is a drama that lifts you right out of your seat. That Warners had a lucky break in the progress of world events that put the name of Casablanca on everyone's lips is the answer to the surefire box-office smash the Hal B. Wallis production will enjoy. But in addition to its present timeliness, the picture has exceptional merits as absorbing entertainment, reflecting the fine craftsmanship of all who had hands in the making. Certainly a more accomplished cast of players cannot be imagined, and their direction by Michael Curtiz is inspired."

Showmen's Trade Review, a journal written for hard-nosed exhibitors, published a surprisingly emotional review. "It may be the prominence that Casablanca enjoys in current news but, somehow or other, the picture takes a stranglehold on the emotions in the opening scene. As sweet a package of grand all around entertainment as has been seen in a long time . . . a pulse-tingling story of activities in the underground where death strikes at Nazi command—but love lives."

Prominent among the reviews were critics' praise for the emergence of Humphrey Bogart as a tough-yet-romantic star of the first order.

"Bogart is, as usual, the cool, cynical, efficient and super-wise guy who operates his business strictly for profit but has a core of sentiment and idealism inside," the *Times* wrote.

The *Hollywood Reporter* said, "Bogart has in Rick one of the most powerful roles of his film career and plays it for all it's worth."

All of the frustrations over the script, the arguments on the set, and the machinations about the production schedule proved worthwhile. *Casablanca* was a certified hit; the picture would, as the *New York World-Telegram* reported, "settle down for quite a stay."

But in *Casablanca* audiences found more than just another entertaining show—the emotion and patriotism on screen spilled over into the audience, and formed the foundation of the film's legacy. Reporters noted that when Paul Henreid led the café customers in singing "La Marseillaise," audiences all over the United States spontaneously rose to their feet and applauded. (Two decades later, college audiences of the 1960s, a new generation of viewers seeing *Casablanca* for the first time, continued the tradition by rising and singing along.) When Strasser asks Rick if he can imagine the Nazis attacking New York, and Rick replies, "Well, there are certain sections of New York, Major, that I wouldn't advise you to try to invade," Manhattan audiences roared their approval. Already, the melding of patriotic fervor, romance, and intrigue were guiding *Casablanca* toward the stature of film legend.

As if the happy coincidence of the invasion's timing and the film's release wasn't enough, Warner Bros. would benefit from yet another astonishing coincidence that would again focus the attention of the world on the capital of French Morocco, and at the same time, the studio's newest hit.

For nearly two months, *Casablanca* screened in a limited number of theaters; the film's rushed release also forced rescheduling of the general distribution of the film to a dead-of-winter, postholiday Saturday in January 1943.

Meanwhile, unknown to the world, President Franklin Roosevelt, British Prime Minister Winston Churchill, and Soviet Premier Joseph Stalin were planning a week of secret meetings to sketch out a plan of action for the remainder of the war (amazingly enough, during World War II it was actually possible for three world leaders to leave their countries and meet in secret without anyone other than their closest confidants knowing their whereabouts). Besides providing an important opportunity to set strategy for the management of the war effort, the meetings would ultimately go down in history as the platform for Roosevelt's declaration that "unconditional surrender" was the only acceptable terms for Axis defeat.

The timing and location of the meeting was perhaps the most closely guarded secret of the war to that date. When the Casablanca conference was announced to the world on January 24, all at Warner Bros. were as surprised as everyone else, but a great deal happier—*Casablanca* had opened nationwide the day before.

Casablanca was, of course, as beloved by audiences in its initial release as it was by the critics. Among the smash hits of 1943, the picture was touted by Warners for the "split-second timing" of its subject matter; after the double dose of publicity bonus the picture had already received from the Allied invasion and the Casablanca conference, Warners continued the momentum with its own advertising. "The army's got Casablanca—and so have Warner Bros.," cried the studio's publicity bulletin to exhibitors. "Warners does it again!" One trade ad for *Casablanca* stated simply, "Was there ever a picture more timely?"

Not all of the advertising for *Casablanca* was handled with such a high degree of marketing acumen; in February 1943, while the picture packed theaters across the country, a studio ad featured three young tuxedoed ushers, clearly dubious about their appearance in print, each wearing various forms of athletic protective equipment over their tuxedos as they guarded a theater door: one wore football shoulder pads and helmet, another sported a hockey goalie's gear, and the third donned catcher's pads. The caption read, "They're ready for *Casablanca*."

The picture received yet another publicity boost in December 1942 when Gen. Charles De Gaulle, head of the Free French government in exile, requested a special showing of the picture in London for his staff and other anti-Vichy leaders. The film broke all attendance records of the day in its New York run, and industry insiders reported that many theaters screening *Casablanca* were racking up triple their normal business. In the days after the Roosevelt-Churchill-Stalin conference, Warners reported that ticket sales for *Casablanca* jumped 50 percent above average at the Hollywood, and also increased substantially at forty other spots across the country. "Exhibitors jammed the Warner exchanges yesterday for prints and some houses pulled their attractions to put *Casablanca* on," said the *Hollywood Reporter*.

A month after the film's premiere, it was voted one of the ten best films of 1942, along with such memorable pictures as *Yankee Doodle Dandy*, *Mrs. Miniver*, *Woman of the Year*, and *Sullivan's Travels*. "This tough and exciting melodrama possesses the sure virtue of being both highly entertaining and intellectually stimulating to boot," the *New York Times* wrote of *Casablanca* in its article announcing the top ten. The film was also voted to "ten best" lists by *Film Daily* and several other publications; however, *Casablanca*'s recognition in *Film Daily* came a year later. At the time, some publications determined a film's "official" release date based on the timing of its general distribution, not when it began a limited run in a handful of theaters. *Casablanca* thus holds an unusual, but not unique, distinction of being voted to "ten best" list in two different years.

While *Casablanca* was considered a 1942 release—at least as far as the *New York Times* ranking was concerned—the picture would have to wait another year before it became eligible for the Academy Awards. The film's limited run in 1942, besides delaying its recognition on "ten best" lists, also classified it as a 1943 release for Oscar consideration.

Rules about determining release dates have changed considerably over the years; now a film's date of release for Academy Award consideration is based on the year in which a theatrical release lasts longer than one week. But in 1943, the decision to include *Casablanca* with 1943 releases for Academy Award consideration was indeed fortunate for Warner Bros.; had the film been classified as a 1942 picture, the Wallis production would have been forced to compete for Academy honors against MGM blockbuster, *Mrs. Miniver*, which swept through the Academy Awards ceremony, winning seven Oscars, including Best Picture.

But when the Academy Award nominations for 1943 were announced on February 7, 1944, *Casablanca* was clearly the picture to beat. The picture was nominated for eight Academy Awards: best picture, actor (Humphrey Bogart), supporting actor (Claude Rains), director (Michael Curtiz), screenplay (Julius Epstein, Philip Epstein, and Howard Koch), black-and-white cinematography (Art Edeson), film editing (Owen Marks), and music scoring of a dramatic or comedy picture (Max Steiner).

Ingrid Bergman received a nomination for best actress, but not for her work at Warner Bros. Instead, she was nominated for a romantic role of a different sort, and the part she coveted throughout the production of *Casablanca*—her performance as Maria in Paramount's version of *For Whom the Bell Tolls*.

Even though *Casablanca* avoided an awards showdown with *Mrs. Miniver*, it still faced stiff competition for best picture of 1943 with nine other nominees, among them Columbia's delightful wartime comedy *The More the Merrier*, Fox's powerful moral drama *The Ox-Bow Incident*, plus *For Whom the Bell Tolls*, *Heaven Can Wait*, *The Human Comedy*, *In Which We Serve*, *Madame Curie*, *The Song of Bernadette*, and *Watch on the Rhine*.

On awards night, March 2, *Casablanca* would emerge the big winner with three major Oscars. During the course of the evening, yet another controversy over the film would emerge—and this conflict Wallis would later cite as the beginning of the end of his two decades of association with Warner Bros. Pictures.

First, the Academy voted its award for best screenplay to *Casablanca*. The months of frustration, confusion, and last-minute panic were vindicated with Oscars for Julius Epstein, Philip Epstein, and Howard Koch.

But absent from the list of Oscar-winning writers was Casey Robinson, the last writer assigned to the script. Why was Robinson not included in the Oscar nominations? Even though Robinson contributed key scenes and character development to the script, his few weeks of involvement in the project probably did not entitle him to screen credit according to Writer's Guild rules had he sought it.

But Robinson remembered the incident as his own decision to decline screen credit. If so, that choice cost him a place in film history.

"I was pretty smart-assed in those days," he recalled. "I wouldn't put my name on the screen with another writer. I was very proud of the fact of my solo screenplays. But to go on the screen with three other writers . . . I wouldn't put my name on the screen. It was a very bad mistake."

Whether or not Robinson actually chose to have his name removed from the screen credits of *Casablanca,* and thus eliminating himself for Academy Award consideration, will probably never be known for certain. While Robinson most certainly added crucial material that developed the script, his involvement in the project, despite his claims to the contrary, was far more limited than that of the Epsteins and Koch.

The target budget set just after filming began provides a more tangible indication of responsibility for the principal elements of the script. By June 2, 1942, some $47,281 of expense for contract writer's time was assigned to *Casablanca*'s budget; the Epsteins accounted for more than $30,000, Koch another $4,200, and the remainder divided among Wally Kline ($1,983), Aeneas MacKenzie ($2,150), and Lenore Coffee ($750).

Although Robinson, who often claimed that *Casablanca* was "my piece," had by this point in the production already contributed his lengthy memo that outlined new directions for the romantic elements in the script, his $3,000 per week salary had not yet been assigned to the production's books. Whether by his own design or not, Robinson's participation in the creation of the film would be recalled only in the history books, and not in the screen credits.

Casablanca received its second honor on Oscar night when Michael Curtiz, after three previous nominations without a win, was named best director. With no expectation of ever taking home an Oscar, the very surprised director blurted a spontaneous crowd-pleasing Curtizism.

"So many times I have a speech ready, but no dice," Curtiz told the Academy audience at Grauman's Chinese Theater. "Always a bridesmaid, never a mother. Now I win, I have no speech."

Unfortunately, Humphrey Bogart was not one of the beneficiaries of the film's success on awards night. Bogart, nominated for best actor for what would become his most beloved role, lost to Paul Lukas for his stirring performance in *Watch on the Rhine*, another Warner production. Bogart's moment to shine on Oscar night would come in 1952, when he won the Academy Award for his role as Charley Allnutt, the crusty river sailor in *The African Queen*.

Finally, with director Sidney Franklin presenting the Oscar, came the announcement of the winner of the Academy Award for best picture. *Casablanca* won, and with the presentation of the award came the biggest shock of the night.

Hal Wallis rose from his seat to claim the Oscar that, as producer, he deserved to collect. To the surprise of all in the theater, studio chief Jack Warner scrambled to the stage first and accepted the award on behalf of the studio.

"I couldn't believe it was happening," Wallis recalled in his memoirs. "I had no alternative but to sit down, humiliated and furious." In his memoirs, Wallis even accused Warner relatives of conspiring against him. "I tried to get out of the row of seats and into the aisle, but the entire Warner family sat blocking me."

Wallis's "humiliation" as recalled decades later would differ substantially from his public action at the time, especially after *Los Angeles Times* columnist Edwin Schallert mentioned the incident in his column two days after the Oscar ceremony.

"The question is being vigorously debated in Hollywood whether J. L. Warner or Hal B. Wallis should have accepted the award tendered for *Casablanca*," wrote Schallert in a column titled "Warner-Wallis 'Rivalry' Intrigues at Film Fete."

"The issue probably never will be solved any more than the various executive setups cooked up in movieland may be penetrated. Producer, associate producer, executive in charge of production, executive producer—these indeed constitute a roundelay of titles that may signify much or little, according to who swings the biggest wallop at the moment in rampageous studio politics."

The same day, an "angry" Wallis fired off a telegram to Schallert to protest—not agree with—the column. "I have been with Warner Bros. for twenty years, and during this time it has been customary here as elsewhere for the studio head to accept the Academy Award for the best production. Naturally, I was glad to see Jack Warner accept the award for *Casablanca*. Your comment in your column this morning on rivalry at Warner Bros. is totally unjustified. I would be grateful if you would correct the misleading impression."

Wallis's telegram provides an interesting counterpoint to the producer's real feelings, especially when knowing that later he would often say, "*Casablanca* had been my creation; Jack had absolutely nothing to do with it."

The film world would soon discover that "angry" protests to the press notwithstanding, feelings of rivalry at Warner Bros. were running high indeed.

In his memoirs, Warner would call the Oscar a "little piece of hardware [that] too often turns into a cave-man club in the belligerent hands of ambitious agents." But on Oscar night 1944, the studio chief himself used an Oscar to bludgeon the ego of his lead producer.

Even though Wallis had been Jack Warner's fair-haired boy since 1923, and the producer was given near carte blanche creative control at the studio, he found out that night who the real boss was at Warner Bros.

Before Warner grabbed up the Oscar for best picture, Wallis received the Irving G. Thalberg Memorial Award, his second such honor for distinguished production. Academy officials would deliver another Oscar to Wallis, but it was hardly a substitute for the public honor of which he had been deprived for producing the best picture of 1943. Wallis would recall the incident as yet another fissure in the already strained relations between the producer and his studio chief, an unavoidable clash of personalities that would result in Wallis's departure from Warner Bros. in 1944 to become an independent filmmaker.

With *Casablanca* earning universal critical praise while generating truckloads of cash for the Warner coffers, it was inevitable that the studio would consider producing a sequel.

"There has been considerable discussion" about a follow-up production, wrote Wallis aide Ralph Butler to a fan of *Casablanca*. "The forces for and against a sequel are about evenly divided."

The studio certainly tried to find an acceptable plot that could be used for the further adventures of Richard Blaine. As early as spring 1943, Wallis was soliciting story treatments for a possible sequel; the producer asked contract writer Frederick Faust (better known as western novelist and screenwriter Max Brand) to report on a treatment by Frederick Stephani.

But with Ilsa's departure with Victor in the closing scene, it was obvious that the romance so perfectly captured in the original film could not be re-created in a sequel; the magic of *Casablanca* would firmly and forever remain in the scenes shot at a make-believe fogbound airport on Stage 1 at Warner Bros. In planning a potential script for *Casablanca II*, the studio would have been able to salvage only Rick's character, ample though it may have been, and insert it into other adventures and romances.

"The main point," Brand wrote in his report on a sequel, "is that Rick made the first picture. I would stick to the original lines of his character and keep him the same man."

Warner Bros. had no need to recycle the character of Richard Blaine for Humphrey Bogart's expanding abilities and star status. With plenty of other material to draw upon for its new king of the lot, Warner Bros. canceled its plans for a sequel to *Casablanca*.

Casablanca has persevered through the decades with the endurance of a cinematic colossus. Although not a wildly overwhelming success in its initial release, the picture did solid box-office business, grossing more than $3 million—perhaps a pittance when compared to today's mega-hits but a strong performance (more than three times the total cost of the picture) by 1942 standards. The picture was rereleased in 1949 to a second round of solid box-office business.

For Humphrey Bogart, *Casablanca* was the final catapult to the pinnacle of Hollywood success. His popularity skyrocketed after the film, boosted by appearances in such Warner blockbusters as *To Have and Have Not*, *The Big Sleep*, *The Treasure of the Sierra Madre*, and *Key Largo*. Finally, after years of the endless grind, the studio gave Bogart a breather; instead of appearing in four to six pictures a year, after *Casablanca* he was top-billed in only two or three films annually—and with a renegotiated contract, at a substantial increase in salary that made him one of Hollywood's best-paid performers. Bogart's status among Hollywood's most durable and popular stars continued to flourish until his death in 1957.

Although *Casablanca*'s popularity never wavered during its original distribution or rerelease, it has achieved a far loftier status in the decades since it first appeared on screen. In the growing market for revival screenings during the 1950s and 1960s, the film was a box-office favorite, and remains so today. College audiences in particular adopted the movie as their own; it ranks just under *Citizen Kane* as one of the most frequently screened motion pictures in classes on film history, theory, and criticism, and stands at the top of the list of films in demand for public showings on university campuses and revival theaters across the country.

Television brought *Casablanca* to new generations of audiences, and beginning in the late 1950s, the film became a broadcast staple on network television and local channels; the movie's airing on local channels consistently outdrew viewership of competing network broadcasts.

Thanks to television, several performers from the original cast would find new work in other vehicles featuring spin-offs of the *Casablanca* story. In 1955, *Casablanca* came to television on ABC as a three-way series alternating with *King's Row* and *Cheyenne*, all featured under the title *Warner Bros. Presents* (in 1983, NBC would also attempt a brief revival of the series, but it lasted only a few episodes).

In the 1955 series, Charles MacGraw appeared in the lead role of Rick ; Marcel Dalio, Emil the croupier in the film version, appeared as the prefect of police played by Claude Rains in the film, and Dan Sey-

Casablanca's *quartet of stars*.

mour, Abdul the doorman in the original, became Señor Ferrari. Clarence Muse, who missed the opportunity to appear as Sam in the film because "he seemed too much of a caricature," finally got the opportunity to play the part on the small screen. Curiously, another performer who was denied the opportunity to appear in the original production of *Casablanca* had already found a role in a spin-off. Hedy Lamarr, who would have been an early candidate to play Ilsa if Louis Mayer had consented to her loan-out, did indeed get the chance to appear in the role—on radio. On January 24, 1944, the Lux Radio Theater hosted by Cecil B. DeMille aired its version of *Casablanca*, starring Lamarr as Ilsa and Alan Ladd as Rick.

More recently, *Casablanca* has expanded into new markets, with broadcasts on cable and purchase or rental on videotape or laserdisc. One of the first pictures transferred to videotape, the movie still tops lists of the most popular videos sold.

No one associated with the frantic production of *Casablanca* would have guessed that decades after their work during the spring and summer of 1942, their efforts would have produced a film that retained such universal and lasting appeal while reaching the status of cinematic masterwork. By any measure—Hal Wallis's careful stewardship of the entire production; the direction by Michael Curtiz; the writing of Julius and Philip Epstein, Howard Koch, and Casey Robinson; the music of Max Steiner; the off-camera contributions by literally hundreds of technicians and craftsmen; and the performances by Humphrey Bogart, Ingrid Bergman, Paul Henreid, Claude Rains, and the others in the superb cast—*Casablanca* has become the ultimate standard of the creative power of the studio system, the motion picture often called the finest product of Hollywood at its peak.

But *Casablanca* remains much more than a motion picture milestone. After fifty years, Hal Wallis's "toughest assignment" remains a beloved film for the ages, a movie that the boundaries of time or taste cannot change. *Casablanca* is the product of another era in America, that brief moment as the 1930s ended and the 1940s began, before the world became a vastly different place. Those years mark an age in America and in American cinema that will never come again but will be remembered forever. Hollywood has moved in new directions, and so have its motion pictures. But we shall always have *Casablanca*.

Compendium

Casablanca

A Warner Bros.-First National Picture
Jack L. Warner, Executive Producer

A Hal B. Wallis Production

*Premiered in New York at the Warner Hollywood Theater,
November 26, 1942*

The Cast

Richard Blaine	Humphrey Bogart
Ilsa Lund	Ingrid Bergman
Victor Laszlo	Paul Henreid
Captain Louis Renault	Claude Rains
Major Heinrich Strasser	Conrad Veidt
Señor Ferrari	Sydney Greenstreet
Ugarte	Peter Lorre
Carl the Headwaiter	S. Z. Sakall
Yvonne	Madeleine LeBeau
Sam	Dooley Wilson
Annina Brandel	Joy Page
Berger	John Qualen

Sascha	Leonid Kinskey
Jan Brandel	Helmut Dantine
Dark European	Curt Bois
Emil the Croupier	Marcel Dalio
Singer	Corinna Mura
Mr. Leuchtag	Ludwig Stossel
Mrs. Leuchtag	Ilka Gruning
Señor Martinez	Charles De La Torre
Arab Vendor	Frank Puglia
Abdul the Doorman	Dan Seymour
Heinze	Richard Ryen
Blue Parrot Waiter	Oliver Prickett
German Banker	Gregory Gaye
Friend	George Meeker
Contact	William Edmunds
Banker	Torben Meyer
Waiter	Gino Corrado
Casselle	George Dee
Englishwoman	Norma Varden
Fyodor	Leo Mostovoy
Headwaiter	Martin Garralaga
Prosperous Man	Olaf Hytten
American	Monte Blue
Vendor	Michael Mark
Dealer	Leon Belasco
Native	Paul Porcasi
German Officer	Hans von Twardowski
French Officer	Albert Morin
Customer	Creighton Hale
German Officer	Henry Rowland
Smuggler	Louis Mercier
Narrator	Lou Marcelle
Stand-in (Ingrid Bergman)	Betty Brooks
Stand-in (Humphrey Bogart)	Russ Lewellyn

Crew

Producer	Hal B. Wallis
Director	Michael Curtiz
Screenplay	Julius J. Epstein, Philip G. Epstein, and Howard Koch, based on the play *Everybody Comes to Rick's*, by Murray Burnett and Joan Alison (additional material by Casey Robinson)
Music	Max Steiner
Orchestrations	Hugo Friedhofer
Songs	Herman Hupfield ("As Time Goes By"), M: K. Jerome and Jack Scholl ("Knock on Wood" and brief excerpts of other songs)
Director of Photography	Arthur Edeson
Special Effects	Lawrence Butler (Director) and Willard Van Enger
Gowns	Orry-Kelly
Montages	Don Siegel and James Leicester
Unit Manager	Al Alleborn
Editor	Owen Marks
Art Director	Carl Jules Weyl
Set Dresser	George James Hopkins
Technical Adviser	Robert Aisner
Assistant Director	Lee Katz
Second Assistant Director	George Tobin
Dialogue Director	Hugh MacMullan
Script Clerk	Alma Dwight
Pianist	Elliott Carpenter
Gaffer	William Conger
Best Boy	William Studeman
Grip	E. F. Dexter
Head Prop Man	Herbert "Limey" Plews
Assistant Prop Man	Robert Turner
Sound	Francis Scheid
Makeup	Frank McCoy
Make-up Artist	Perc Westmore (listed in the credits for the film
Hairdresser	Jean Burt
Wardrobe (Men)	Leon Roberts
Wardrobe (Women)	Marie Blanchard

Reviews of Casablanca

Author's Note: To give you a sense of the excitement that accompanied the premier of Casablanca, four reviews of the film are included here: the first, from The New York Times, *provides an appraisal of the film directed at a general audience; and the other three, from publications directed at the film industry—*Film Daily, Hollywood Reporter, *and* Showmen's Trade Review—*provide their own unique perspective on the picture.*

All of the following reviews appeared in print in the weeks following the Allied invasion of North Africa, and text that speaks of events in that region of the world are referring to the military successes there.

Readers who have not seen Casablanca *(don't scoff—some movie buffs have never seen it) should use caution reading reviews from* Film Daily *and the* Showmen's Trade Review. *While reviews of the feature geared toward the general public didn't give away the conclusion or other important details of the plot—*The New York Times *even pointed out that to do so would be "the rankest sabotage"—industry publications told all, an understandable practice for readers who are far more interested in why a movie will make money than in being surprised by the story.* Film Daily *and* Showmen's Trade Review *gave up most of the important plot details—in only two paragraphs,* Film Daily *manages to cover all of the key plot details, including the ending. However, the* Hollywood Reporter *skirts around most of the important points without revealing too much of the story. Unfortunately, the* Hollywood Reporter *misidentified the writers of "As Time Goes By," described as the "song that recalls the romance," as M. K. Jerome and Jack Scholl. Herman Hupfield wrote "As Time Goes By"; Jerome and Scholl write "Knock on Wood."*

The New York Times

Against the electric background of a sleek cafe in a North African port, through which swirls a background of connivers, crooks, and fleeing European refugees, the Warner Brothers are telling a rich, suave, exciting and moving tale in their new film, *Casablanca*, which came to the Hollywood [Theater] yesterday. They are telling it in the high tradition of their hard-boiled romantic-adventure style. And to make it all the more tempting they have given it a top-notch thriller cast of Humphrey Bogart, Sydney Greenstreet, Peter Lorre, Conrad Veidt and even Claude Rains, and have capped it magnificently with Ingrid Bergman, Paul Henreid and a Negro "find" named Dooley Wilson.

Yes, indeed, the Warners here have a picture which makes the spine tingle and the heart take a leap. For once more, as in recent Bogart pictures, they have turned the incisive trick of draping a tender love story within the folds of a tight topical theme. They have used Mr. Bogart's personality, so well established in other brilliant films, to inject a cold point of tough resistance to evil forces afoot in Europe today. And they have so combined sentiment, humor and pathos with taut melodrama and bristling intrigue that the result is a highly entertaining and even inspired film.

Don't worry; we won't tell you how it all comes out. That would be the rankest sabotage. But we will tell you that the urbane detail and the crackling dialogue which has been packed into this film by the scriptwriters, the Epstein brothers and Howard Koch, is of the best. We will tell you that Michael Curtiz has directed for slow suspense and that his camera is always conveying grim tension and uncertainty. Some of the significant incidents, too, are affecting—such as that in which the passionate Czech patriot rouses the customers in Rick's cafe to drown out a chorus of Nazis by singing the Marseillaise, or any moment in which Dooley Wilson is remembering past popular songs in a hushed room.

We will tell you also that the performances of the actors are all of the first order, but especially those of Mr. Bogart and Miss Bergman in the leading roles. Mr. Bogart is, as usual, the cool, cynical, efficient and super-wise guy who operates his business strictly for profit but has a core of sentiment and idealism inside. Conflict becomes his inner character, and he handles it credibly. Miss Bergman is surpassingly lovely, crisp and natural as the girl and lights the romantic passages with a warm and genuine glow.

Mr. Rains is properly slippery and crafty as a minion of Vichy perfidy, and Mr. Veidt plays again a Nazi officer with cold and implacable resolve. Very little is demanded of Mr. Greenstreet as a shrewd black-market trader, but that is good, and Mr. Henreid is forthright and simple as the imperiled Czech patriot. Mr. Wilson's performance as Rick's devoted friend, though rather brief, is filled with a sweetness and compassion which lends a helpful mood to the whole film, and other small roles are played by S. Z. Sakall, Joy Page, Leonid Kinskey and Mr. Lorre.

In short, we will say that *Casablanca* is one of the year's most exciting and trenchant films.

Casablanca

206

Film Daily

SMASHING MELODRAMA OF TIMELY IMPORT
SHOULD CLICK HEAVILY AT BOX-OFFICES
EVERYWHERE

*C*asablanca! A magic word, that. A word that will open theater doors wide and keep them open. For the movement of humanity into houses where this Warner film is played will be constant and heavy.

Yes, Casablanca is a word that piques the interest and stirs the imagination. The lightning developments in the North African theater of war have brought that name vividly into the consciousness of America. As a result, this Warner picture should have the impact of a bombshell on film audiences of the country. The film's timeliness is its most priceless virtue. It is difficult to see how exhibitors can fail to clean up on so screaming a subject.

The entire action of the picture transpires in the French Moroccan city which in recent days has bulked so prominently in the news out of Africa. The film is an exciting and suspense-laden melodrama of Nazi intrigue. The events in the picture are so close to fact as to give *Casablanca* a fascination that is irresistible. Whirled about in the maelstrom of action are Humphrey Bogart, Ingrid Bergman and Paul Henreid. Bogart is an American with a shady past who operates a cafe and gambling joint peopled by a strange collection of characters.

Miss Bergman is his onetime love, now married to Henreid, a Czech whose work as head of the European underground has placed a price on his head. Bogart and Miss Bergman take up their romance where they left off. For a long time the man is torn between love and a sense of duty. After a lot of romantic torture Bogart turns sacrificial and makes it possible for Miss Bergman to get safely out of the country with her husband, who needs her moral aid to carry on his noble work in behalf of freedom.

The story, which deals heavily with the operation of the black market in Casablanca, has been skillfully contrived by Julius J. and Philip G. Epstein and Howard Koch from a play by Murray Burnett and Joan Alison. Their script has been directed by Michael Curtiz with a fine flow of movement and a punch that make *Casablanca* extremely gripping entertainment. The film, a Hal Wallis production, has been produced with a high regard for showmanship and photographed by Arthur Edeson in highly commendable fashion. Max Steiner's music is a definite asset to the film.

Bogart, Miss Bergman and Henreid perform capably. Their acting points up beautifully the human drama of the story. Claude Rains does a swell job as a French officer who turns against the Nazis at the end when he fully realizes the enormity of their villainy. Conrad Veidt couldn't have been better as the head Nazi officer. Sydney Greenstreet, Peter Lorre, S. Z. Sakall, [and] Madeleine LeBeau reap considerable honor in supporting roles.

Casablanca

Hollywood Reporter

Inspired Casting, Curtiz Direction, Give Wallis Winner

*H*ere is a drama that lifts you right out of your seat. That Warners had a lucky break in the progress of world events that put the name of Casablanca on everyone's lips is the answer to the surefire box-office smash the Hal B. Wallis production will enjoy. But in addition to its present timeliness, the picture has exceptional merits as absorbing entertainment, reflecting the fine craftsmanship of all who had hands in its making. Certainly a more accomplished cast of players cannot be imagined, and their direction by Michael Curtiz is inspired.

Casablanca brings to vivid reality on the screen the melting pot that this Moorish port has become since the Nazis overran Europe. There flock the refugees, escaped political prisoners, and those opportunists who prey on people in trouble. Visas to the Americas, via Lisbon, are obtainable through the black market at exorbitant prices. Corruption rules the town and nearly all those in it. And through these people, the story of *Casablanca* is told with expert intensity.

Humphrey Bogart has, in Rick, the cafe proprietor, one of the most powerful roles of his film career and plays it for all it's worth. The fascinating Ingrid Bergman is the wife of Paul Henreid, leader of the vast underground movement on the Continent. During the year he was imprisoned in a German concentration camp, and reported dead, the girl and Rick met and loved in Paris, details of their romance being projected in flashback. Meeting again in Rick's popular Casablanca cafe, the triangle is intelligently developed and superbly performed, Miss Bergman is lending rare beauty to the girl and Henreid taking another long step forward with his restrained portrayal. A choice assignment falls to Claude Rains as the prefect of police who describes himself as "a poor, corrupt official," and Rains makes every second of it count. Conrad Veidt does a German major with the authority expected of him, Sydney Greenstreet distinguishes his very brief part of the black market head, and Dooley Wilson creates something joyous as Rick's faithful Negro piano player.

Peter Lorre is in and out of the picture in the first reel, yet the impression he makes is remembered. Others who score memorably with what they have to do include Madeleine LeBeau as a hanger-on who may "someday be a second front," S. Z. Sakall as a loyal waiter, Joy Page as the refugee bride of Helmut Dantine, Curt Bois as a pickpocket, Marcel Dalio as a croupier, Corinna Mura as a singer, and Ludwig Stossel and Ilka Gruning as a charming old couple on their way to Lisbon.

There are only minutes with some of these characters, yet all are outstanding. Wallis really wisely invested in the spectacular casting with the soundest of showmanly results.

It was obviously a bewildering task that Curtiz faced in balancing the wealth of contributing material that was placed at his disposal, but he meets the challenge with directorial skill of Academy Award calibre. The events are shot with sharp humor and delightful touches of political satire.

In a show that is admirable in every department, the long list of technical achievements are headed by the photography of Arthur Edeson, the art direction of Carl Jules Weyl, the music of Max Steiner, the dialogue direction by Hugh McMullan and Joan Hathaway, and the editing by Owen Marks. The song that recalls the romance was clefted by M. K. Jerome and Jack Scholl.

Casablanca

Showmen's Trade Review

AUDIENCE SLANT: (Family) As sweet a package of grand all around entertainment as has been seen in a long time.

BOX OFFICE SLANT: Title, cast, story and production all presage stratospheric receipts.

PLOT: Into the intrigue-ridden city of Casablanca (prior to its recent capitulation to the Allied cause) comes the leader of the hidden and hunted patriots who flaunt and obstruct Nazi rule throughout the conquered nations of Europe. He is accompanied by his pretty wife who, during a period when he had been reported killed while escaping a Nazi concentration camp, had fallen in love with an American adventurer in Paris and had, in turn, left the American when she heard of her husband's safety. In Casablanca, they accidentally visit the saloon and gambling casino owned and run by the American, who has escaped Paris with a price on his head and managed to inject himself into a position of questionable prominence and popularity in the refugee-filled Vichy French city. Nazi pressure to maneuver her husband's death forces the wife to seek the help of her old sweetheart who smothers his own desire for her freely offered favors, tricks the authorities, and arranges their passage in a plane bound for neutral Lisbon.

COMMENT: It may be the prominence that Casablanca enjoys in current news but, somehow or other, the picture takes a stranglehold on the emotions in the opening scene. The character backgrounds are quickly established to show the vicious intrigue, black market operatives, thieves and vandals who prey on the unfortunates willing to relinquish virtue, wealth and position in order to secure the coveted privilege of passage to America. Onto this vividly colorful and highly interesting tapestry of circumstance is laid a captivating array of heart tugs, thrills, suspense, pathos, terror, glamour, excitement and revelry, masterfully embellished with lilting songs and leavening sidelights.

Throughout, the spectator is kept aware of the fact that the inner workings of a woman's heart and the torment of a man's soul are being laid bare. Each of the dominant screen characters cleverly avoid any cue as to the exact position they will assume as the story unfolds and many surprising and pleasing reversals of expected performance take place before the highly satisfactory climax.

Casablanca probably gives as fine an example of the care and secrecy that prevails in the widely publicized but little known "underground" as it is possible for pictures to portray. Humphrey Bogart chalks up another ace performance as a fellow with a world-hardened front and a soft heart, while Ingrid Bergman's performance as the heroine gives new understanding to the complexities of the feminine nature. Paul Henreid does a swell job as the understanding husband; Claude Rains is, as usual, without fault as the Vichy prefect of police; and Sydney Greenstreet and Peter Lorre score in the menace department.

The subordinate players, the direction, the technical departments and all other factors, including a song they will be whistling, contribute to make this an absorbing and entertaining photoplay.

CATCHLINE: A pulse-tingling story of activities in the "underground" where death strikes at Nazi command—but love lives.

Casablanca

212

Bibliography

*A*uthor's Note: *Two different spellings are shown here for Humphrey Bogart's nickname, "Bogie." The actor himself spelled it with an "ie" ending; however, book titles below are spelled as published.*

Also, several authors chose to use the spelling "Warner Brothers" in the titles of their books, even though the studio's official name was "Warner Bros." Titles listed here have been included as originally published, regardless of their accuracy.

ARCHIVAL MATERIAL

Warner Bros. Files (*Casablanca* production files, studio legal records, business correspondence, publicity releases, advertising material, internal memoranda), University of Southern California, School of Cinema-Television

SCRIPTS

Casablanca, Julius J. Epstein, Philip G. Epstein, and Howard Koch, additional material by Casey Robinson
Everybody Comes to Rick's, Murray Burnett and Joan Alison

REFERENCE VIEWINGS OF CASABLANCA

Laserdisc (standard play version), MGM/UA-Turner Entertainment Co.
Laserdisc (Collector's Edition version), Criterion Collection.
Videotape, MGM/UA-Turner Entertainment Co.

PERIODICALS

Hollywood Reporter, 1941–44, selected issues.
Variety (weekly edition), 1941–44, selected issues.

Los Angeles Times, 1941–43, selected issues.
New York Times, 1941–43, selected issues.
Life, 1941, selected issues; fall 1991, Pearl Harbor Collector's Edition.
Time, 1941, selected issues; December 2, 1991, Pearl Harbor 50th Anniversary Special.

MAPS

Collier's World Atlas and Gazetteer, P.F. Collier and Sons Corporation, 1945.
The New Matthews-Northrup Global Atlas of the World at War, The World Publishing Company, 1943.

BOOKS

About Humphrey Bogart

Bogart, Allen Eyles, Doubleday, 1975.
Bogart, Richard Gehman, Fawcett, 1965.
Bogart, David Hanna, Leisure Books, 1976.
Bogart and Bacall: A Love Story, Joe Hyams, David McKay 1975.
Bogey, Jonah Ruddy and Jonathan Hill, Tower, 1965.
Bogey: The Films of Humphrey Bogart, Clifford McCarty, Citadel Press, 1965.
Bogey: The Good-Bad Guy, Ezra Goodman, Lyle Stuart, 1965.
Bogie: The Biography of Humphrey Bogart, Joy Hyams, New American Library 1967.
Humphrey Bogart, Alan G. Barbour, Pyramid Publications, 1973.
Humphrey Bogart, Nathaniel Benchley, Little, Brown, 1975.
Humphrey Bogart, Alan G. Frank, Exeter, 1982.
Humphrey Bogart: Take It & Like It, Jonathan Coe, Grove Weidenfeld, 1991.
Humphrey Bogart: The Man and His Films, Paul Michael, Bobbs-Merrill, 1965.

About Ingrid Bergman

As Time Goes By: The Life of Ingrid Bergman, Laurence Leamer, Harper & Row, 1986.
The Films of Ingrid Bergman, Lawrence J. Quirk, Citadel Press, 1970.
Ingrid Bergman, Curtis F. Brown, Pyramid Publications, 1973.
Ingrid Bergman: An Intimate Portrait, Joseph Henry Steele, David McKay Co., 1959.
Ingrid Bergman: My Story, Ingrid Bergman and Alan Burgess, Delacorte Press, 1980.

About Casablanca

Casablanca (includes dialogue and key frame stills), Richard J. Anobile, New York Universe Books, 1974.

Casablanca

214

About Michael Curtiz

The American Films of Michael Curtiz, Roy Kinnard and R. J. Vitone, Scarecrow Press, 1986.
Casablanca and Other Major Films of Michael Curtiz, Sidney Rosenzweig, UMI Research Press, 1982.

About Paul Henreid

Ladies' Man: An Autobiography, Paul Henreid with Julius Fast, St. Martin's Press, 1984.

About Max Steiner/Film Composition

The Composer in Hollywood, Christopher Palmer, Marion Boyars/Rizzoli International, 1990.
Film Music, A Neglected Art: A Critical Study of Music in Films, Roy Prendergast, W. W. Norton, 1973.
Music for the Movies, Tony Thomas, A. S. Barnes, 1973.

About Conrad Veidt

Conrad Veidt: From Caligari to Casablanca, J. C. Allen, Boxwood Press, 1987.

About Hal Wallis

Starmaker: The Autobiography of Hal Wallis, Hal Wallis and Charles Higham, Macmillan Publishing Co., 1980.

About Jack Warner

Clown Prince of Hollywood: The Antic Life and Times of Jack L. Warner, Bob Thomas, McGraw-Hill, 1990.
My First Hundred Years in Hollywood, Jack L. Warner, Random House, 1965.

About Warner Bros. Pictures

Inside Warner Bros., Rudy Behlmer, Simon & Schuster, 1987.
A New Deal in Entertainment: Warner Brothers in the 1930s, Nick Roddick, British Film Institute, 1983.
The Warner Bros. Story, Clive Hirschhorn, Crown Publishers, 1979.
The Warner Brothers, Michael Freedland, St. Martin's Press, 1983.
Warner Brothers, Charles Higham, Scribner's, 1975.
The Warner Brothers Directors: The Hard-Boiled, the Comic, and the Weepers, William R. Meyer, Arlington House, 1978.

Other Books

All My Yesterdays: An Autobiography, Edward G. Robinson with Leonard
     Spigelgass, Hawthorn Books, 1973.
America's Favorite Movies: Behind the Scenes, Rudy Behlmer, Ungar, 1982.
Cagney by Cagney, James Cagney, Doubleday, 1976.
The Complete Films of Edward G. Robinson, Alvin H. Marill, Citadel Press,
     1990.
The Dame in the Kimono, Leonard J. Leff and Jerold L. Simmons, Grove
     Weidenfeld, 1990.
The Film Encyclopedia, Ephraim Katz, Perigee, 1982.
Hollywood Goes to War, Clayton R. Koppes and Gregory D. Black, The Free
     Press/Macmillan, 1987.
The Hollywood Story, Joel Finler, Crown, 1988.
Leonard Maltin's Movie Guide 1992, Signet, 1991.
The Lonely Life: An Autobiography, Bette Davis, G.P. Putnam's Sons, 1962.
Memo From: David O. Selznick, Edited by Rudy Behlmer, Evergreen, 1981.
My Wicked, Wicked Ways, Errol Flynn, G.P. Putnam's Sons, 1959.

Casablanca
_____

216

Index